NO MENTOR BUT MYSELF

Kennikat Press
National University Publications
Literary Criticism Series

General Editor
John E. Becker

JACK LONDON

NO MENTOR
BUT MYSELF

A Collection of Articles, Essays, Reviews, and Letters
on
WRITING AND WRITERS

edited by
DALE L. WALKER

Foreword by Howard Lachtman

National University Publications
KENNIKAT PRESS // 1979
Port Washington, N.Y. // London

2/1980
Am. Lit.

The publisher acknowledges, with gratitude, the cooperation of Mr. I. Milo Shepard in permitting the use of the material incorporated in this book.

Manufactured in the United States of America

Published by
Kennikat Press Corp.
Port Washington, N.Y. / London

Library of Congress Cataloging in Publication Data

London, Jack, 1876–1916
    No mentor but myself.

    (Literary criticism series)
    Includes bibliographical references
    I. Walker, Dale L. II. Title.
PS3523.046A6   1979   818'.5'209   78-21238
ISBN 0-8046-9227-0

.

CONTENTS

JACK LONDON: The Office Under the Hat

Foreword by
HOWARD LACHTMAN

"A writer does well to place himself in such conditions that he may experience as many as possible of the vicissitudes which occur to men. . . . I would have him be in turns tinker, tailor, soldier, sailor; I would have him love and lose, go hungry and get drunk, play poker with roughnecks in San Francisco, bet with racing touts at Newmarket, philander with duchesses in Paris and argue with philosophers in Bonn, ride with bullfighters in Seville and swim with Kanakas in the South Seas."

W. Somerset Maugham, *A Writer's Notebook*

"First, there must be talent, much talent. Talent such as Kipling had. Then there must be discipline. The discipline of Flaubert. Then there must be the conception of what it can be and an absolute conscience as unchanging as the standard meter in Paris, to prevent faking. Then the writer must be intelligent and disinterested and above all he must survive. Try to get all these in one person and have him come through all the influences that press on a writer. The hardest thing, because time is so short, is for him to survive and get his work done. But I would like us to have such a writer and to read what he would write.

Ernest Hemingway, *Green Hills of Africa*

"My desire to write is the most vital thing in me."

Jack London, *Martin Eden*

Despite the glamor with which posterity has endowed him as a symbol of robust living and romantic mythmaking, Jack London was a workaday professional who wrote for his daily bread and allowed nothing to interfere with the performance of his highly disciplined writing routine.

"No matter how alluring the situation," his wife observed of him, "how novel, how exciting, at nine of the clock down he sits, peppers the plain before him with little note pads, some already scribbled, some black, squares his manuscript tablet, selects an ink pencil from the half dozen that we keep filled, reads over the previous day's thousand words and then, with a little swooping bob that seems to shake him free of all eternal bother, and a busy wise little smile, he settles for two hours of creation—of bread and butter, he will have it. Sometimes he looks up, with a big smile in his eyes and says to me, 'Funny way to make a living, isn't it, Mate Woman?'"

What struck London as "funny" about his enormous success as a writer was that he never quite understood how it had happened. He had known educated derelicts, unrewarded literary geniuses, and unsuccessful writers blessed with talent but cursed by chance or circumstance. He found it difficult to account for the fact that a craft based on the fickle tastes of editors and readers had given him not merely wealth and respectability, but a legend which promised to provide him with the enduring life of a literary immortal.

So well did he succeed in his chosen profession, however, that he seemed, to the majority of his admirers, to have stepped forth from out of the pages of his own stories. Whether he intended it or not, his name soon became synonymous with a "heroic" style of living and a way of writing that seemed to be a direct transcript of that adventurous life. Indeed, the name "Jack London" continues to evoke in the public mind a distinct picture, or series of pictures, of the writer as literary hero: clad in a fur-lined parka or able-bodied seaman's blouse, exploring the wide wilderness or crowded urban slums, chasing a war or a Kanaka wave, describing the efficiency of a boxer's ring style or the necessity of social reform.

The sum of these personas is a writer who has moved beyond literary history into the realm of popular mythology. As such, London persists in the collective imagination of the universal reading public which has adopted him as permanently as Sherlock Holmes, Mark Twain, Don Quixote, Dr. Johnson, the wonderful wizard of the Emerald City, Hemingway, or Tarzan. To this day, more than sixty years after his death, he continues to receive enthusiastic fan mail from his newest readers, while contemporary critics and biographers have just as eagerly begun to "rediscover" him.

London's public role, typically perceived as that of a daring man of action and swashbuckling freelancer of fortune, has often obscured the shrewd, disciplined, and methodical writer whose work helped to shape the myth. That elusive, authorial "self" is by far the least known of all London identities, and it is precisely with the aim of detecting it (and, thereby, of discovering the man behind the myth) that Dale Walker has compiled this remarkable collection.

As *No Mentor But Myself* makes clear, Jack London was one of the first American writers to express himself candidly on such issues as the economics of authorship, the demands of editors, the expectations of readers, and the specifications of critics. In these practical reflections and meditations on his profession, London the elusive adventurer gives way to London the passionate philosopher. Engaged in the act of self-scrutiny, standing both in his work and beyond it, he opens his mind and art to us. Through his first-person perspective, we gain access to the literary industry in turn-of-the-century America and to an intimate view of literary life during the golden age of the mass circulation magazine, newspaper, and short story. It may have been the best time of all to be a writer in America.

Any author who has made the transition from literary aspirant to popular writer, from public figure to enduring legend, is certainly worth reading for what he can reveal to us about the nature of his trade. This is especially true in the case of Jack London. Apart from the semiautobiographical *Martin Eden,* it is not commonly known what London had to say about the business, the philosophy, and what we might call the role of the writer. Judging by the contents of this seminal anthology, he was hardly as silent on the subject as some of his interpreters have supposed. In fact, his views disclose a great deal about his personal and professional activities, and about the temper of the era in which he won prominence as a participant, chronicler, and "first-hand theorist" of adventurous experience.

The scope of *No Mentor But Myself* extends from the "all work and no pay" life of the struggling freelancer to the success-trap of the acclaimed professional. Here, for the first time, and in his own voice, London speaks to us at length about a subject dear to his heart and never far, if one can judge, from his thoughts. His "voice" is preserved in a surprising variety of literary forms: articles, essays, fictions, letters, prefaces, and reviews. By collecting these various points of view, many gathered from rare or arcane sources, and arranging them in a revealing order of flow, Dale Walker has produced a book which transcends the usual collection of odds and ends. For *No Mentor* is in reality a unique mosaic, enabling us to trace the evolution of Jack London's literary theory and practice. At the time of his death, London himself was planning to treat that very subject, not in another article or essay, but in the full-length format of a book. The present anthology includes all the most important source materials on which, undoubtedly, he would have drawn for use in his projected work. The sum of these pieces approximates the book London did not live to write: the autobiography of his adventures in the writing game.

Readers are always naturally curious about successful writers—the more so if those readers also happen to be aspiring authors—and their curiosity sometimes weaves compensatory and explanatory myths about the heads of their literary heroes. Because London's rise to fame appeared swift and apparently effortless, his readers forgot (if they ever knew) that the writer had gone hungry, pawned his typewriter and personal goods, received a heartbreaking sheaf of rejection slips, and lacked money and hope for longer than he cared to remember. The popular view had London taking a direct shortcut to literary success, whereas London was always quick to point out to those who asked him for it that no such shortcut existed. Even in a new and "impatient" age of writing, the literary apprentice still had to serve his apprenticeship. There were factors of literary success, but no "magic formula" for it.

"You want some short cut that, to save my soul, I have no knowledge exists," he told one ambitious young man. "If I could short-cut men to success, I'd quit writing for a living and go out and make millions at teaching it. I'd put all the universities out of business if I only had such a magic formula for short cutting. No, I'll be darned if I can help you."

Prospective writers who took their trade seriously and asked London's help seldom failed to receive it. But that, too, created problems for him. Plagued with the manuscripts and appeals of literary hopefuls whose requests he was seldom able to refuse, London found that his typewriter pep talks never had the desired effect of producing better stories—or grateful correspondents. If anything, such efforts to teach the tricks of the trade were exercises in futility.

"You have a lot to learn in the trick of making stories," he advised one aspiring storyteller. "Now, I cannot teach you this trick. I have possibly five hundred proposals a year from men and women to have me teach them that trick. When I was younger and more rash than I am now, I did endeavor to teach a few the trick, with the only result that I hurt their feelings and lost their friendship. Not one of them ever got the trick. On the other hand, were I as patient as Job, did I have forty-eight hours to spare out of each day, I would not have time enough to teach or guide the many who appeal to me for that form of assistance—namely, learning the trick of successful authorship."

One of the few who did "learn the trick" was San Francisco newsboy and amateur boxer Louis Stevens, later a successful screenwriter and novelist. Stevens remembered his mentor as "a man of warm friendship and unstinting generosity. Furiously though he worked to meet his writing deadline, he never failed to read my too-frequent attempts at writing. Always he came through with encouraging words, suggestions. . . ." Such as the time when, in the course of a story, Stevens scoffed at the finer emotions, drawing this warning from his teacher: "No man can succeed at writing who is not sincere in the things he is writing about. You cannot sneer at a thing and write about it successfully. You don't know love. Don't write about love until you do know love."

But Louis Stevens was one of the rare exceptions. The majority of London's pupils were evidently inept thinkers and writers who would have benefited immensely by reading most of the contents of this book before setting pen to paper. Indeed, one wonders why London simply didn't send reprints of his own pertinent articles and essays on "successful authorship" to those five hundred annual time-wasters. He had once gone so far as to compose a standard letter of regret to ward them off, but this was soon discarded in favor of an indefatigable willingness to befriend, admonish, and encourage younger writers.

Why did London, already a literary idol, desire to take on the thankless and ill-rewarded role of literary mentor? Over and above their public relations value, the only explanation I can offer is that he *enjoyed* these personal contacts with his otherwise faceless and voiceless audience. He had a need to reach out, to communicate with the world at large, to be in touch with his public. Then too, he could never quite manage to hold in check his literary interests and enthusiasms. That much is evident in *No Mentor But Myself,* along with a rarely seen view of London as a critic, analyst, and reviewer of other writers' work. These efforts in particular reveal much of London's own essential personality—his freedom from envy, his lack of malice, his gifts of sympathy and patience, his occasional fits of indignation, his generosity, his firm intelligence, and his pawky sense of humor.

Dale Walker's broad and richly evocative text offers us a close-up view of the literary process as well as an entertaining account of a life in letters. Here are Jack London's motives and rationales for writing, his self-contemplated image of himself, his reaction to charges of "nature-faking" and plagiarism, his study of reader psychology, his comments on the conflict between truth and fiction, his inquiry into the relationship between personality and art, and his recognition of the special communion between the isolated writer and the mass reading audience he serves ("He would be one of the eyes through which the world saw," London describes the aim of the aspiring Martin Eden, "one of the ears through which it heard, one of the hearts through which it felt").

Here, too, we learn London's feelings about the "mercenary craft" by which the literary artist must support himself and sustain himself in pursuit of a higher vision. We gain insight into the divided consciousness of the professional author who discovered that, after all, "bread and glory are divorced; and where he dreamed of serving one master he found two masters. The one master he must serve that he may live; the other that his work may live."

In these pages the panorama of London's developing prose style unfolds before us from the imitative and sententious utterances of his late Victorian literary apprenticeship to his own recognizably crisp and compact personal idiom. Throughout, there is the lively interplay of didacticist and experimentalist, of spontaneous writer and prudent counselor. Much of London's counsel remains eminently useful. "As I, myself, began a writing career," one successful young American writer has recently explained, "I began to appreciate the craftsmanship of other writers, and one of my most admired persons was Jack London. His style was aggressive and rich, active and inspiring. In many respects I tried to emulate London's technique."

One suspects that there are many such emulators. Although the literary market has undergone radical change since London's day, his practical advice to aspirants on getting into print has lost neither its tang nor truth. His "words to the wise" can still benefit and instruct the fledgling wordsmith:

"Don't quit your job in order to write unless there is none dependent upon you."

"Don't dash off a six-thousand word story before breakfast."

"Don't write too much. Concentrate your sweat on one story rather than dissipate it over a dozen."

"Don't loaf and invite inspiration; light out after it with a club, and if you don't get it you will nonetheless get something that looks remarkably like it."

"Set yourself a 'stint,' and see that you do that 'stint' every day."

"Study the tricks of the writers who have arrived. They have mastered the tools with which you are cutting your fingers."

To those who had "cut their fingers," London invariably offered the bandages of constructive criticism. He understood the impact of the rejection slip. He knew at first-hand the fierce resentment of the rejected writer who feels he has been dismissed by some inhuman process ("Surely there were no live, warm editors at the other end. It was all wheels and cogs and oil-cups—a clever mechanism operated by automatons.") But he also insisted that self-pity is a luxury no writer can afford, and that most manuscripts defeat themselves by the haste, the vanity, the absence of sensibility, the omission of objectivity, and the lack of sincerity which stamp them as unmarketable.

"You wrote your story at white heat," he chides one young woman whose sense of narrative urgency has overwhelmed her sense of narrative plausibility. "Hell is kept warm by unpublished manuscripts that were written in white heat. Develop your locality. Get in your local color. Develop your characters. Make your characters real to your readers. Get out of yourself and into your readers' minds and know what impression your readers are getting from your written words. Always remember that you are not writing for yourself but that you are writing for your readers."

A writer could be guided by worse rules and by less honest teachers. London's lessons are drawn directly from his own experience and given with a minimum of fanfare or self-consciousness. He appreciates the difference Hemingway later defined between talking about writing and writing without talking about it, but in him the critical urge seems to be almost as powerful as the creative one, and the two impulses have the mutually beneficial interaction of a literary symbiosis. He himself writes with fine dash and infectious verve, but the crux of his critical advice for young literary horsemen eager to ride is that one must sit before one can gallop. Because there are already too many riderless horses in view, he has a horror of such impulsive, slovenly cavalry. The illusion of effortlessness and spontaneity, he warns his students, is not the result of free rein, but of curb and bit.

If his myth is to be believed, London lived dangerously and wrote as dangerously as he lived. And yet, as Walker's anthology shows us, the truth was that London considered writing a far greater hazard than freezing in the Klondike, riding the rails, or bluffing man-hungry Solomon Island headhunters. The adventurer, at least, did not have to worry about such things as "editorial crimes," the question of acquiring a name and the burden of maintaining it, the slings and arrows of outrageous critics, the unsolicited manuscripts of literary aspirants, the fear of declining popularity, and the writer's "bread or glory" dilemma of whether to write to please himself or satisfy the formula-bound expectations of the market. No wonder London sometimes lost patience and declared his loathing of his profession. What writer has not?

But London was also a man who cherished the consolations of his craft: the total absorption in creative work which makes a writer able to shut off the outside world and forget his troubles; the pleasure of shaping a plausible and profitable tale; and the liberty to do with his life as he sees fit. It was this last which London appears to have prized above cash or acclaim. "Personally," he observed late in his career, "it strikes me that the one great special advantage of authorship as a means of livelihood is that it gives one more freedom than is given any person in business or in the various other professions. The author's office and business is under his hat and he can go everywhere and write anywhere as the spirit moves him."

The spirit of Jack London, private man and literary businessman, is in this book. It may not take us "everywhere," but it can lead us in many unexpected and intriguing directions. Among other things, it shows us an American writer engaged in analyzing the problems and pleasures of his calling both as literary apprentice and literary success, opening the mysteries of his profession to public examination, and taking as a subject for his fiction the dream, decline and fall of an ambitious author whose fate clearly anticipates Gatsby's.

These "portraits of the artist" by the artist himself make London's literary counsel and criticism of use to us today and help define his value in the sense that V. S. Pritchett has remarked: "It is an enormous comfort to a writer and one of the great rewards of writing to find that what you've written has meant something to another writer or writers or to other people and that you're part of the continuity of literature.... I think that every writer is valuable insofar as he helps other writers."

London continues to be a helpful mentor to writers who seek to discover, as did his own Martin Eden, "the trick of expression, of making words obedient servitors, and of making combinations of words mean more than the sum of their separate meanings."

But beyond merely providing insight into the successful market strategies of the literary craftsman, London offers his reader a direct, primary view of the actual *experience* of writing, recorded with such painstaking fidelity to his own practice that one can almost hear the sound of his pen scratching paper or see the "busy wise little smile" of the author at play over his manuscript tablet.

There is also a special fascination in the way that the successful London, obsessed with the genesis of his career, waxes nostalgic and wistful for the lean days of struggle, the unrewarded days of promise. "You look back," he reminisced to his daughter, who herself would later become a writer and one of her father's biographers, "you look back and see how hard you worked, and how poor you were, and how desperately anxious you were to succeed, and all you can remember is how happy you were. You were young, and you were working at something you believed in with all your heart, and you knew you were going to succeed!"

London's "first aid to rising authors" and his revelations about himself as a writer in search of his own identity and integrity of vision will no doubt come **as** a surprise to those who continue to regard him as a narrowly limited teller of tales about "boys, boats, and dogs." But Dale Walker's book is an indication that the mind of Jack London was as manifold as his experience, and that his experience as a writer, from apprentice to mature artist, is the great untold tale of his life. In the following pertinent and provocative examples of London's literary voice, we can hear the accents not only of the mythic author we expected to meet, but of the man we did not.

ACKNOWLEDGEMENTS

Among the Jack London scholars to whom I owe a debt of gratitude are these: Richard Weiderman, editor of Wolf House Books in Grand Rapids, Mich., for originating the idea for this collection of London's writings on writing; Howard Lachtman of Stockton, Calif., for his foreword, for reading the manuscript, and for his advice through all phases of its preparation; Dennis Hensley of Muncie, Ind., and Russ Kingman of Glen Ellen, Calif., for locating many of the rare pieces for me and for their encouragement; and Earle Labor of Shreveport, La., Franklin Walker of Oakland, Calif., Sal Noto of Cupertino, Calif., Hensley Woodbridge of Carbondale, Ill., and Milo Shepard, executor of the London estate in Glen Ellen, Calif., for their invariably generous advice and aid.

I am also grateful to Margaret Burlingame and Julie Sears of the El Paso Public Library for help in locating obscure works of London's for examination and for their interest in the project; to El Paso writer Elroy Bode for his reading of the material and pertinent comments on it; and to Sue Wimberly, my secretary, and Dianne Walker, my daughter, for their reading and typing and developing along the way a keen interest in Jack London.

NO MENTOR BUT MYSELF

Dale L. Walker is Director of the Office of News and Information at the University of Texas at El Paso. He is the author of six books, numerous magazine and journal articles, and hundreds of book reviews. Walker's interest in Jack London is of nearly thirty years duration, and he has written extensively about London in journals such as *American Literary Realism,* and in book-length studies.

A book reviewer for the San Francisco *Chronicle* and Los Angeles *Times,* Howard Lachtman is the author of *A Reader's Guide to Jack London,* to be published in 1979, and is at work on a biography of London. Dr. Lachtman is a member of the civic arts commission in Stockton, California, in addition to being contributing editor for *Contemporary Quarterly.*

INTRODUCTION

The Jack London revival is now at least a dozen years old; its birth perhaps coinciding with the 1965 Odyssey Press volume, *Letters from Jack London.* This five-hundred-page *sui generis* production, Andrew Sinclair claims, "made most of the critical and biographical writing about him appear absurd,"[1] and most dedicated London students would agree. The revival, launched so auspiciously, shows no sign of diminishing; indeed, each year since 1965 has added new impetus to the awakening world interest in this signal figure of American letters. Among the most noteworthy developments are these:

1977 produced the most dramatic birth of Jack London studies since the author's death: Andrew Sinclair's provocative scholarly biography, *Jack* (first full-length biography since Richard O'Connor's *Jack London* in 1964); another biography by a British writer, Robert Barltrop's *Jack London: The Man, The Writer, The Rebel;* Joan Sherman's *Jack London: A Reference Guide,* containing over sixteen hundred annotated entries of works about London; and a new edition of Irving Stone's *Sailor on Horseback: A Biography of Jack London,* revised for the first time since its original publication in 1938.

Scholarly academic journals are rediscovering London and some of the innovative ones—*Modern Fiction Studies* (Purdue), *Western American Literature* (Utah State), and *The Pacific Historian* (University of the Pacific)—have devoted entire issues to London studies, as have several international journals.

Twayne Publishers added Jack London as number 230 in their "U.S. Author Series" in 1974—a path-marking critical study by Earle Labor of Centenary College.

New editions of London's works have appeared in England, Denmark, Norway, Portugal, Italy, Mexico, Japan, France (where all of London's works are being reprinted), and the Soviet Union. (The Russians have always loved Jack London and an estimated 30 million copies of his books have been published there.)

The number of languages into which London has now been translated stands at nearly seventy.

New films and television versions of the Californian's stories are being produced following the successful television adaptation by poet James Dickey of London's 1903 novel, *The Call of the Wild.*

Book-length scholarly keys to London's works are proliferating: *Jack London: A Bibliography* (1966; revised edition, 1971); *Jack London & The Klondike* (1966); *The Fiction of Jack London: A Chronological Bibliography* (1972); *White Logic: Jack London's Short Stories* (1975); *Jack London: A Reference Guide* (1977); and such collections of scarce London works as *Jack London Reports* (1970), and *Curious Fragments: Jack London's Tales of Fantasy Fiction,* which Kennikat Press published in 1975.

Books-in-the-works include a multivolumed new collection of London's letters, a pictorial biography, a biography of London's wife, Charmian Kittredge, a bibliography of his nonfiction works, a Jack London reader's guide, and a collection of London's prizefight and sports writings.

Why all this commotion over a writer who for sixty-one years has been at rest under that volcanic boulder in the Valley of the Moon in northern California? Andrew Sinclair strikes at the heart of this protean figure in writing:

As he thought himself larger than life, he tried to do more than other men did. For a man who has a heroic vision can do more than a man who knows himself too well and is afraid to move. To deny weakness, to insist on excess and success is to live at full stretch. Jack London lived nine lives and wrote more than fifty books and founded a ranch and died at forty. A man like that is worth his own myths.[2]

It is a small irony that in all the reappraising of Jack London in the revival period these past dozen years, he is rarely viewed in one of his principal roles: writer on writing, friend of writers—"writer's writer."

His biographers have been touched by London's lifelong compassion for struggling writers, his open-handed, open-hearted attempts to help them, and the endless hours he devoted to their work.

Richard O'Connor wrote in 1964:

The way he gave himself to other people, his patience and generosity even with complete strangers, his unquenchable sympathy for struggling writers, or strugglers of any kind, was the most remarkable virtue he possessed.

And O'Connor adds the melancholy observation:

He kept pouring his energy, enthusiasm and experience into other people's lives, even though most of his supplicants possessed little talent and few exhibited even the faintest signs of gratitude; his efforts were taken for granted, yet were continued with unflagging zeal.[3]

In 1938, Irving Stone said, with a bit more hyperbole: "His greatest generosity was to the aspiring writers who descended upon him in staggering numbers, their manuscripts darkening his sky like a locust plague. Not a day of his life passed without his receiving a manuscript from a hopeful author, asking him to criticize, rewrite, sell it." Stone also wrote that London received letters from nearly every successful writer of his time, hearing their troubles, mental and spiritual anguish, and giving in turn his sympathy, encouragement, understanding and love.[4]

Jack London launched writers by guiding them and launched books by praising them; for writers—once-was, would-be, never-to-be, obscure and renowned, young and old—he was ever the available man.

And, from the beginning of his career to the end he wrote about writing and writers in his novels, short stories, autobiography, articles, reviews, and letters. He wrote on his struggle against the odds to win success—life for Jack London was always the grand struggle—and with no mentor but himself, poured out what he had learned: serve your apprenticeship, develop a working philosophy of life, learn the markets, absorb the punishment of disappointment and failure that is in store, temper determination with patience, master the tools, see that your pores are open and your digestion is good, have something to say, be sincere in saying it, read, hustle, WORK!

There remains much to learn from Jack London's writings on writing and writers. The writer today can benefit from the timeless truths they contain and one can perceive in them London's own inner disunion about his craft.

The forty-three selections in this volume are arranged chronologically, 1899–1917, with the single exception of the long *Martin Eden* excerpt. *Martin Eden* quite simply belongs at the end of this book: it is a culminating work, an epitome, and all that London says about writing in the forty-two selections that precede it are distilled in this quintessential story of a writer who writes himself into success and, ironically, out of existence. And, while only a fraction of this important novel is included, it is a fraction with a beginning, a middle, and an end.

No Mentor But Myself is made up of eight essays on various aspects of the writer's craft, seven reviews and book introductions, five literary essays, twenty-one letters, and excerpts from two of London's most important autobiographical works.

Twenty of the forty-three selections have never been collected in book form; indeed, most of these have never been reprinted since their original periodical appearance. The selections include London's little-known essays on writing for such magazines as *The Editor, The Bookman, The Critic, Dilettante, Impressions, Ability,* and *The Reader;* essays on Poe, Kipling, and Dana's *Two Years Before the Mast;* reviews of books by Maxim Gorky, Upton Sinclair, and Frank Norris; controversies such as the "nature-faker" charge against London by President Theodore Roosevelt, and plagiarism charges against such works as *The Iron Heel* and *The Call of the Wild;* and letters which range from instructive ones to struggling writers, to a sensitive exchange in 1915 with Joseph Conrad. The excerpts from *John Barleycorn* and *Martin Eden* depict London's view of himself, seen through his autobiographical fiction.

Taken together, Jack London's works on writing and writers illuminate the man and his contradictions. In reading these works, one begins to understand what he meant when he wrote Cloudesley Johns early in his career: "Between you and me, I wish I had never opened the books. That's where I was the fool."[5] But it is difficult to imagine him *not* opening them and more difficult to believe he would ever have willingly closed them, for, as Andrew Sinclair remarks: "He wrote continuously for himself and for his causes, for the market and for his spirit."[6]

NOTES

1. *Jack: A Biography of Jack London,* p. 250.
2. *Jack,* p. 252.
3. *Jack London: A Biography,* p. 377.
4. *Sailor on Horseback: The Biography of Jack London,* p. 298.
5. Charmian K. London, *The Book of Jack London,* vol. 1, p. 378.
6. *Jack,* p. 134.

THE SELECTIONS

ON THE WRITER'S PHILOSOPHY OF LIFE

(The Editor, October, 1899)

⊕ ⊕ ⊕ ⊕ ⊕ ⊕ ⊕ ⊕ ⊕ ⊕ ⊕ ⊕

Here, on the eve of his first great triumphs—the *Atlantic*'s publication of "An Odyssey of the North" (January, 1900) and Houghton Mifflin's publication of his first book, *The Son of the Wolf* (April, 1900)—Jack London sounds some familiar notes of advice to the aspiring writer: develop a philosophy of life, put a stamp of "self" on your work, have something to say, use your time wisely, learn how to read, how to absorb and discard.

⊕ ⊕ ⊕ ⊕ ⊕ ⊕ ⊕ ⊕ ⊕ ⊕ ⊕ ⊕

The literary hack, the one who is satisfied to turn out "pot boilers" for the rest of his or her life, will save time and vexation by passing this article by. It contains no hints as to the disposing of manuscript, the vagaries of the blue-pencil, the filing of material, nor the innate perversity of adjectives and adverbs. Petrified "Pen-trotters," pass on! This is for the writer—no matter how much hack-work he is turning out just now— who cherishes ambitions and ideals, and yearns for the time when agricultural newspapers and home magazines no more may occupy the major portion of his visiting list.

How are you, dear sir, madam, or miss, to achieve distinction in the field you have chosen? Genius? Oh, but you are no genius. If you were you would not be reading these lines. Genius is irresistible; it casts aside all shackles and restraints; it cannot be held down. Genius is a *rara avis,* not to be found fluttering in every grove as are you and I. But then you are talented? Yes, in an embryonic sort of way. The biceps of Hercules was a puny affair when he rolled about in swaddling-clothes. So with you—your talent is undeveloped. If it had received proper nutrition and were well matured, you would not be wasting your time over this. And if you think your talent really has attained its years of discretion, stop right here. If you think it has not, then by what methods do you think it will?

By being original, you at once suggest; then add, *and by constantly strengthening that originality.* Very good. But the question is not merely being original—the veriest tyro knows that much—but now can you become original? How are you to cause the reading world to look eagerly for your work? to force the publishers to pant for it? You cannot expect to become original by following the blazed trail of another, by reflecting the radiations of some one else's originality. No one broke ground for Scott or Dickens, for Poe or Longfellow, for George Eliot or Mrs. Humphrey Ward, for Stevenson and Kipling, Anthony Hope, Stephen Crane, and many others of the lengthening list. Yet publishers and public have clamored for their ware. They conquered originality. And how? By not being silly weather-cocks, turning to every breeze that flows. They, with the countless failures, started even in the race; the world with its traditions was their common heritage. But in one thing they differed from the failures; they drew straight from the source, rejecting the material which filtered through other hands. They had no use for the conclusions and the conceits of others. They must put the stamp of "self" upon their work—a trade mark of far greater value than copyright. So, from the world and its traditions—which is another term for knowledge and culture—they drew at first hand, certain materials, which they builded into an individual philosophy of life.

Now this phrase, "a philosophy of life," will not permit of precise definition. In the first place it does not mean a philosophy on any one thing. It has no especial concern with any one of such questions as the past and future travail of the soul, the double and single standard of morals for the sexes, the economic independence of women, the possibility of acquired characters being inherited, spiritualism, reincarnation, temperance, etc. But it is concerned with all of them, in a way, and with all the other ruts and stumbling blocks which confront the man or woman who really lives. In short, it is an ordinary working philosophy of life.

Every permanently successful writer has possessed this philosophy. It was a view peculiarly his own. It was a yardstick by which he measured all things which came to his notice. By it he focused the characters he drew, the thoughts he uttered. Because of it his work was sane, normal, and fresh. It was something new, something the world wished to hear. It was his, and not a garbled mouthing of things the world had already heard.

But make no mistake. The possession of such a philosophy does not imply a yielding to the didactic impulse. Because one may have pronounced views on any question is no reason that he assault the public ear with a novel with a purpose, and for that matter, no reason that he should not. But it will be noticed, however, that this philosophy of the writer rarely manifests itself in a desire to sway the world to one side or the other of any problem. Some few great writers have been avowedly didactic, while some, like Robert Louis Stevenson, in a manner at once bold and delicate, have put themselves almost wholly into their work, and done so without once imparting the idea that they had something to teach.

And it must be understood that such a working philosophy enables the writer to put not only himself into his work, but to put that which is not himself but which is viewed and weighted by himself. Of none is this more true than of that triumvirate of intellectual giants—Shakespeare, Goethe, Balzac. Each was himself, and so much so, that there is no point of comparison. Each had drawn from this store his own working philosophy. And by this individual standard they accomplished their work. At birth they must have been very similar to all infants; but somehow, from the world and its traditions, they acquired something which their fellows did not. And this was neither more nor less than *something to say*.

Now you, young writer, have you something to say, or do you merely think you have something to say? If you have, there is nothing to prevent your saying it. If you are capable of thinking thoughts which the world would like to hear, the very form of the thinking is the expression. If you think clearly, you will write clearly; if your thoughts are worthy, so will your writing be worthy. But if your expression is poor, it is because your thought is poor, if narrow, because you are narrow. If your ideas are confused and jumbled, how can you expect a lucid utterance? If your knowledge is sparse or unsystematized, how can your words be broad or logical? And without the strong central thread of a working philosophy, how can you make order out of chaos? how can your foresight and insight be clear? how can you have a quantitive and qualitative perception of the relative importance of every scrap of knowledge you possess? And without all this how can you possibly be yourself? how can you have something fresh for the jaded ear of the world?

The only way of gaining this philosophy is by seeking it, by drawing the materials which go to compose it from the knowledge and culture of the world. What do you know of the world beneath its bubbling surface? What can you know of the bubbles unless you comprehend the forces at work in the depths of the cauldron? Can an artist paint an "Ecce Homo" without having a conception of the Hebrew myths and history, and all the varied traits which form collectively the character of the Jew, his beliefs and ideals, his passions and his pleasures, his hopes and fears! Can a musician compose a "Ride of the Valkyries" and know nothing of the great Teutonic epics? So with you—you must study.

You must come to read the face of life with understanding. To comprehend the characters and phases of any movement, you must know the spirit which moves to action individuals and peoples, which gives birth and momentum to great ideas, which hangs a John Brown or crucifies a Savior. You must have your hand on the inner pulse of things. And the sum of all this will be your working philosophy, by which, in turn, you will measure, weigh, and balance, and interpret to the world. It is this stamp of personality of individual view, which is known as individuality.

What do you know of history, biology, evolution, ethics, and the thousand and one branches of knowledge? "But," you object, "I fail to see how such things can aid me in the writing of a romance or a poem." Ah, but they will. They broaden your thought, lengthen out your vistas, drive back the bounds of the field in which you work. They give you your philosophy, which is like unto no other man's philosophy, force you to original thought.

"But the task is stupendous," you protest; "I have no time." Others have not been deterred by its immensity. The years of your life are at your own disposal. Certainly you cannot expect to master it all, but in the proportion you do master it, just so will your efficiency increase, just so will you command the attention of your fellows. Time! When you speak of its lack you mean lack of economy in its use. Have you really learned *how* to read? How many insipid short stories and novels do you read in the course of a year, endeavoring either to master the art of story-writing or of exercising your critical faculty? How many magazines do you read clear through from beginning to end? There's time for you, time you have been wasting with a fool's prodigality—time which can never come again. Learn to discriminate in the selection of your reading and learn to skim judiciously. You laugh at the doddering graybeard who reads the daily paper, advertisements and all. But is it less pathetic, the spectacle you present in trying to breast the tide of current fiction? But don't shun it. Read the best, and the best only. Don't finish a tale simply because you have commenced it. Remember that you are a writer, first, last and always. Remember that these are the mouthings of others, and if you read them exclusively, that you may garble them; you will have nothing else to write about. Time! If you cannot find time, rest assured that the world will not find time to listen to you.

LETTER TO HOUGHTON MIFFLIN
(January 31, 1900)

⊕ ⊕ ⊕ ⊕ ⊕ ⊕ ⊕ ⊕ ⊕ ⊕ ⊕ ⊕

In this exuberant letter to his first book publisher, containing the biographical information to be used in connection with publication of *A Son of the Wolf,* Jack London indulges in a bit of myth making: He portrays the Pennsylvanian John London as his father. No serious biographer since 1921 agrees that John London was anything but a good-hearted stepfather who gave young Jack both his given and surname and his love. The evidence is overwhelming that Jack (John Griffith) London was born out-of-wedlock and that his mother, Flora Wellman of Ohio, married John London eight months after Jack was born in Oakland on January 12, 1876. Although the evidence is less overwhelming, it is convincing that the father was William H. Chaney, a wandering astrologer from Maine.

Jack miscalculated on two other matters herein as well: "I have not married—the world is too large and its call too insistent," he wrote his publisher, yet on the following April 6—nine weeks after writing this—he married. As to the sealing voyage he made in 1893 on the *Sophia Sutherland,* he would endure one of much greater length and travail between 1907 and 1909 aboard his ketch *Snark* in the South Seas.

But for all that, there is much truth and great magnetism in this poignant "The world is so very good" letter.

The "Trowbridge" mentioned is John Townsend Trowbridge (1827-1916), novelist, poet and mainstay contributor to *The Youth's Companion* and *Atlantic* for many years, known particularly for his stories for boys. Among his over forty books are *Father Brighthopes* (1853), *Neighbor Jackwood* (1857), and *The Jolly Roger* (1882).

The "Life of Garfield" mentioned was W. M. Thayer's *From Log-Cabin to White House: The Story of President Garfield's Life* (1881).

Paul Belloni du Chaillu (1835-1903) was an explorer and travel writer and probably the first white man to see living anthropoid apes in the wild. In 1861 he published *Explorations and Adventures in Equatorial Africa*—the book Jack refers to as "du Chaillu's *Travels.*"

"Ouida" was the world-famous pen name of Louise de la Ramée (1839-1908), the British novelist and author of such immensely popular works as *Under Two Flags* (1867), *A Dog of Flanders* (1872), and Jack's favorite, *Signa* (1875).

⊕ ⊕ ⊕ ⊕ ⊕ ⊕ ⊕ ⊕ ⊕ ⊕ ⊕ ⊕

Oakland, Calif.
Jan. 31, 1900

Gentlemen:

In reply to yours of January 25th. requesting additional biographical data. I see I shall have to piece out my previous narrative, which, in turn, will make this choppy.

My father was Pennsylvania-born, a soldier, scout, backwoodsman, trapper, and wanderer. My mother was born in Ohio. Both came west independently, meeting and marrying in San Francisco, where I was born January 12, 1876. What little city life I then passed was in my babyhood. My life, from my fourth to my ninth years, was spent upon Californian ranches. I learned to read and write about my fifth year, though I do not remember anything about it. I always could read and write, and have no recollection antedating such a condition. Folks say I simply insisted upon being taught. Was an omnivorous reader, principally because reading matter was scarce and I had to be grateful for whatever fell into my hands. Remember reading some of Trowbridge's works for boys at six years of age. At seven I was reading Paul du Chaillu's *Travels,* Captain Cook's *Voyages,* and *Life of Garfield.* And all through this period I devoured what Seaside Library novels I could borrow from the womenfolk and dime novels from the farm hands. At eight I was deep in Ouida and Washington Irving. Also during this period read a great deal of American History. Also, life on a Californian ranch is not very nourishing to the imagination.

Somewhere around my ninth year we removed to Oakland, which, today, I believe, is a town of about eighty thousand, and is removed by thirty minutes from the heart of San Francisco. Here, most previous to me was a free library. Since that time Oakland has been my home seat. Here my father died, and here I yet live with my mother. I have not married—the world is too large and its call too insistent.

However, from my ninth year, with the exception of the hours spent at school (and I earned them by hard labor), my life has been one of toil. It is worthless to give the long sordid list of occupations, none of them trades, all heavy manual labor. Of course I continued to read. Was never without a book. My education was popular, graduating from the grammar school at about fourteen. Took a taste for the water. At fifteen left home and went upon a Bay life. San Francisco Bay is no mill pond by the way. I was a salmon fisher, an oyster pirate, a schooner sailor, a fish patrolman, a longshoreman, and a general sort of bay-faring adventurer—a boy in years and a man amongst men. Always a book, and always reading when the rest were asleep; when they were awake I was one with them, for I was always a good comrade.

Within a week of my seventeenth birthday I shipped before the mast as sailor on a three top-mast sealing schooner. We went to Japan and hunted along the coast north to the Russian side of Bering Sea. This was my longest voyage; I could not again endure one of such length; not because it was tedious or long, but because life was so short. However, I have made short voyages, too brief to mention, and today am at home in any fore-castle or stokehole—good comradeship, you know. I believe this comprises my travels; for I spoke at length in previous letter concerning my tramping and Klondiking. Have been all over Canada, Northwest Ty., Alaska, etc., etc., at different times, besides mining, prospecting and wandering through the Sierra Nevadas.

I have outlined my education. In the main I am self-educated; have had no mentor but myself. High school or college curriculums I simply selected from, finding it impossible to follow the rut—life and pocket book were both too short. I attended the first year of high school (Oakland), then stayed at home, without coaching, and crammed the next two years into three months and took the entrance examination, and entered the University of California at Berkeley. Was forced, much against my inclinations, to give this over just prior to the completion of my Freshman Year.

My father died while I was in the Klondike, and I returned home to take up the reins.

As to literary work: My first magazine article (I had done no newspaper work), was published in January, 1899; it is now the fifth story in the *Son of the Wolf*. Since then I have done work for *The Overland Monthly*, *The Atlantic*, *The Wave*, *The Arena*, *The Youth's Companion*, *The Review of Reviews*, etc., etc., besides a host of lesser publications, and to say nothing of newspaper and syndicate work. Hackwork all, or nearly so, from a comic joke or triolet to pseudoscientific disquisitions upon things about which I knew nothing. Hackwork for dollars, that's all, setting aside practically all ambitious efforts to some future period of less financial stringence. Thus, my literary life is just thirteen months old today.

Naturally, my reading early bred in me a desire to write, but my manner of life prevented me attempting it. I have had no literary help or advice of any kind—just been sort of hammering around in the dark till I knocked holes through here and there and caught glimpses of daylight. Common knowledge of magazine methods, etc., came to me as revelation. Not a soul to say here you are and there you mistake.

Of course, during my revolutionary period I perpetrated my opinions upon the public through the medium of the local papers, gratis. But that was years ago when I went to high school and was more notorious than esteemed. Once, by the way, returned from my sealing voyage, I won a prize essay of twenty-five dollars from a San Francisco paper over the heads of Stanford and California Universities, both of which were represented by second and third place through their undergraduates. This gave me hope for achieving something ultimately.

After my tramping trip I started to high school in 1895. I entered the University of California in 1896. Thus, had I continued, I would be just now preparing to take my sheepskin.

As to studies: I am always studying. The aim of the university is simply to prepare one for a whole future life of study. I have been denied this advantage, but am knocking along somehow. Never a night (whether I have gone out or not), but the last several hours are spent in bed with my books. All things interest me—the world is so very good. Principal studies are, scientific, sociological, and ethical—these, of course, including biology, economics, psychology, physiology, history, etc., etc., without end. And I strive, also, to not neglect literature.

Am healthy, love exercise, and take little. Shall pay the penalty some day.

There, I can't think of anything else. I know what data I have furnished is wretched, but autobiography is not entertaining to a narrator who is sick of it. Should you require further information, just specify, and I shall be pleased to supply it. Also, I shall be grateful for the privilege of looking over the biographical note before it is printed.

Very truly yours,
Jack London

Reprinted from *Letters From Jack London* (1965).

LETTER TO CLOUDESLEY JOHNS
(June 16, 1900)

⊕ ⊕ ⊕ ⊕ ⊕ ⊕ ⊕ ⊕ ⊕ ⊕ ⊕ ⊕

When *Overland Monthly* published London's "To the Man on the Trail" in January, 1899, Cloudesley Johns, a young post office employee in a small southern California town, wrote a fan letter. The result was a friendship that lasted nearly seventeen years, ending only with London's death.

If Jack had no mentor but himself, Cloudesley had Jack London—a pugnacious mentor who seldom pulled his punches. Jack's advice was born of his own experience and to Johns, as to many other aspiring writers, he gave of it freely.

They met on several occasions. During London's writing of *The Sea Wolf* in 1903, Johns came up to Piedmont and the two men sailed up to the mouth of the Sacramento River on Jack's sloop *Spray*. There they played chess, swam, shot ducks and mudhens, fished, talked and wrote. "The more I see of Cloudesley, the more I like him," Jack wrote. "He is honest and loyal, young and fresh, understands the discipline of a boat, and is a good cook, to say nothing of being a good-natured and genial companion."*

⊕ ⊕ ⊕ ⊕ ⊕ ⊕ ⊕ ⊕ ⊕ ⊕ ⊕ ⊕

Oakland, Calif.
June 16, 1900

Dear Cloudesley:

To commence with, you do me wrong. When you asked if I thought you could do the "Philosophy of the Road," I had no idea of what it was to be, that is, how it was to be treated, and so, did not have the slightest idea concerning whether you could do it or not. Further, when

---

*Quoted in Stone, p. 193.

I wrote you, I overlooked that query—that was all. Had I remembered I would have spoken as I have spoken at the head of this paragraph. I do take a little of it back. I did think at the time that by experience you certainly were fitted for it.

It is a fascinating subject. It has itched me for long, and it is often all I can do to keep away from writing on it. However, I have been and am still laying aside notes on it, so that, some day, saturating myself with the life again, I will go ahead. But as you say, it is infinite.

But Cloudesley, do you think you are handling it just right? I don't forget that they were written for "Stories and Sketches of the Road," nor that you say they will have to be re-written; but still I ask, are you going about it right? You are treating it in much the manner Wyckoff treated the *Workers,* "East and West." But he treated it scientifically, and empirically scientifically, if I may use the phrase. And for that matter, he dealt more with the workers than with the tramps; but the method of treatment still applies. As it seems to me, you are too dry. You are not, from your choice of subjects or topics, treating it as he treated it. Therefore your style should be different. You are handling stirring life, romance, things of human life and death, humor and pathos, etc. But God, man, handle them as they should be. Don't you tell the reader the philosophy of the road (except where you are actually there as participant in the first person). Don't you tell the reader. Don't. Don't. Don't. But HAVE YOUR CHARACTERS TELL IT BY THEIR DEEDS, ACTIONS, TALK, ETC. Then, and not until then, are you writing fiction and not a sociological paper upon a certain sub-stratum of society.

And get the atmosphere. Get the breadth and thickness to your stories, and not only the length (which is the mere narration). The reader, since it is fiction, doesn't want your dissertations on the subject, your observations, your knowledge as your knowledge, your thoughts about it, your ideas—BUT PUT ALL THOSE THINGS WHICH ARE YOURS INTO THE STORIES, INTO THE TALES, ELIMINATING YOURSELF (except when in the first person as participant). AND THIS WILL BE THE ATMOSPHERE, AND THIS ATMOSPHERE WILL BE YOU, DON'T YOU UNDERSTAND, YOU! YOU! And for this, and for this only, will the critics praise you, and the public appreciate you, and your work be art. In short, you will then be the artist; do not do it, and you will be the artisan. That's where all the difference comes in. Study your detestable Kipling; study your Beloved's *Ebb Tide.* Study them and see how they eliminate themselves and create things that live, and breathe, and grip men, and cause reading lamps to burn overtime. Atmosphere stands always for the elimination of the artist, that is to say, the atmosphere is the artist; and when there is no atmosphere and the artist is yet there, it simply means that the machinery is creaking and that the reader hears it.

And get your good strong phrases, fresh, and vivid. And write intensively, not exhaustively or lengthily. Don't narrate—paint! draw! build!—CREATE! Better one thousand words which are builded, than a whole book of mediocre, spun-out, dashed-off stuff.

Think it over and see if you catch what I am driving at. Of course, if you intend what I have called a scientific paper, then don't do anything of these things I have suggested. They would be out of place. But if you intend fiction, then write fiction from the highest standpoint of fiction. Don't be so damnably specific, adding dry detail to dry detail. Put in life, and movement—and for God's sake no creaking. Damn you! Forget you. And then the world will remember you. But if you don't damn you, and don't forget you, then the world will close its ears to you. Pour all yourself into your work until your work becomes you, but nowhere let yourself be apparent. When, in the *Ebb Tide*, the schooner is at the pearl island, and the missionary pearler meets those three desperate men and puts his will against theirs for life or death, does the reader think of Stevenson? Does the reader have one thought of the writer? Nay, Nay. Afterwards, when all is over, he recollects, and wonders, and loves Stevenson—but at the time? Not he.

Do the wheels in Shakespeare creak? When Hamlet soliloquizes, does the reader think at the time that it is Shakespeare? But afterwards, ah afterwards, and then he says, "Great is Shakespeare!"

Do you see what I mean? Now please don't fall upon what I have written in spirit other than with which it was written. I've hammered it out hastily and not done it justice, I know, but it has all been sincere.

I can't speak of the good points in the Mss., for I have devoted my space to generalities. But you show a good grasp of psychology, which will or should be a wonderful aid when you get the right method. But I can't go into that. Haven't time. Have to get ready to go out and want to get this off first.

However, let me thank you for sending me the Mss.

I shall not answer the rest of your short letter, though I appreciated it all and would like to.

Jack London

Reprinted from *Letters From Jack London* (1965).

THE QUESTION OF A NAME
(*The Writer*, December, 1900)

⊕ ⊕ ⊕ ⊕ ⊕ ⊕ ⊕ ⊕ ⊕ ⊕ ⊕ ⊕

"A name is a very excellent thing for a writer to possess," London says in this lighthearted but hardheaded glimpse at the markets and demands of publishers. By the time this piece was published, his own name was gaining stature: He had published in the *Atlantic, McClure's, The Woman's Home Companion, The Smart Set, Harper's Bazar, The Youth's Companion, Outing,* and other important markets of the day, and his second collection of stories, *The God of His Fathers,* would appear in five months from McClure, Phillips & Co.

With nearly forty short stories and a sizable number of essays already published, his pace of writing a thousand words a day was indeed "splendid speed."

⊕ ⊕ ⊕ ⊕ ⊕ ⊕ ⊕ ⊕ ⊕ ⊕ ⊕ ⊕

"The chance of the unknown writer" may be discussed *ad nauseam,* but the unpleasant fact will yet remain that he has not the chance of the known writer. It is a matter that he has knowledge that he cannot compete with the latter on the equal ground of comparative merit. Every first-class magazine is overwhelmed with material (good material), of which it cannot use a tithe; and it will reject an unknown's work, which may possess a value of say, two, and for which it would have paid a price of, say, one, and in place of it accept a known's work with a value of one, for which it will pay a price of ten.

This is not an assumption, but an assertion grounded on the bitter facts of policy and expediency. There are no Utopian magazines on the market; nor are there any which are run primarily for the benefit of the writer class. In the last analysis, commercialism is the basis upon which they are all conducted. Occasionally an editor of pre-eminent position may allow his heart to transgress his business principles in order to give a struggling unknown a lift. But such an act is a transgression, and is permitted only because of the pre-eminence which its perpetrator enjoys. Let him do it always and his magazine will go bankrupt, he will be looking for a new sanctum, and, worst of all (for the writer class), he will have been deprived of his power of occasionally extending the helping hand. In short, the magazine editor must consult first and always the advertisers and the reading public; he must obey the mandates of the business department, and be deaf, very often, to the promptings of his heart. Trade is trade.

But this is just. Every known writer was once an unknown, struggling in the crowded lists for a chance of recognition, toiling early and late and always to lift his small voice above the clamor and obtain a hearing. And at last, by no primrose path of dalliance, having gained a name, it is no more than right that he should enjoy the perquisites of office, namely: the *entree* of the first-class periodicals and publishing houses, and the privilege of continuing to supply his own reading public which he has built up by his own exertions. He has drummed up his trade; let him retain it. If other competitors (the unknowns) attempt to crowd him out, let them expect to encounter the same obstacles which he has overcome. No editor smoothed them away for him; it were unjust to him should the editors make it easier for his new-born rivals. If he be not secured in the position he has attained, what was the use of his striving? and further, what incentive would there be for the unknown? If nothing goes with a name, why strive? Let them leave his trade alone and drum up more for themselves.

A name is a very excellent thing for a writer to possess; and the achievement of a name is an ambition which dominates every normal unknown who ever entered the field. The word "normal" is used understandingly. Whether a materialist or an idealist, no normal writer is insensible to the benefits which accrue from such a possession. To the one it will give greater scope and opportunity for the gathering in of shekels; to the other, a larger hearing and a more authoritative rostrum. The creature is abnormal who claims neither to desire the felicities of existence which gold will purchase, nor to whisper or thunder helpful messages to the weary world. He is an egotist. He would sing his songs in his own ear, dance naked for his own pleasure. There is no place for him in the world, nor shall he retain that to which he was born. Natural selection will settle his account for him, even in the third or the fourth generation. Yet again, this abnormal, inconsistent, and most preposterous personage loads the mails with his wares and seeks publication with ravenous avidity. This is illogical, but tax him with it and he has the audacity to defend himself. He is a sophist and a degenerate, and if he persist in his iniquity, he will perish without posterity, or, at best, with a weak and sickly line.

But let us deal with the normal writer, the new-born, the unknown.

How may he obtain a name? There be divers ways, but simmered down and summed up, there will be found but two: *By writing a successful or popular book, or by excellent magazine work.* Let the weak and wavering attempt it not. But the lion-hearted, let them advance; let them blow, as only such breed can blow: "Childe Harold to the dark tower came!"

Much may be said in favor of attempting the successful book; much may be said against the undertaking. First, however, one must have within him the potentialities of the successful book. Having established this premise of quality, or believe that he has, let him proceed. As regards quantity, he need not work hard. Though many books are shorter and a few longer, the covers of the modern book of fiction shelter from fifty thousand to eighty thousand words—call it sixty thousand for a fair average. Let him do a thousand words a day; but, they must be good words, the very best he has in him. If he writes more, the chances are large that they will deteriorate to second-best and to third-best. A thousand a day is splendid speed—so long as the writer is satisfied with each thousand as he rolls it out. In ninety days he will have worked sixty and lazied thirty, and there will stand his volume complete. If it is successful, how easy! how dazzling! His name is become an open sesame; in a moment he is lifted from the stifling herd. But ah! that dazzle! It leads the many to essay sixty thousand words before they are prepared. They may possess potentiality, but somehow they fail to realize upon it. They would write a classic or the great American novel when they should yet be digging in the rusty pages of their rhetoric, cultivating the art of selection, or polishing up the sister art of expression. Success if just this—retaining the substance and transmuting the potential into the kinetic. That's all. When the trick is discovered the name is assured.

However, our tyro, who possesses potentiality and a lion's heart, has failed to transmute. Let him declare a truce for thirty days, taking this time to recuperate, to study, to incubate, to plan, to meditate upon his own weaknesses, and to measure himself against those who bear the hall-mark of the world's approval. Then at it again, sixty days of work and thirty of loafing (these latter interspersed with the former as his moods dictate), and there is the second volume ready for the test. A failure? Good. He is lion-hearted; he possesses potentiality; he needs only the Midas-touch of transmutation. Another truce of thirty days; another creative effort of ninety days; a third volume; and he may then rest a month, and after all is said and done, have consumed only a year of his life. That's not hard work. A bricklayer will have worked longer and severer hours, while *he*—why, during this time he has soared thrice for a seat with the immortals.

And what if defeat be his portion! Let him work two years, three years—why, he would work five to learn many a manual trade, and in five years he may make fifteen flights for a name and immortality. A name means position, freedom, life! While for immortality, who can measure it?

Excellent magazine work, as a means to the high end, is slower, more discouraging, perhaps, in certain ways, and harder. But it is a training school, and it is surer. Every effort is a written exercise for the editor-teacher. Each acceptance is a reward of merit, to be added one unto another till the sum total is equivalent to the graduation certificate. This certificate is the name which enables one to command the ear and the purse of both the publisher and the public. But the way is beset with pitfalls, and to make the journey more hazardous, they cannot always be avoided. While genius soars it starves. To satisfy the belly-need, the aspirant must often turn his pen to other than excellent work. If his should be steady and his brain clear, this need not harm. Let him clothe his ambition in a hair shirt, and all will go well with him. But if, while still turned to other work, he finds that his ambition no longer hurts him, let him arise in the night and flee away from destruction. Let him also invest in a new hair shirt, more bristly, more peace-destroying. The habitual inebriate is no pleasant sight; but the confirmed hack-writer is a most melancholy spectacle—a gibbering spectre of a once robust manhood; while lucrative mediocrity typifies in these latter days those ancient, muck-wallowing swine who were once brave men in Ulysses' band.

Knowing good from evil, we must presuppose that our young lionheart can safely thread these various dangers. Excellent work is all that stands between him and the name, but oh, how excellent it must be! The farm or home papers, the second and third-class magazines, and all sorts and conditions of erratic periodicals, will receive his second and third rate work; but it is to the first-class magazines that his ambition must appeal for a hearing; and this he finds an almost hopeless task, which would appall any but his own stout heart. Such publications are rich. They can afford the best—from a business point of view—and the chiefs of the business departments demand that they buy the best. The "star" system of the American stage is equally in vogue with the American editors. Here are knights, true and tried, who have long since received the world's accolade. With them the unknown must compete, but on most unequal ground. What if he does as well? The business department will say him nay. A certain intrinsic value attaches to a name. To his work what name may they append? Pshaw! Nonsense! Why, there's a host of nameless who can do as good as the named are doing. That is not what is wanted. They want better, better work than even the named are turning out.

Most unfair! Most impossible! Ah, but that's the very point. Our unknown must do the impossible; by that means only may he become known. The impossible? Precisely. No man ever became great who did not achieve the impossible. It is the secret of greatness. It is what the unknown must do, and what he will do. Mark that well—what he will do. Else he is one of the weak and wavering, masquerading under the guise of a lion-heart, and we have pinned our faith to a shadow.

But not only must he do the impossible, he must continue to do it. Having chosen to carve a name in this manner, instead of by the sudden flight of a successful book, he must abide by the issue. His first impossible performance is almost sure to fall flat. Most likely little notice will be taken of it. The critics, moving along their well-greased grooves, will hardly notice him. Many people are capable of doing the impossible only once. The critics know this. They will keep silent; but bear this in mind, they will remember him. Let him continue to do the impossible, and they will gather faith in him—likewise those arbiters of success, the editors. They are always on the lookout for budding genius. Too often they have been fooled. They will not be hasty, but they will keep an eye upon him, and suddenly, one day, like a bolt out of a clear sky, they will swoop down upon him and carry him away to Olympus. Then will he possess a name, prestige, be a Somebody. The pinnacle upon which he sits will have been built, brick by brick, slowly, tediously, and through great travail; but the foundation will be deep and sure, the masonry honest. He may precipitate himself from his perch, but it will never crumble beneath him. The perch will remain, though he be forgotten.

And so, in these two ways, lie the paths to success: Either by the writing of a successful or popular book, or by excellent magazine work. One is more brilliant; the other sounder. Some are better fitted for the one; some for the other. A favored few are capable of either. But none may be permitted so to classify himself until he has tried. Ay, until he has tried, and tried, and tried many times. Brows are not laureled for the asking, nor is the earth a heritage to any save to the sons of toil.

FIRST AID TO RISING AUTHORS

(The Junior Munsey Magazine, December, 1900)

⊕ ⊕ ⊕ ⊕ ⊕ ⊕ ⊕ ⊕ ⊕ ⊕ ⊕ ⊕

Ever seeming the literary mammonist, London's cry for "cash" and selling even messages on the ills of the world for "goodly sums" disguised his serious literary endeavors and his expressed hatred of writing purely for monetary return.

Dr. S. Weir Mitchell, M.D. (1829–1914) was a Philadelphia medical writer, poet and novelist. He was author of *Hugh Wynne: Free Quaker* (1898) and *Adventures of François* (1899), the latter a picaresque novel. His best-known poem was "Ode on a Lycian Tomb," written on the death of his daughter at age twenty-two, of diphtheria.

The British philosopher Herbert Spencer (1820–1903), who generalized evolutionary theory outside the confines of biology, was chief among the "teachers" of Jack London's self-education. Thomas Henry Huxley (1825–95), biologist and teacher, was the leading proponent of Darwinism and agnosticism of the nineteenth century.

Sir John Lubbock, Lord Avebury (1834–1913) was a British naturalist and writer; Edward L. Youmans (1821–87) was an editor and science writer who edited several volumes of Spencer's works and attempted to popularize him in America.

⊕ ⊕ ⊕ ⊕ ⊕ ⊕ ⊕ ⊕ ⊕ ⊕ ⊕ ⊕

Many are the motives which drive men into setting foot on the thorny paths of literature; and among these impelling forces may be chiefly noted ambition.

Ambition is a very vague term. Let us get right down to the root of the matter, strip off all foolish fancies and cunning deceits and resolve the word into something more definite. Ambition for what? For fame? For notice? For an audience? For power? For a living? Indeed, for what?

Now, let it be remarked at this juncture that the discussion only appertains to individuals who really enter the arena and burden the mails in quest of a market. We have no concern with the true poet, who sings for the song's sake; who sings because force moves along the line of least resistance; who sings, in short, because he cannot help singing. Such a one does not send his songs between glued flaps to the uttermost ends of the earth, to harrow the souls of countless editors. At the best (or it may be the worst), after due persuasion, he gets out a private edition for gratuitous distribution among his nearest and dearest friends; but he does nothing more. Of course, should the note he strikes be pure and sweet and true, should it have the strong, deft, indefinable eternal touch, he cannot escape a constant increase in the number of his listeners. But it is they that bring him his market; for each warbles his songs to the other, and one to another, till at last all the world is divided 'twixt warbling and clamoring for warbles, and wires and cables are hot with offers from anxious eyed publishers. In this case, it is the market which came to him; not he to the market.

But we are engaged in analyzing that ambition which leads men to make commodities of their written thoughts, and to send them forth, like turnips and cabbages, to be bought and sold. When a man does this thing, it is fair to ask why. Does he do it for fame? Let us see. In the first place, the question arises, does a man, solely impelled by a hungering for distinction or glory, ever become distinguished or glorious? It does not seem so. He may achieve notoriety, but never renown. The great men of the world become so because they had work to do in the world, and did it; because they worked busily and mightily, and lost themselves in their work, till they were surprised, one day, when honors fell thick upon them, and their names were on all men's lips. And, further, for the one who would sell his thoughts merely for the reward of sitting in the high places, is it not a ridiculous way to chase fame through publishers' offices and editorial sanctums, pestering a thousand busy coat tails, the owners of which he does not even know? Surely, laurels are not for such as he is!

Then, there are other men, ambitious just to see themselves in print. Just to have their friends say, "There's Soandso. Clever fellow, don't you know? Writes for the magazines." Such a man desires to have people speak of him; to sneak for a moment into the shilling gallery, and then walk proudly among those who know him as one who has sat among the writer people; to possess a caste distinction to which he was not born, and which, because of his innate asininity, he never can earn. There are such men—buttonhole the next editor you are introduced to, and ask him—petty, vain, and foolish creatures; but, while we weep for them, we cannot discuss as ambitious their misbegotten desires. Let us be charitable, lay the blame upon their ancestors, and pass on.

There are many others to be eliminated from the proposition; the specialists, for instance—doctors, lawyers, professors, historians, and scientists. These men write in their professional capacity, as men who have something to say. But their ambitions have been realized in the careers already chosen, and the literary work they do is only a modern phase of their careers. There are also the dabblers—people who are not abubble with some great word for the world, who are not swayed by vanity; who, by luck of birth or circumstance, have been removed from the struggle for existence, and their desire to be doing something; people who write for the same reason that they hunt, fish, travel, or attend the opera.

With all these, ambition, as a distinctive term, plays no part. To whom, then, does it apply? To two classes—those who have, or think they have, a message the world needs or would be glad to hear; and those whose lives have been cast on hard ground and in barren places, striving to make the belly need. The first is the smaller class. They are the heavenly, fire flashing, fire bringing creatures, so made that they must speak though ears be deaf and the heavens fall. History is full of them, and attests that they have spoken, whether on the graven tablets of Mount Sinai, in the warring pamphlets of a later period, or in the screaming Sunday newspaper of today. Their ambition is to teach, to help, to uplift. Self is no determining factor. They were not created primarily for their own good, but for the good of the world. Honor, glory, and power do not attract them. A crust of bread and a beggar's garb meet all their material desires. Existence is an episode; a means to an end. The world's comfort and happiness is their comfort and happiness. And, being helpers and advisers, they do not ask help or advice; nor will they take it if proffered them, for their courses are predestined, like the stars. And when all is said and done, who would have it otherwise?

But there yet remains the second class, and since it is the larger class, composed of clay born creatures like you and me, let us see the part played by ambition in rushing us into print. Ask the editors, the publishers, the booksellers, the reading public, and the answer will be, "Cash." Now, the idealist or the dreamer who has strayed thus far would better return. The question at issue is becoming brutal. Cash? Yes, cash! So put your head back among the clouds, and leave us alone. It's too bad, we know, that we are not to be satisfied with a crust of bread and a beggar's garb; but then, you see, we are only the clay born. Our sins be upon the heads of our progenitors, or whosoever had the shaping of us.

We are the ones who suffer from the belly need. We are joy loving, pleasure seeking, and we are ever hungry for the things which we deem the compensation of living. The world owes us something, and we intend dunning until we get it. True, most of the debts seem bad; wherefore, the more reason that we dun the harder. Some of us do not hold the bills to be very large, and will sign off for the most ridiculous sums. Others are more insistent; while not a few are sure they never can be paid enough for having been born. But we all consider ourselves creditors, and have early learned that we must do our own collecting.

We want good food, and plenty of it; meat as often as we feel inclined —not skirt steaks, but porterhouses; fruits; and, when the call is for cream, cream and not skim milk. We want nice houses, with sanitary plumbing and tight roofs, and we do not want to be cramped or stifled, either. We want high ceilings, big windows, and lots of sunshine; room outside for flowers to grow, and vines, and fig trees, and walks, wherein to wander in the cool of the day. And we want all kinds of nice things inside those houses—books, pictures, pianos, and couches with no end of cushions. We want good tobacco, and we want plenty of it, so that our friends may come and help us smoke it. And if their lips turn dry, we want to give them something better to drink than the ill tasting liquid for which we are so often mulcted by bloated corporations.

And we want to marry and multiply, and we want our multiplications to be pleasures, not worries. We want them to breathe good air, to eat things which befit an animal which walks upright, to see and hear things which give soul and right understanding. We want them to grow up fat and strong, with big muscles and large lungs and clear eyes. We want them to become men and women, strong of breed and big of heart, with a knowledge of things and a power of doing. We also want for ourselves saddle horses, bicycles, and automobiles; cameras, shot guns, and jointed rods; canoes, catboats, and yawls. We want railway tickets, tents, and camping outfits. We want to climb mountains, to walk barefoot on sandy shores, to plow the salt seas in whatever way most pleases us. We are tired of poring over illustrated atlases and guide books, and we want to go and see for ourselves. We are sick of weak photographs and worse copies of the masterpieces men have done. We want to see with our own eyes these paintings and sculptures, to hear with our own ears these singers and musicians. When India starves, or the town needs a library, or the poor man in our neighborhood loses his one horse and falls sick, we want to put our hands in our pockets and help. And to do all this, we want cash!

Because we want these things, and because we are going to rush into print to get them, it were perhaps well to know which kind of print to rush into in order to get most of them. We have chosen print because we thought we were better adapted for it; and, further, because we preferred it to pulling teeth, mending broken bones, adding up figures, or working with pick and shovel. Many men, paddling in the same boat with us, took up with literature for precisely similar reasons; but, unfortunately, they did not choose their particular field with due deliberation. So they suffered sore, and only learned of their mistake after the weary travail of years.

Grant Allen, who certainly achieved literary success, had such an experience. Returning from Jamaica to England in 1876, out of work, he decided to make his living with his pen. Prior to this, in spare moments, he had written a hundred or more magazine articles on philosophical and scientific subjects, not one of which had ever brought him in a penny. But he now devoted himself to writing a book, *Physiological Esthetics*, the publication of which cost him six hundred dollars. The reviews were favorable, and so good was it that it won him the friendship of men like Darwin and Spencer, and actually sold to the tune of nearly three hundred copies. When everything was cleaned up, he had lost, plus his time, a paltry hundred and fifty dollars. His next book was *The Color Sense*. This involved between five and six thousand references, required a year and a half to complete, and in the course of ten years netted him something like one hundred and fifty dollars. Does anybody ask why Grant Allen came to write fiction in his latter days?

So deeply did this mistake affect him, that he said, in 1893: "I had a ten years' struggle for bread, into the details of which I don't care to enter. It left me broken in health and spirit, with all the vitality and vivacity crushed out of me. If the object of this paper is to warn off ingenious and aspiring youth from the hardest worked and worst paid of all professions, I should say earnestly: 'Brain for brain, in no market can you sell your abilities to such poor advantage. Don't take to literature if you've capital enough to buy a good broom, and energy enough to annex a vacant crossing.'"

Whether this be so or not, is not the question at stake. The point is, that in the high tide of success Grant Allen was yet able to speak thus because of what he had suffered and undergone. As he saw it, no success under the sun could atone for the ten years' struggle. No monetary reward, no material comfort, no boundless demand for his wares, none of the satisfactions of life which were his, could compensate for what he had lost. The fact that a man should feel so when tasting the sweets of living, with the struggle all behind him, serves to show the bitterness of that struggle; and, further, to illustrate the enormity of the mistake.

So it were well that we, moved towards literature by belly need, should judiciously decide what part of us is the best to put on paper.

Frankly, which pays the best—fiction, poetry, essay, history, philosophy, or science? The circulating library is an artery where one may feel the pulse of the market. That which is most read is most in demand, and was there ever a circulating library which did not put forth more fiction than all other forms of printed thought combined? The bookseller will tell the same story; likewise the publisher. Many an editor has advised a contributor to turn from the more serious fields to fiction; but rarely has the opposite advice been given. And why so? Surely not because the contributor was unfitted for the other and more serious fields. There are no end of fiction writers who could turn their hands to such, and turn them well. But they do not.

Dr. Weir Mitchell is undoubtedly capable of most important and well constructed medical tomes; but he prefers to write *The Adventures of François*. John Uri Lloyd was guilty of various works on chemistry; but now we are all reading his *Stringtown on the Pike*. Mr. Kipling could discourse profoundly on mechanical engineering and other technical subjects; yet we are pleasuring in *Captains Courageous* and *Stalky and Company*. And Grant Allen, aforementioned, who wrote the *Color Sense*, later wrote *The Tents of Shem* and *The Woman Who Did*. Not that we would infer that these gentlemen, and a myriad others, are sufferers from the belly need. No, no; no doubt it is simply inclination and temperament which lead them into paths where the primroses are more thickly sprinkled.

Let us, however, seek more concrete evidence, taking, for instance, the case of Herbert Spencer. Mr. Spencer's contribution to the world's knowledge is so great that we cannot really appreciate it. We lack perspective. Only future centuries may measure his work for what it is; and when a thousand generations of fiction writers have been laid away, one upon another, and forgotten, Spencer will be even better known than in this day. Yet he was forced to publish his philosophy at his own expense. By 1865, because of this, he owed fifty-five hundred dollars, and was driven into making the announcement that he would discontinue issuing his work. In America, Youmans raised seven thousand dollars, and in England, Huxley and Lubbock attempted to increase artificially the list of subscribers, by inducing people to take the work—not because they intended reading it, but in order to help support it. But the death of his father so increased Spencer's income that he declined to advantage by the kindness of his friends, and went on as before, bearing the loss himself.

A glance at the other side is quite apropos. Alphonse Daudet is said to have received two hundred thousand dollars for his *Sappho*. The *Pall Mall Gazette* paid Kipling seven hundred and fifty dollars for each of his "Barrack Room Ballads." For his short stories, he has received as high as a dollar per word. What scientist or philosopher ever achieved the like? Anthony Hope reserves the copyright, and receives four hundred and fifty dollars for a magazine article. Frank R. Stockton sells the shortest of his tales for something like five hundred dollars. The Harpers are said to have paid General Lew Wallace a hundred thousand dollars for his *Prince of India.* They also bought the American rights of *Trilby* for ten thousand dollars; but they afterwards, out of the largeness of their hearts, voluntarily sent Du Maurier forty thousand dollars more.

But, though fiction does pay best, it should go without saying that the same is not true of all fiction. The poorer class periodicals pay for stories anywhere from forty cents to a dollar per thousand words, and even then they sometimes pay under protest. Not infrequently, the major portion of such pittance is spent for stamps and stationery wherewith to dun for the remainder. There are publishers who never pay. And, so black is iniquity, some periodicals force the writer to subscribe ere they will publish his work without pay. But we who want the good things of the world will not be unwise enough to put our hands to this kind of work— unless we are incapable of better.

Then, again, there is another class of fiction to avoid, especially perilous to those of us who titubate between Grub Street and a country house flung about with twenty woodland acres. This consists of the inanely vapid sort which amuses the commonplace souls of the commonplace public, and the melodramatic messes which tickle the palates of the sensation mongers, who otherwise spend their time neurotically wandering through the yellow journals. Witness Charlotte M. Braeme and Laura Jean Libbey on the one hand, and Albert Ross and Archibald Clavering Gunter on the other. Of course it pays; but because we happen to be mercenarily inclined, there is no reason why we should lose our self respect. A man material enough of soul to work for his living is not, in consequence, so utterly bad as to be incapable of exercising choice. If scavenging be not to his liking, the more honor when he becomes a wood chopper. So with us. Though the dreamers and idealists scorn us because of our close contact with the earth, no disgrace need attach to that contact. The flesh may sit heavily upon us, yet may we stand erect and look one another in the eyes.

And in this connection we may well take a lesson from those same dreamers and idealists. Let us be fire bringers in a humble way. Let us have an eye to the ills of the world and its needs; and if we find messages, let us deliver them. Ah, pardon me, purely for materialistic reasons. We will weave about with our fictions, and make them beautiful, and sell them for goodly sums.

Of course there is a danger in this. It is liable to be catching. We may become possessed by our ideas, and be whisked away into the clouds. But we won't inoculate. Honor bright, we won't inoculate. And in the meantime, let us add to the list a few more of the good things we want.

Some things do not change. The vexations of writers working in the marketplace—ruinous and maddening delays, mutilation of manuscripts, delays in payment—these are nearly as familiar today as in Jack London's time, three-quarters of a century ago.

On Jack's dealings with editors, Irving Stone has written that "He was gentle, courteous, and easy to get along with—until he decided that someone was cheating him or injuring his work. Then he descended upon the offender with the ferocity of an enraged grizzly."*

⊕ ⊕ ⊕ ⊕ ⊕ ⊕ ⊕ ⊕ ⊕ ⊕ ⊕ ⊕

Now the majority of editors are excellent men, courteous and sympathetic to a degree hardly to be expected under the circumstances. But there is no disguising the fact that there are unscrupulous editors, and it were well that the beginner be made acquainted with a few of their crimes and misdemeanors; for the results of such editorial wrong-doing are often cruel and always vexatious. And there is no reason for the perpetration of these crimes, except in the pitiable case of the medicant journals, at the sanctum door of which the wolf of bankruptcy is always growling. To them all things are permissible. They are brilliant exponents of the law of self-preservation.

Not so with the rest of the fraternity. They can present no valid excuse for their misconduct. For instance: A writer spends his spare time in stamping and addressing countless envelopes and in keeping a large miscellany of manuscripts on the road. It behooves him to keep a short lookout against their being lost, strayed, or stolen. With a newspaper,

---

*Stone, p. 300.

after the dispatch of the manuscript, he probably permits a month of silence to elapse; with a second rate magazine, six weeks; and with a first rate magazine, possibly two months. At the end of these respective periods, in the meantime having received no news of the wandering child of his head and hand, he sends off a "trailer." As a rule, this either brings him the return of the manuscript, or a note of acceptance. In either case the editor has been guilty of a misdemeanor. The manuscript is a commodity. The "time element" of the political economist enters into the determination of its value, though, forsooth, the writer is denied any monetary consideration on the same. A manufacturer, selling shoes on ninety days, demands and receives—and justly so—a larger price than if he sells for cash. Since the writer is denied this, it is the plain duty of the editor to cause as little possible delay in the examination of his wares. The very fact that the "trailer" elicited so prompt an editorial decision, proves that the editor was sinning.

But when, after long holding of the article, the editor takes no notice of the trailer, he is positively criminal. Common ethics demands a reply. And again, after several months of anxious waiting, a trailer will bring back the manuscript in the company of a stereotyped slip, upon which may be noted, among other things, the following: *Should a manuscript be held as presenting features worthy of additional consideration for a longer period than suits the convenience of the author, it will be immediately returned upon a request from the author.* Now the trailer distinctly stated that it did not wish the return of the manuscript, but was merely what it purported to be—an enquiry after its welfare and a desire to guard against its loss. Surely, the magazine in question could not in the practical nature of things have been holding more than a very limited number of manuscripts for "additional consideration;" and it would have been a light task to inform the authors interested of the state of affairs.

Having had such an experience, the present writer, fearing a repetition, allowed a manuscript to remain six months with another magazine editor. But lack-a-day, it took four trailers, thirty days apart, to compass its return. So, under such circumstances, the writer finds himself 'twixt the devil and the deep sea; on the one hand the touchiness of the editor, on the other the loss of the manuscript.

From another editor, after four months of holding, a trailer resurrected the manuscript and the accompanying note: It has merit but is too long. *While it does not suit our paper you will doubtless find a market.* In the name of common idiocy, did it take four months to reach this conclusion?

The return of manuscript written over and scrawled upon is not so unusual an occurance in the course of marketing one's wares. And it is in no pleasant spirit that a writer sits down to re-type an article mutilated by a criminal editor. But even then, compensation sometimes plays its small part. I once submitted an afternoon's hack-work, in the form of a fifteen hundred word skit, to a New York weekly paper. If accepted, my fondest dreams could not picture a check of greater magnitude than five dollars. After two months of silence, I trailed it; and back it came by return mail. It was OK'd and signed with the editor's name across the face, and edited for the press, and blue-pencilled throughout. Utterly ruined—so I thought; but in sheer despair, without removing one of the barbarian's ravages, I dispatched it to the most prominent boy's paper in the United States. Four weeks later came a check for twenty-five dollars. My maledictions upon the head of the barbarian turn to blessings. Even now my heart goes out to him. My benefactor!

The question of payment is another matter which involves much criminality. An editor, whose rates are extremely low, has no right in dealing with a new contributor, to rush his work into print without first ascertaining whether these low rates are agreeable to the vendor of manuscripts. Yet this is often done. There is also the newspaper editor who accepts and pays for work, and when the writer asks for the number in which it was published, advises him to buy the files, or asks why did he not subscribe. Then there is the editor who writes one a pleasant little note of acceptance, saying nice little things about the "contribution," but omitting to make mention of that important little matter of payment. It will be noticed that he has inserted the thin end of the wedge when he refers to the manuscript as a "contribution." Keep an eye on him! Some day he will express unholy surprise at your daring to ask for your pay. Likewise, there is the editor one has always to dun. There is a custom among the "silent, sullen people who run the magazines," to make payment within thirty days after publication. With this no fault can be found. But there certainly can be with the editor who waits sixty or ninety days, or a year, or any other length of time after publication; and who, at any time past the thirty day limit, in reply to a dun, makes instant payment and profuse apology. It is too bad, but one sometimes has to deal with such fellows. But don't be bashful with them. Give them the limit, and then dun. If it turns out to be only a mistake on their part, why, nobody is hurt and everything is rectified. If it is no mistake, then rest assured that you have made no mistake either.

⊕ ⊕ ⊕ ⊕ ⊕ ⊕ ⊕ ⊕ ⊕ ⊕ ⊕ ⊕

This glowing review is of the first volume of Frank Norris's *Epic of the Wheat*. *The Octopus,* published by Doubleday, Page & Co. in 1901, dealt with the production of wheat; *The Pit* (1903) with the distribution. For the third volume of the trilogy, Norris hoped to travel to India to study and write on the consumption of wheat during a great famine. He also planned a trilogy of novels around the battle of Gettysburg but died suddenly in San Francisco on October 25, 1902, of peritonitis. He was thirty-two.

Although contemporaries (Norris was born in Chicago but moved to the Oakland–San Francisco area in 1884), the two writers never met. They had much in common, from experiences at the University of California to literary Darwinism, and London was such a fan of Norris's work they would no doubt have gotten on famously had Norris lived longer.

⊕ ⊕ ⊕ ⊕ ⊕ ⊕ ⊕ ⊕ ⊕ ⊕ ⊕ ⊕

There it was, the Wheat, the Wheat! The little seed long planted, germinating in the deep, dark furrows of the soil, straining, swelling, suddenly in one night had burst upward to the light. The wheat had come up. It was before him, around him, everywhere illimitable, immeasurable. The winter brownness of the ground was overlaid with a little shimmer of green. The promise of the sowing was being fulfilled. The earth, the loyal mother who never failed, who never disappointed, was keeping her faith again.

Very long ago, we of the West heard it rumored that Frank Norris had it in mind to write the *Epic of the Wheat.* Nor can it be denied that many of us doubted—not the ability of Frank Norris merely, but the ability of the human, of all humans. This great, incoherent, amorphous

West! Who could grip the spirit and the essence of it, the luster and the wonder, and bind it all, definitely and sanely, within the covers of a printed book? Surely we of the West, who knew our West, may have been pardoned our lack of faith.

And now Frank Norris has done it; has, in a machine age, achieved what has been peculiarly the privilege of the man who lived in an heroic age; in short, has sung the *Epic of the Wheat.* "More power to his elbow," as Charles F. Lummis would say.

On first sight of the Valley of the San Joaquin, one cannot help but call it the "new and naked land." There is apparently little to be seen. A few isolated ranches in the midst of the vastness, no timber, a sparse population—that is all. And the men of the ranches, sweating in bitter toil, they must likewise be new and naked. So it would seem; but Norris has given breadth to both, and depth. Not only has he gone down into the soil, into the womb of the passionate earth, yearning for motherhood, the sustenance of nations; but he has gone down into the heart of its people, simple, elemental, prone to the ruder amenities of existence, growling and snarling with brute anger under cruel wrong. One needs must feel a sympathy for these men, workers and fighters, and for all of their weakness, a respect. And, after all, as Norris has well shown, their weakness is not inherent. It is the weakness of unorganization, the weakness of the force which they represent and of which they are a part, the agricultural force as opposed to the capitalistic force, the farmer against the financier, the tiller of the soil against the captain of industry.

No man, not large of heart, lacking in spontaneous sympathy, incapable of great enthusiasms, could have written *The Octopus.* Presley, the poet, dreamer and singer, is a composite fellow. So far as mere surface incident goes, he is audaciously Edwin Markham; but down in the heart of him he is Frank Norris. Presley, groping vaguely in the silence of the burning night for the sigh of the land; Presley, with his great Song of the West forever leaping up in his imagination and forever eluding him; Presley, wrestling passionately for the swing of his "thundering progression of hexameters"—who is this Presley but Norris, grappling in keen travail with his problem of *The Octopus,* and doubting often, as we of the West have doubted?

Men obtain knowledge in two ways: by generalizing from experience; by gathering to themselves the generalizations of others. As regards Frank Norris, one cannot avoid pausing for speculation. It is patent that in this, his last and greatest effort, he has laid down uncompromisingly the materialistic conception of history, or, more politely, the economic interpretation of history. Now the question arises: Did Frank Norris acquire the economic interpretation of history from the printed records of the thoughts of other men, and thus equipped, approach his problem of *The Octopus?* or, rather, did he approach it, naive and innocent? and from direct contact with the great social forces was he not forced to so generalize for himself? It is a pretty question. Will he someday tell us? Did Norris undergo the same evolution he has so strongly depicted in Presley? Presley's ultimate sociological concept came somewhat in this fashion: Shelgrim, the president and owner of the Pacific and Southwestern, laid "a thick, powerful forefinger on the table to emphasize his words. 'Try to believe this—to begin with—that railroads build themselves. Where there is a demand, sooner or later there will be a supply. Mr. Derrick, does he grow his wheat? The wheat grows itself. What does he count for? Does he supply the force? What do I count for? Do I build the railroad? You are dealing with forces, young man, when you speak of wheat and the railroads, not with men. There is the wheat, the supply. It must be carried to feed the people. There is the demand. The wheat is one force, the railroad another, and there is the law that governs them— supply and demand. Men have only little to do in the whole business. Complications may arise, conditions that bear hard on the individual— crush him, maybe—but the wheat will be carried to feed the people as inevitably as it will grow.'"

One feels disposed to quarrel with Norris for his inordinate realism. What does the world care whether Hooven's meat safe be square or oblong; whether it be lined with wire screen or mosquito netting; whether it be hung to the branches of the oak tree or to the ridgepole of the barn; whether, in fact, Hooven has a meat safe or not? "Feels disposed" is used advisedly. In truth, we cannot quarrel with him. It is confession and capitulation. The facts are against us. He *has* produced results, Titanic results. Never mind the realism, the unimportant detail, minute description, Hooven's meat safe and the rest. Let it be stated flatly that by no other method could Frank Norris or anybody else have handled the vast Valley of the San Joaquin and the no less vast-tentacled *Octopus.* Results? It was the only way to get results, the only way to paint the broad canvas he has painted, with the sunflare in his brush.

But he gives us something more than realism. Listen to this:

Once more the pendulum of the seasons swung in its mighty arc.
Then, faint and prolonged, across the levels of the ranch, he heard the engine whistling for Bonneville. Again and again, at rapid intervals in its flying course, it whistled for road crossings, for sharp curves, for trestles; ominous notes, hoarse, bellowing, ringing with the accents of menace and defiance; and abruptly Presley saw again, in his imagination, the galloping monster, the terror of steel and steam, with its single eye, cyclopean, red, shooting from horizon to horizon; but saw it now as

the symbol of a vast power, huge, terrible, flinging the echo of its thunder over all the reaches of the valley, leaving blood and destruction in its path; the leviathan, with tentacles of steel clutching into the soil, the soulless Force, the iron-hearted Power, the monster, the Colossus, the Octopus.

The direct brutality of ten thousand acres of wheat, nothing but wheat as far as the eye could see, stunned her a little. There was something vaguely indecent in the sight, this food of the people, this elemental force, this basic energy, weltering here under the sun in all the unconscious nakedness of a sprawling, primordial Titan.

Everywhere throughout the great San Joaquin, unseen and unheard, a thousand ploughs up-stirred the land, tens of thousands of shears clutched deep into the warm, moist soil. It was the long, stroking caress, vigorous, male, powerful, for which the Earth seemed panting. The heroic embrace of a multitude of iron hands, gripping down into the brown, warm flesh of the land that quivered responsive and passionate under this rude advance, so robust as to be almost an assault, so violent as to be veritably brutal. There, under the sun and under the speckless sheen of the sky, the wooing of the Titan began, the vast primal passion, the two world-forces, the elemental Male and Female, locked in a colossal embrace, at grapples in the throes of an infinite desire, at once terrible and divine, knowing no law, untamed, savage, natural, sublime.

Many men, and women, too, pass through the pages of *The Octopus*, but one, greatest of all, we cannot forbear mentioning in passing—Annixter. Annixter, rough almost to insolence, direct in speech, intolerant in his opinions, relying upon absolutely no one but himself; crusty of temper, bullying of disposition, a ferocious worker, and as widely trusted as he was widely hated; obstinate and contrary, cantankerous, and deliciously afraid of "feemale women"—this is Annixter. He is worth knowing. In such cunning fashion has Norris blown the breath of life into him, that his death comes with a shock which is seldom produced by deaths in fiction. Osterman, laying his head on his arms like a tired man going to rest, and Delaney, crawling instinctively out of the blood-welter to die in the growing wheat; but it is Annixter, instantly killed, falling without movement, for whom we first weep. A living man there died.

Well, the promise of *Moran* and *McTeague* has been realized. Can we ask more? Yet we have only the first of the trilogy. *The Epic of the Wheat* is no little thing. Content with *The Octopus*, we may look forward to *The Pit* and *The Wolf*. We shall not doubt this time.

REVIEW OF "FOMÁ GORDYÉEFF"

(*Impressions*, November, 1901)

⊕ ⊕ ⊕ ⊕ ⊕ ⊕ ⊕ ⊕ ⊕ ⊕ ⊕ ⊕

In a letter to Anna Strunsky in the spring of 1902, London wrote: "I am to proceed right now to a review of 'Foma Gordyeeff' for *Impressions*. Have you read it yet? . . . It is a wonderful book. I wish I could allow myself the freshness of a whole day to do it instead of going at it as I now shall, jaded and tired."*

Maxim Górky (1868-1936) lived the life of a vagabond in his native Russia after leaving home at age fourteen. His early short stories were romanticized accounts of people he met in his wanderings. In about 1900, at the time London's professional writing career began, Górky abandoned romanticism for works of social protest—such as *Fomá Gordyéeff* (later published as *The Man Who Was Afraid*), his first novel. The review appeared in London's *Revolution & Other Essays* (1910).

⊕ ⊕ ⊕ ⊕ ⊕ ⊕ ⊕ ⊕ ⊕ ⊕ ⊕ ⊕

"What, without asking, hither hurried *Whence?*
And, without asking, *Whither* hurried hence!
Oh, many a Cup of this forbidden Wine
Must drown the memory of that insolence!"

Fomá Gordyéeff is a big book—not only is the breadth of Russia in it, but the expanse of life. Yet, though in each land, in this world of marts and exchanges, this age of trade and traffic, passionate figures rise up and demand of life what its fever is, in *Fomá Gordyéeff* it is a Russian who so rises up and demands. For Górky, the Bitter One, is essentially a Russian in his grasp on the facts of life and in his treatment.

---

*Charmian K. London, vol. 1, p. 375.

All the Russian self-analysis and insistent introspection are his. And, like his brother Russians, ardent, passionate protest impregnates his work. There is a purpose to it. He writes because he has something to say which the world should hear. From that clenched fist of his, light and airy romances, pretty and sweet and beguiling, do not flow, but realities— yes, big and brutal and repulsive, but real.

He raises the cry of the miserable and the despised, and in a masterly arraignment of commercialism, protests against social conditions, against the grinding of the faces of the poor and weak, and the self-pollution of the rich and strong, in their mad lust for place and power. It is to be doubted strongly if the average bourgeois, smug and fat and prosperous, can understand this man Fomá Gordyéeff. The rebellion in his blood is something to which their own does not thrill. To them it will be inexplicable that this man, with his health and his millions, could not go on living as his class lived, keeping regular hours at desk and stock exchange, driving close contracts, underbidding his competitors, and exulting in the business disasters of his fellows. It would appear so easy, and, after such a life, well appointed and eminently respectable, he could die. "Ah," Fomá will interrupt rudely,—he is given to rude interruptions,—"if to die and disappear is the end of these money-grubbing years, why money-grub?" And the bourgeois whom he rudely interrupted will not understand. Nor did Mayákin understand as he labored holily with his wayward godson.

"Why do you brag?" Fomá bursts out upon him. "What have you to brag about? Your son—where is he? Your daughter—where is she? Ekh, you manager of life! Come, now, you're clever, you know everything— tell me, why do you live? Why do you accumulate money? Aren't you going to die? Well, what then?" And Mayákin finds himself speechless and without answer, but unshaken and unconvinced.

Receiving by heredity the fierce, bull-like nature of his father plus the passive indomitableness and groping spirit of his mother, Fomá, proud and rebellious, is repelled by the selfish, money-seeking environment into which he is born. Ignát, his father, and Mayákin, the godfather, and all the horde of successful merchants singing their paean of the strong and the praises of merciless, remorseless *laissez faire,* cannot entice him. Why? he demands. This is a nightmare, this life! It is without significance! What does it all mean? What is there underneath? What is the meaning of that which is underneath?

"You do well to pity people," Ignát tells Fomá, the boy, "only you must use judgment with your pity. First consider the man, find out what he is like, what use can be made of him; and if you see that he is a strong and capable man, help him if you like. But if a man is weak, not inclined to work—spit upon him and go your way. And you must know that when a man complains about everything, and cries out and groans,— he is not worth more than two kopéks, he is not worthy of pity, and will be of no use to you if you do help him."

Such the frank and militant commercialism, bellowed out between glasses of strong liquor. Now comes Mayákin, speaking softly and without satire:

"Eh, my boy, what is a beggar? A beggar is a man who is forced, by fate, to remind us of Christ; he is Christ's brother; he is the bell of the Lord, and rings in life for the purpose of awakening our conscience, of stirring up the satiety of man's flesh. He stands under the windows and sings, 'For Christ's sa-ake!' and by that chant he reminds us of Christ, of His holy command to help our neighbor. But men have so ordered their lives that it is utterly impossible for them to act in accordance with Christ's teaching, and Jesus Christ has become entirely superfluous to us. Not once, but, in all probability, a thousand times, we have given Him over to be crucified, but still we cannot banish Him from out lives so long as His poor brethren sing His name in the streets and remind us of Him. And so now we have hit on the idea of shutting up the beggars in such special buildings, so that they may not roam about the streets and stir up our consciences."

But Fomá will have none of it. He is neither to be enticed nor cajoled. The cry of his nature is for light. He must have light. And in burning revolt he goes seeking the meaning of life. "His thoughts embraced all those petty people who toiled at hard labor. It was strange—why did they live? What satisfaction was it to them to live on the earth? All they did was to perform their dirty, arduous toil, eat poorly; they were miserably clad, addicted to drunkenness. One was sixty years old, but he still toiled side by side with young men. And they all presented themselves to Fomá's imagination as a huge heap of worms, who were swarming over the earth merely to eat."

He becomes the living interrogation of life. He cannot begin living until he knows what living means, and he seeks its meaning vainly. "Why should I try to live life when I do not know what life is?" he objects when Mayákin strives with him to return and manage his business. Why should men fetch and carry for him? be slaves to him and his money?

"Work is not everything to a man," he says; "it is not true that justification lies in work. . . . Some people never do any work at all, all their lives long—yet they live better than the toilers. Why is that? And what justification have I? And how will all the people who give their orders justify themselves? What have they lived for? But my idea is that everybody ought, without fail, to know solidly what he is living for. Is it possible that a man is born to toil, accumulate money, build a house, beget children, and—die? No; life means something in itself. ... A man has been born, has lived, has died—why? All of us must consider why we are living, by God, we must! There is no sense in our life—there is no sense at all. Some are rich—they have money enough for a thousand men all to themselves—and they live without occupation; others bow their backs in toil all their life, and they haven't a penny."

But Fomá can only be destructive. He is not constructive. The dim groping spirit of his mother and the curse of his environment press too heavily upon him, and he is crushed to debauchery and madness. He does not drink because liquor tastes good in his mouth. In the vile companions who purvey to his baser appetites he finds no charm. It is all utterly despicable and sordid, but thither his quest leads him and he follows the quest. He knows that everything is wrong, but he cannot right it, cannot tell why. He can only attack and demolish. "What justification have you all in the sight of God? Why do you live?" he demands of the conclave of merchants, of life's successes. "You have not constructed life—you have made a cesspool! You have disseminated filth and stifling exhalations by your deeds. Have you any conscience? Do you remember God? A five-kopék piece—that is your God! But you have expelled your conscience!"

Like the cry of Isaiah, "Go to, now, ye rich men, weep and howl for your misfortunes that shall come upon you," is Fomá's: "You bloodsuckers! You live on other people's strength; you work with other people's hands! For all this you shall be made to pay! You shall perish—you shall be called to account for all! For all—to the last little teardrop!"

Stunned by this puddle of life, unable to make sense of it, Fomá questions, and questions vainly, whether of Sófya Medýnsky in her drawing-room of beauty, or in the foulest depths of the first chance courtesan's heart. Linboff, whose books contradict one another, cannot help him; nor can the pilgrims on crowded steamers, nor the verse writers and harlots in dives and boozing-kens. And so, wondering, pondering, perplexed, amazed, whirling through the mad whirlpool of life, dancing the dance of death, groping for the nameless, indefinite something, the magic formula, the essence, the intrinsic fact, the flash of light through the murk and dark,—the rational sanction for existence, in short,—Fomá Gordyéeff goes down to madness and death.

It is not a pretty book, but it is a masterful interrogation of life—not the life universal, but of life particular, the social life of today. It is not nice; neither is the social life of today nice. One lays the book down sick at heart—sick for life with all its "lyings and its lusts." But it is a healthy book. So fearful is its portrayal of social disease, so ruthless its stripping of the painted charms from vice, that its tendency cannot but be strongly for good. It is a goad, to prick sleeping human consciences awake and drive them into the battle for humanity.

But no story is told, nothing is finished, some one will object. Surely, when Sásha leaped overboard and swam to Fomá, something happened. It was pregnant with possibilities. Yet it was not finished, was not decisive. She left him to go with the son of a rich vodka-maker. And all that was best in Sófya Medýnsky was quickened when she looked upon Fomá with the look of the Mother-Woman. She might have been a power for good in his life, she might have shed light into it and lifted him up to safety and honor and understanding. Yet she went away next day, and he never saw her again. No story is told, nothing is finished.

Ah, but surely the story of Fomá Gordyéeff is told; his life is finished, as lives are being finished each day around us. Besides, it is the way of life, and the art of Górky is the art of realism. But it is less tedious realism than that of Tolstoy or Turgenev. It lives and breathes from page to page with a swing and dash and go that they rarely attain. Their mantle has fallen on his young shoulders, and he promises to wear it royally.

Even so, but so helpless, hopeless, terrible is this life of Fomá Gordyéeff that we would be filled with profound sorrow for Górky did we not know that he has come up out of the Valley of the Shadow. That he hopes, we know, else would he not now be festering in a Russian prison because he is brave enough to live the hope he feels. He knows life, why and how it should be lived. And in conclusion, this one thing is manifest: Fomá Gordyéeff is no mere statement of an intellectual problem. For as he lived and interrogated living, so, in sweat and blood and travail, has Górky lived.

Piedmont, California
November, 1901

REVIEW OF "LINCOLN AND OTHER POEMS"

(*San Francisco Sunday Examiner Magazine,* November 10, 1901)

⊕ ⊕ ⊕ ⊕ ⊕ ⊕ ⊕ ⊕ ⊕ ⊕ ⊕ ⊕

Edwin Markham (1852-1940) was an Oregon-born California poet best known, as London indicates in this review, for the poem "The Man With the Hoe" (1899), written as a protest against the degradation and exploitation of labor and inspired by a painting by Jean François Millet.

⊕ ⊕ ⊕ ⊕ ⊕ ⊕ ⊕ ⊕ ⊕ ⊕ ⊕ ⊕

When "The Man With the Hoe" took the world by storm it was deemed by many a rocket-like flare, the one spark of genius flashing up and out, the one song of the man Markham and a song that was sung. Comes now his second volume, *Lincoln and Other Poems,* a sheaf of songs to give the lie to hasty opinion and false judgment. For Mr. Markham's voice is strong and clear. He pipes no quavering lays; nor does he sing half-heartedly; nor does he wistfully remember the greatness and the glory of the things that were. His theme is the Here and Now and Yet to Be. Passion and prophecy are in his utterance, joy and a great gladness; and his words are winged with messages of Love and Hope, of Comradeship and Brotherhood.

He believes in the youth of the world, and it is all a wonder and delight. All things are yet young. Men and the world have but achieved their adolescence; they are just beginning to realize themselves. The dawn has a marvelous fascination for him. Throughout his poems he revels in the beauty of it and the glow. In it he finds a fair and radiant promise, as in this twentieth century he finds the world just coming to its dawn. As "the Muse of Labor" sings for him, so is it with him:

> The warm first rush of rapture in my song,
> The first faint light of morning on my hair.

Next to "The Man With the Hoe," certainly "Lincoln, the Man of the People," the initial poem in his new volume, is the most remarkable thing

Mr. Markham has done. For the man Lincoln, who said, "God must have loved the common people, he made so many of them," it required a man Markham to voice full appreciation and understanding. When the Norn-mother made Lincoln, "A man to meet the mortal need":

> She took the tried clay of the common road—
> Clay warm yet with the genial heat of Earth,
> Dished through it all a strain of prophecy;
> Then mixed a laughter with the serious stuff.
>
> . . . .
>
> The color of the ground was in him, the red earth;
> The tang and odor of the primal things—
> The rectitude and patience of the rocks;
> The gladness of the wind that shakes the corn;
> The courage of the bird that dares the sea;
> The justice of the rain that loves all leaves. . .

What more splendid characterization of the "Great Commoner" is possible? And we who know and love our Lincoln, how it comes home to our hearts and brings the gush of warm tears to our eyes. "Then mixed a laughter with the serious stuff."

> He held his place—
> Held the long purpose like a growing tree—
> Held on through blame and flattered not at praise.
> And when he fell in whirlwind, he went down
> As when a kingly cedar green with boughs
> Goes down with a great shout upon the hills,
> And leaves a lonesome place against the sky.

Not forgetting Walt Whitman's "O Captain, My Captain," wet with tears and halting with half-sobs, it is not too much to state that in Mr. Markham's "Lincoln" the last word has been said. The poem itself is a "stuff to wear for centuries." In the centuries to come it is inevitable that it shall be coupled with the name of Lincoln. If its author had made no other bid for fame, this one bid would suffice. It is an inspired biography, an imperishable portraiture of a man, and so long as the memory of Lincoln endures will it endure.

But there are other poems, and big poems, in this book. There is "The Sower," written after seeing Millet's painting of the same title, which opens so wonderfully:

> Soon will the lonesome cricket by the stone
> Begin to hush the night; and lightly blown
> Field fragrances will fill the fading blue—
> Old furrow-scents that Ancient Eden knew.
> Soon in the upper twilight will be heard
> The winging whisper of a homing bird.

Surely the true poetic quality is poured in large measure into "The Witness of the Dust" as witness these four stanzas:

> Voices are crying from the dust of Tyre,
>   From Baalbec and the stones of Babylon—
> "We raised our pillars upon Self-Desire,
>   And perished from the large gaze of the sun."
>
> Eternity was on the pyramid,
>   And immortality on Greece and Rome,
> But in them all the ancient Traitor hid,
>   And so they tottered like unstable foam.
>
> There was no substance in their soaring hopes;
>   The voice of Thebes is now a desert cry;
> A spider bars the road with filmy ropes,
>   Where once the feet of Carthage thundered by.
>
> A bittern booms where once fair Helen laughed;
>   A thistle nods where once the Forum poured;
> A lizard lifts and listens on a shaft,
>   Where once of old the Coliseum roared.

Mr. Markham looked into "The Wallstreet Pit" when Northern Pacific went skyward and the market went mad:

> I see a hell of faces surge and whirl
> Like maelstrom in the ocean—faces lean
> And fleshless as the talons of a hawk—
> Hot faces like the faces of the wolves
> That track the traveler fleeing through the night—
> Grim faces shrunken up and fallen in,
> Deep-ploughed like weather-eaten bark of oak—
> Drawn faces like the faces of the dead,
> Grown suddenly old upon the brink of Earth.
>   . . . .

Oh, saner are the hearts on stiller ways!
Thrice happier they who, far from these wild hours,
Grow softly as the apples on a bough.
Wiser the ploughman with his scudding blade,
Turning a straight fresh furrow down a field—
Wiser the herdsman whistling to his heart
In the long shadows at the break of day—
Wiser the fisherman with quiet hand,
Slanting his sail against the evening wind.

By many mouths had Mr. Markham been branded pessimistic. But one can hardly read his poems and accept this judgment. His words are warm with Faith and Hope. He has an unwavering belief in a new heaven and a new earth, a new humanity, a fuller democracy, a broader brotherhood. Either Mr. Markham is no pessimist, or else pessimism has lost its evil and become a goodly thing to strive after.

First and last, above and beneath and throughout, he is an optimist. But his is not the smug complacent optimism of the little soulless, selfish men, but the big-hearted optimism of the doer and fighter, of the doer and fighter who strives to overcome hurts and hindrances. It is a very good world, Mr. Markham holds, but it may still be a better world. Let us then make it a better world.

This is discontent, but it is not the discontent of pessimism. It is a noble discontent which is the secret of progress. Only the pusillanimous are content. Heart's desires are divine discontents. Only the unsatisfied do things. The satisfied do nothing. Unsatisfaction is the stimulus to achievement. Satisfaction is destruction and leads down to the chamber of death.

And because of this, Mr. Markham has a sublime faith in the soil. There he finds the inchoate deeds, the nascent captains, the power and glory of man and of life. He feels a finer delight in the cowherd or the plowman than in the pomps and pageants of courts and kings—in the one the strength and virtue of the soil, in the other the emptiness of sham and the impotence of age. Old men and old ideas are not good in the young world of a young humanity. There must be freshness and newness; there must be vigor and virility, stout blows for the Cause and doughty deeds; and there must be golden dreams and luring ideals into living facts. The tough Teutonic fiber of his being, chastened and sublimated by the heats of twenty centuries, still finds the world a field for fighting, not for lust and conquest, but for Right and Justice.

> There is a new Sphinx watching by the road!
> Its name is Labor, and the world must hear—
> Must hear and answer its dread question—yes,
> Or perish as the tribes of yesterday.

He believes in the common man, and in bright destiny, and that whoso stands between must perish. What he believes he breathes into his poetry, and Purpose is writ large. He is no "idle singer of an empty day." Life is not life without purpose and is death in the midst of life. Whoso stands between is dead, dead and foredoomed and damned. As for the common man: dead, dead and foredoomed and damned. As for the common man:

> Not his the lurching of an aimless clod,
> For with the august stare of a god—
> A gesture that is question and command—
> He hurls the bread of nations from his hand;
> And in the passion of the gesture flings
> His fierce resentment in the face of kings.
> . . . .
> This is the Earth-god of the latter day,
> Treading with solemn joy the upward way;
> Democracy whose sure insurgent stride
> Jars kingdoms to their ultimate stone of pride.

Every master is supposed to have had a master, but in style what master has Mr. Markham had? It were a difficult and probably bootless task to seek him out. Mr. Markham is himself, or as nearly so, as gregarious as man can possibly be. His power is his own, his treatment his own. While he is remarkable for his largeness of grasp, a vivid concreteness characterizes his work. His phrases ring like trumpet calls; and there is an epic sweep in his conceptions and his figures. And his figures, always clean, clear-cut, have in them all the primitiveness of the elements and the earth. "With wind of laughter and with rain of joy," "Thunder and earthquake crouch beyond the gate"—so he grips and uses the great natural forces, all potent to please or terrify, which have registered themselves in the heritage of the race.

We have had laureates of kings and emperors, of heroes and of races, and now comes Mr. Markham, laureate of the common man. We have had Shelley's "Men of England," and Morris' "Songs of Labor," but their most ardent admirers must grant that they have never sung the song of labor as Mr. Markham sings it. He himself is "The Muse of Labor," and full well he preaches the gospel and the dignity of work. To him:

More than white incense rising to the dome,
Is a field well furrowed or a nail sent home.

And as he somewhere says, "The Book of Kings is closed, and the Book of the People is opening."

One cannot better conclude this appreciation of Mr. Markham's work than with his own words to himself:

> Give me heart-touch with all that live,
>   And strength to speak my word;
> But if that be denied me, give
>   The strength to live unheard.

⊕ ⊕ ⊕ ⊕ ⊕ ⊕ ⊕ ⊕ ⊕ ⊕ ⊕ ⊕

By the time this piece was published on the work of modern editors "expressing literature in terms of cash," London's third book, *Children of the Frost,* and his sixty-third short story had been published. He was a month away from seeing his first adult novel, *A Daughter of the Snows,* in print and he very clearly knew the nature of the magazines and book-publishers and what they must publish for circulation and life.

⊕ ⊕ ⊕ ⊕ ⊕ ⊕ ⊕ ⊕ ⊕ ⊕ ⊕ ⊕

The literary aspirant these days, or rather the literary artist-aspirant, or rather the literary artist-aspirant with active belly and empty purse, finds himself face to face with a howling paradox. Being an aspirant, he is conclusively a man who has not arrived, and a man who has not arrived has no pull on popularity. Being a man, and empty-pursed, he must eat. Being an artist, possessing the true artist-soul, his delight is to pour out in printed speech the joy of his heart. And this is the paradox he faces and must compass: *How and in what fashion must he sing the joy of his heart that the printed speech thereof may bring him bread?*

This does not appear a paradox. At least it does not appear a paradox to the merely literary aspirant; nor does it so appear to the man with the artist-soul and the full purse. The one, unwitting of artistry, finds it simple enough to supply public demand. The other, unwitting of sordid necessity, is satisfied to wait till he has created public demand. As for the man who has arrived, he does not count. He has compassed the paradox. But the man dreaming greatly and pressed by sordid necessity, he is the man who must confront the absolute contradiction. He is the man who cannot pour his artist-soul into his work and exchange that work for bread and meat. The world is strangely and coldly averse to his exchanging the joy of his heart for the solace of his stomach. And to him is it given to discover that what the world prized most it demands least, and that what it clamors the loudest after it does not prize at all.

It is a way the world has, and it is especially the way of the twentieth century, at least so far as printed speech is concerned. The streak of yellow which is condemned in journalism crops out in the magazines. Popularity is the key-note. The advertisements bring the cash; the circulation brings the advertisements; the magazine brings the circulation; problem: what must be printed in the magazine so that it may bring the circulation that brings the advertisements that bring the cash? Wherefore the editor is dominated by the business manager, who keeps his eye on the circulation, or else the editor is sufficiently capable of keeping his own eye on the circulation. And the circulation must be large, in order that the advertisements be many, in order that the cash be much. So the editor prints in the pages of his magazine that which a large number of people want to read. He does not print what they ought to read, for his function is to pander, not to propagandize.

This is frankly commercial. And why should it not be frankly commercial in a commercial age? The deepest values of life are today expressed in terms of cash. That which is most significant today is the making of money. When our late chief magistrate was laid to rest, the deepest respect New York City could show was to stop its railways for five minutes, to stop the sending of its telegraph messages for half a minute—to stop, respectively, making money for five minutes and for half a minute. And New York City was sincere. The depth of her grief can be plumbed only by the length of her act. So vital, so significant, was the making of money to her, that to cease making money for five minutes and for half a minute was the profoundest possible expression of her sympathy and sorrow—vastly profounder than fifty-two weeks of resolution and fast. It was the undiminished essence of the spirit of sacrifice which lurks in the well-springs of being, which impelled the shepherd of a pastoral age to offer up the fat firstlings of his flock; which impelled Abraham in the land of Moriah to offer up Isaac, the son of his loins, as a burnt offering of his fealty to God; which impelled New York City to cease making money for five minutes and for half a minute.

This being so—the making of money the most vital fact in life today— it is only fair that literature be expressed in terms of cash. And it is not only fair but it is good business sense for an editor to print in the pages of his magazine that which a large number of people want to read. This comes of admitting the mass into living, or of being forced to admit the mass into living (which is the same thing); of giving the mass good houses, good clothes, free public schools, and civil and religious liberty. It is the penalty of democracy. Poise of power cannot be expected of the newly manumitted, of the newly made powerful. The uncultured mass cannot become cultured in a twinkling of an eye. The mass, totally without art-concepts, cannot, in the instant of achieving freedom, achieve the loftiest of art-concepts. And wherever the mass is admitted into living, wherever the common men for the first time grip hold of life, there must follow a falling away from all that is fine of tone and usage, a diminishing, a descending to a something which is average, which is humanly average.

The Athenians of two thousand years ago present the remarkable spectacle of a cultured people. But in contemplating this spectacle we are prone to forget that each Athenian stood on the head and shoulders of ten slaves. We are prone to forget that, had every slave been given equal voice and vote in Athenian affairs, the culture of the Athenians would have presented quite another and unremarkable spectacle. And today we are likewise prone to forget that we have but yesterday admitted to equal voice and vote our own peasants and serfs, our villains and clouts and clowns. For as surely as a clout or clown is made into a free man, taught to read and write and to think somewhat dimly, and given three dollars a day for the labor of his head and hand, just so surely will that clout or clown, with ten cents in his hand and a desire for a magazine in his heart, become a power in the land. His free and equal voice will be heard, and the editor will listen to it; for of a majority of such is a large number of people composed.

And because a large number of people have ten cents in their hands—or twenty-five cents, the sum matters not—the editor must express literature, not merely in terms of cash, but in terms of the cash of the large number of people. In other words, the immediate appraisement of literature is made by the large number of people. The newly manumitted and artless determine what manner of speech the business manager may permit the editor to print on the pages of his magazine. The editor becomes the mouthpiece of the newly manumitted and artless. What they want, he wants. He is the purveyor, the middleman, the purchaser of goods for a large number of people who have not the time and training to dicker and bicker for themselves. And he goes into the highways and byways, where men hawk the wares of their brain, and selects his stock in trade. And, as the editor receives his bread from the hands of the large number of people, so, through the editor, the writers hawking their wares receive their bread. The large number of people feed them, and whosoever feeds a man is that man's master. And as masters, making the immediate appraisement of literature, the large number of people demand literature that is immediate.

Now the ultimate appraisement of literature is none of their business.

They, with their dimes and quarters in their hands, and their free and equal thumbs turned up or down, determine what shall live for today and for this month; and, consequently, with their dimes and quarters (which are bread and meat), they determine what writers are to live for this day and month.

But while the large number of people are the masters so far as immediate appraisement is concerned, a different and small number of people make the ultimate appraisement. These men, figuratively, stand upon the heads and shoulders of the others. These final arbiters, using the word in its largest sense, may be called the "critics." They are not to be confounded with the men who review books, so many a week, for publications in the advertising pages of which the same books appear. Nor are they necessarily the men who speak professionally, nor need they speak through print at all. But they are the men, 'spite of deaf ears, who say the good word for the worthy thing and damn balderdash, and who continue to say the good word and to damn balderdash until they attract a crowd. They may be likened to the schoolmaster in the average classroom. The boys may find greater delight in a buzzing bottlefly than in cube root; but the schoolmaster hammers, hammers, hammers, until he has painfully hammered cube root into their heads. Theirs is the immediate appraisement of knowledge, his the ultimate. And so with the large number of people and the critics. The critic hammers, hammers, hammers, praising and blaming, interpreting, explaining, making clear and plain, on his own responsibility guerdoning the artist and forcing the large number of people finally to guerdon him.

But the critics, who may be called the discerning, are the small number of people; and though they, too, hold dimes and quarters in their hands, the dimes and quarters are not many, and the editor, busily expressing literature in terms of cash, can give them little heed. Not that the editor does not slip in a worthy thing now and again. But he does it sometimes through mistake, and ofttimes without mistake and in fear and trembling, tentatively, anxiously, with a flutter of many doubts.

Comes now the artist-aspirant to spill his unsung song on the typewritten page, to exchange the joy of his heart for the solace of his stomach, to make stuff that shall live and at the same time to live himself. Unless he be an extremely fortunate artist-aspirant, he quickly finds that singing into a typewriter and singing out of a magazine are quite unrelated performances; that soul's delights and heart's desires, pressed into enduring art-forms, are not necessarily immediate literature; in short, that the master he seeks to serve for bread and glory will have none of him. And while he sits down to catch his breath he sees the merely literary aspirants forging past him, droves of them, content to take the bread and let the glory go. People in general differentiate into the large number of people and the small number of people; bread and glory are divorced; and where he dreamed of serving one master he finds two masters. The one master he must serve that he may live, the other that his work may live, and what the one demands most of all the other has little or no use for.

"Go ahead," say the discerning, patting him on the shoulder. "We're with you. Turn out your masterpieces and we'll write your name high in the temple of fame." But they are the small number of people, their dimes and quarters few, and the editor does not listen to them. "I don't want masterpieces," says the editor. "I cater to a large number of people of a certain calibre. Give me something, anything, never mind what it is so long as it fits that calibre, and I'll write the figures high for you on the national bank."

"Truth alone endures," whisper the discerning. "Be a far-visioner and we shall remember you, and our children and our children's children shall remember you." And the artist-aspirant sits him down and gives form and substance to eternal and beautiful truth. "Too strong," says the editor. "Which is another way of saying 'Too true,'" the artist-aspirant objects. "Quite true," the editor replies. "It would cost me a thousand subscribers. Learn, O bright-browed youth, that I want no far-visioning; my subscribers are loth to part with their honest money for far-visioning." "You ... don't ... want ... truth ... ?" the artist-aspirant quavers. "Not so," says the editor, "but it were well to learn that there be truth and truth and yet again truth. We do want truth, but it must be truth toned down, truth diluted, truth insipid, harmless truth, conventionalized truth, trimmed truth. There you have it! Trim your truth, young man. Get out your shears and clip, and I'll do business with you." "But I clip my immortality," cries the artist-aspirant. "You have made a mistake." says the editor finally and firmly; "I do not run an immortality market. Goodday."

And so the artist-aspirant sits down to generalize afresh upon his unsung songs and his sordid necessities. How and in what fashion must he sing the joy of his heart that the printed speech thereof may bring him bread? And he is puzzled at the men who have arrived, who (within limits), month after month, are running the truth that is in them in the magazines. And he is more puzzled when he realizes that they have compassed the paradox which confronts him. There's the sketch by Jones, the GREAT JONES, and the study by the IMMORTAL JENKINS; and yet the editor distinctly told him that such sketches and studies were not at all in demand. And there's another somewhat daring bit of verse by Mrs.

Maybelle, the ONLY MRS. MAYBELLE. He struck the same note in fresher and more vigorous song, yet the same editor sent it back.

"My dear sir," says the editor in answer to his plaint, "these noted writers you mention speak with authority. They have reputations. The large number of people will always listen to the one who speaks with authority, even though they do not understand him. Go and get a reputation and I'll publish anything you write, that is—er—almost anything, and at least all the rot. I'll even go so far as to publish some of the very things I am now refusing." "But if you refuse to publish them now," demands the artist-aspirant, "how under the sun am I ever to get a reputation?" "That," says the editor, "is your business, not mine."

And the artist-aspirant either subsides, taking the bread and letting the glory go, or, without dying, he compasses the paradox, even as Jones, Jenkins, and Maybelle compassed it. As to how he compasses it? That, dear reader, as the editor told him, is his business. Yours to be grateful that he does compass it.

⊕ ⊕ ⊕ ⊕ ⊕ ⊕ ⊕ ⊕ ⊕ ⊕ ⊕ ⊕

London's early struggles as a writer are seen again in *Martin Eden* (1909), *John Barleycorn* (1913)—excerpts from both of which are included in this volume—and elsewhere.

The incident involving the $5 for a four-thousand-word story is true: *Overland Monthly* promised that sum for Jack's "To the Man on the Trail" which they published in January, 1899. To get even the $5, London had to storm the *Overland* office and almost literally shake the money from the pockets of the impecunious editors. The editors apparently did not hold the incident against the young writer, and upped his pay to $7.50 for "The White Silence" which they published the following month.

The life-saving, career-deciding $40 from *The Black Cat* was for the story "A Thousand Deaths."* See London's introduction to *The Red Hot Dollar & Other Stories From The Black Cat* in this volume.

⊕ ⊕ ⊕ ⊕ ⊕ ⊕ ⊕ ⊕ ⊕ ⊕ ⊕ ⊕

As soon as a fellow sells two or three things to the magazines, or successfully inveigles some publisher into bringing out a book, his friends all ask him how he managed to do it. So it is fair to conclude that the placing of books and of stories with the magazines is a highly interesting performance.

I know it is highly interesting to me; vitally interesting, I may say. I used to run through endless magazines and newspapers, wondering all the time how the writers of all that stuff managed to place it. To show that the possession of this knowledge was vitally important to me, let me state that I had many liabilities and no assets, no income, several mouths to feed, and for landlady a poor widow woman whose imperative necessities

---

*Reprinted in Dale L. Walker, *Curious Fragments: Jack London's Tales of Fantasy Fiction.* Port Washington, N.Y.: Kennikat Press, 1975.

demanded that I should pay my rent with some degree of regularity. This was my economic situation when I buckled on the harness and went up against the magazines.

Further, and to the point, I knew positively nothing about it. I lived in California, far from the great publishing centers. I did not know what an editor looked like. I did not know a soul who had ever published anything; nor yet again, a soul, with the exception of my own, who had ever tried to write anything, much less tried to publish it.

I had no one to give me tips, no one's experience to profit by. So I sat down and wrote in order to get an experience of my own. I wrote everything—short stories, articles, anecdotes, jokes, essays, sonnets, ballads, vilanelles, triolets, songs, light plays in iambic tetrameter, and heavy tragedies in blank verse. These various creations I stuck into envelopes, enclosed return postage, and dropped into the mail. Oh, I was prolific. Day by day my manuscripts mounted up, till the problem of finding stamps for them became as great as that of making life livable for my widow landlady.

All my manuscripts came back. They continued to come back. The process seemed like the working of a soulless machine. I dropped the manuscript into the mail box. After the lapse of a certain approximate length of time, the manuscript was brought back to me by the postman. Accompanying it was a stereotyped rejection slip. A part of the machine, some cunning arrangement of cogs and cranks at the other end (it could not have been a living, breathing man with blood in his veins) had transferred the manuscript to another envelope, taken the stamps from the inside and pasted them outside, and added the rejection slip.

This went on for some months. I was still in the dark. I had not yet gained the smallest particle of experience. Concerning which was the more marketable, poetry or prose, jokes or sonnets, short stories or essays, I knew no more than when I began. I had vague ideas, however, dim and hazy ideas to the effect that a minimum rate of ten dollars a thousand words was paid; that if I only published two or three things the editors would clamor for my wares; that a manuscript held in some editor's hands for the small matter of four or five months did not necessarily mean a manuscript that was sold.

Concerning this minimum rate of ten dollars a thousand words, a thing in which I fondly believed, I must confess that I had gleaned it from some Sunday supplement. Likewise I must confess the beautiful and touching modesty with which I aspired. Let other men, thought I, receive the maximum rate, whatever marvelous sum it may be. As for myself, I shall always be content to receive the minimum rate. And, once I get started, I shall do no more than three thousand words a day, five days only in the week.

This will give me plenty of recreation, while I shall be earning six hundred dollars a month without overstocking the market.

As I say, the machine worked on for several months, and then, one morning, the postman brought me a letter, mark you, not a long thick one but a short thin one, and from a magazine. My stamp problem and my landlady problem were pressing me cruelly, and this short, thin letter from a magazine would of a certainty solve both problems in short order.

I could not open the letter right away. It seemed a sacred thing. It contained the written words of an editor. The magazine he represented I imagined ranked in the first class. I knew it held a four-thousand-word story of mine. What will it be? I asked. The minimum rate, I answered, modest as ever; forty dollars of course. Having thus guarded myself against any possible kind of disappointment, I opened the letter and read what I thought would be blazed in letters of fire on my memory for all time. Alas! the years are few, yet I have forgotten. But the gist of the letter was coldly to the effect that my story was available, that they would print it the next summer, and that they would pay me for it the sum of five dollars.

Five dollars! A dollar and a quarter a thousand! That I did not die right there and then convinces me that I am possessed of a singular ruggedness of soul which will permit me to survive and ultimately qualify for the oldest inhabitant.

Five dollars! When? The editor did not state. I didn't have even a stamp with which to convey my acceptation or rejection of his offer. Just then the landlady's little girl knocked at the back door. Both problems were clamoring more compellingly than ever for solution. It was plain there was no such thing as a minimum rate. Nothing remained but to get out and shovel coal. I had done it before and earned more money at it. I resolved to do it again; and I certainly should have, had it not been for the *Black Cat.*

Yes, the *Black Cat.* The postman brought me an offer from it of forty dollars for a four-thousand-word story, which same was more lengthy than strengthy, if I would grant permission to cut it down half. This was equivalent to a twenty-dollar rate. Grant permission? I told them they could cut it down two-halves if they'd only send the money along, which they did, by return mail. As for the five dollars previously mentioned, I finally received it, after publication and a great deal of embarrassment and trouble. I forgot my coal shoveling resolution and continued to whang away at the typewriter—"to drip adjectives from the ends of my fingers," as some young woman has picturesquely phrased it.

In closing this brief narrative of experience, let me give a few painfully acquired generalizations. Don't quit your job in order to write unless there is none dependent upon you. Fiction pays best of all, and when it is of fair quality is more easily sold. A good joke will sell quicker than a good poem, and, measured in sweat and blood, will bring better remuneration. Avoid the unhappy ending, the harsh, the brutal, the tragic, the horrible—if you care to see in print the things you write. (In this connection don't do as I do, but do as I say.)

Humor is the hardest to write, easiest to sell, and best rewarded. There are only a few who are able to do it. If you are able, do it by all means. You will find it a Klondike and a Rand rolled into one. Look at Mark Twain.

Don't dash off a six-thousand-word story before breakfast. Don't write too much. Concentrate your sweat on one story, rather than dissipate it over a dozen. Don't loaf and invite inspiration; light out after it with a club, and if you don't get it you will nonetheless get something that looks remarkably like it. Set yourself a "stint," and see that you do that "stint" each day; you will have more words to your credit at the end of the year.

Study the tricks of the writers who have arrived. They have mastered the tools with which you are cutting your fingers. They are doing things, and their work bears the internal evidence of how it is done. Don't wait for some good Samaritan to tell you, but dig it out for yourself.

See that your pores are open and your digestion is good. That is, I am confident, the most important rule of all. And don't fling Carlyle in my teeth, please.

Keep a notebook. Travel with it, eat with it, sleep with it. Slap into it every stray thought that flutters up into your brain. Cheap paper is less perishable than gray matter, and lead pencil markings endure longer than memory.

And work. Spell it in capital letters, WORK. WORK all the time. Find out about this earth, this universe; this force and matter, and the spirit that glimmers up through force and matter from the magnet to Godhead. And by all this I mean WORK for a philosophy of life. It does not hurt how wrong your philosophy of life may be, so long as you have one and have it well.

The three great things are: GOOD HEALTH; WORK; and a PHILOSOPHY OF LIFE. I may add, nay, must add, a fourth— SINCERITY. Without this, the other three are without avail; and with it you may cleave to greatness and sit among the giants.

THE TERRIBLE AND TRAGIC IN FICTION
(The Critic, June, 1903)

⊕ ⊕ ⊕ ⊕ ⊕ ⊕ ⊕ ⊕ ⊕ ⊕ ⊕ ⊕

Using Poe as his example, London here examines the terrible-tragic-horror tale, its travail but secret popularity among readers everywhere. London had already written a sociological horror story in *The People of the Abyss* (1903) and would soon produce a horror story of the high seas, *The Sea Wolf* (1904). Both were "terrible" and yet had the noble dimensions of the tragic.

"Mr. Morrow" was William Chambers Morrow (1853-1923); "Without Benefit of Clergy" is the Kipling tale, found in *Life's Handicap* (1891); and "A Lodging for the Night" is Robert Louis Stevenson's "Tale of François Villon" (1877).

⊕ ⊕ ⊕ ⊕ ⊕ ⊕ ⊕ ⊕ ⊕ ⊕ ⊕ ⊕

I am anxious that your firm should continue to be my publishers, and, if you would be willing to bring out the book, I should be glad to accept the terms which you allowed me before—that is, you receive all profits, and allow me twenty copies for distribution to friends.

So wrote Edgar Allan Poe, on August 13, 1841, to the publishing house of Lee & Blanchard. They replied:

We very much regret to say that the state of affairs is such as to give little encouragement to new undertakings. . . . We assure you that we regret this on your account as well as our own, as it would give us great pleasure to promote your views in relation to publication.

Five years later, in 1846, Poe wrote to Mr. E. H. Duyckinck:

For particular reasons I am anxious to have another volume of my tales published before the first of March. Do you think it possible to accomplish it for me? Would not Mr. Wiley give me, say $50, in full for the copyright of the collection I now send?

Measured by the earnings of contemporaneous writers, it is clear that Poe received little or nothing for the stories he wrote. In the autumn of 1900, one of the three extant copies of his *Tamerlane and Other Poems* sold for $2050—a sum greater, perhaps, than he received from the serial and book sales of all his stories and poems.

On the one hand, he was more poorly rewarded than even the mediocre of his contemporaries; while, on the other hand, he produced a more powerful effect than the great majority of them and achieved a fame more brilliant and lasting.

Cooke, in a letter to Poe, says:

"The Valdemar Case" I read in a number of your *Broadway Journal* last winter—as I lay in a Turkey blind, muffled to the eyes in overcoats, &c., and pronounce it without hesitation the most damnable, vraisemblable, horrible, hair-lifting, shocking, ingenious chapter of fiction that any brain ever conceived, or hands treated. That gelatinous, viscous sound of man's voice! there never was such an idea before. That story scared me in broad day, armed with a double-barrel Tyron Turkey gun. What would it have done at midnight in some old ghostly country-house? I have always found some one remarkable thing in your stories to haunt me long after reading them. The *teeth* of Berenice—the changing eyes of Morella—that red and glaring crack in the House of Usher—the pores of the deck in "The MS. Found in a Bottle"—the visible drops falling into the goblet in "Ligeia," &c., &c.—there is always something of this sort to stick by the mind—by mine at least.

About this time Elizabeth Barrett Browning, then Miss Barrett, wrote to Poe:

Your "Raven" has produced a sensation, a "fit horror," here in England.... I hear of persons haunted by the "Nevermore," and one acquaintance of mine who has the misfortune of possessing a "bust of Pallas" never can bear to look at it in the twilight.... Then there is a tale of yours ... which is going the round of the newspapers, about mesmerism, throwing us all into "most admired disorder," and dreadful doubts as to whether "it can be true," as the children say of ghost stories. The certain thing in the tale in question is the power of the writer, and the faculty he has of making horrible improbabilities seem near and familiar.

Though his stories threw people into "most admired disorders" and scared men in broad day in "Turkey blinds," and though his stories were read, one might say, universally, there seemed at the time a feeling against them which condemned them as a class of stories eminently repulsive and unreadable. The public read Poe's stories, but Poe was not in touch with that public. And when that public spoke to him through the mouths of the magazine editors, it spoke in no uncertain terms; and, rebelliously aspiring, he dreamed of a magazine of his own—no "namby-pamby" magazine, filled with "contemptible pictures, fashion-plates, music, and love-tales," but a magazine which uttered the thing for the thing's sake and told a story because it was a story rather than a hodgepodge which the public might claim it liked.

James E. Heath, writing to Poe concerning "Fall of the House of Usher," said:

He [White, editor of the *Southern Literary Messenger*] doubts whether the readers of the *Messenger* have much relish for tales of the German School, although written with great power and ability, and in this opinion, I confess to you frankly, I am strongly inclined to concur. I doubt very much whether tales of the wild, improbable, and terrible class can ever be permanently popular in this country. Charles Dickens it appears to me has given the final death-blow to writings of that description.

Nevertheless, the writer-men of that day, who wrote the popular stories and received readier sales and fatter checks, are dead and forgotten and their stories with them, while Poe and the stories of Poe live on. In a way, this side of Poe's history is a paradoxical tangle. Editors did not like to publish his stories nor people to read them, yet they were read universally and discussed and remembered, and went the round of the foreign newspapers. They earned him little money, yet they have since earned a great deal of money and to this day command a large and steady sale. It was the common belief at the time they appeared that they could never become popular in the United States, yet their steady sales, complete editions, and what-not, which continue to come out, attest a popularity that is, to say the least, enduring. The sombre and terrible "Fall of the House of Usher," "Ligeia," "Black Cat," "Cask of Amontillado," "Berenice," "Pit and the Pendulum," and "Masque of the Red Death" are read today with an eagerness as great as ever. And especially is this true of the younger generation, which ofttimes places the seal of its approval on things the graybeards have read, approved, forgotten they have approved, and finally censured and condemned.

Yet the conditions which obtained in Poe's time obtain just as inexorably today. No self-respecting editor with an eye to the subscription-list can be bribed or bullied into admitting a terrible or tragic story into his magazine; while the reading public, when it does chance upon such stories in one way or another—and it manages to chance upon them somehow—says it does not care for them.

A person reads such a story, lays it down with a shudder, and says:

"It makes my blood run cold. I never want to read anything like that again." Yet he or she will read something like that again, and again, and yet again, and return and read them over again. Talk with the average man or woman of the reading public and it will be found that they have read all, or nearly all, of the terrible and horrible tales which have been written. Also, they will shiver, express a dislike for such tales, and then proceed to discuss them with a keenness and understanding as remarkable as it is surprising.

When it is considered that so many condemn these tales and continue to read them (as is amply proved by heart-to-heart experience and by the book sales such as Poe's), the question arises: Are folk honest when they shudder and say they do not care for the terrible, the horrible, and the tragic? Or are they afraid that they do like to be afraid?

Deep down in the roots of the race is fear. It came first into the world, and it was the dominant emotion in the primitive world. Today, for that matter, it remains the most firmly seated of the emotions. But in the primitive world people were uncomplex, not yet self-conscious, and they frankly delighted in terror-inspiring tales and religions. Is it true that the complex, self-conscious people of today do not delight in the things which inspire terror? or is it true that they are ashamed to make known their delight?

What is it that lures boys to haunted houses after dark, compelling them to fling rocks and run away with their hearts going so thunderously pit-a-pat as to drown the clatter of their flying feet? What is it that grips a child, forcing it to listen to ghost stories which drive it into ecstasies of fear, and yet forces it to beg for more and more? Is it a baleful thing? a thing his instinct warns him as unhealthy and evil the while his desire leaps out to it? Or, again, what is it that sends the heart fluttering up and quickens the feet of the man or woman who goes alone down a dark hall or up a winding stair? Is it a stirring of the savage in them?—of the savage who has slept, but never died, since the time the river-folk crouched over the fires of their squatting-places, or the tree-folk bunched together and chattered in the dark?

Whatever the thing is, and whether it be good or evil, it is a thing and it is real. It is the thing Poe rouses in us, scaring us in broad day and throwing us into "admired disorders." It is rarely that the grown person who is afraid of the dark will make confession. It does not seem to them proper to be afraid of the dark, and they are ashamed. Perhaps people feel that it is not proper to delight in stories that arouse fear and terror. They may feel instinctively that it is bad and injurious to have such emotions aroused, and because of this are impelled to say that they do not like such stories, while in actuality they do like them.

The great emotion exploited by Dickens was fear, as Mr. Brooks Adams has pointed out, just as courage was the great emotion exploited by Scott. The militant nobility seemed to possess an excess of courage and to respond more readily to things courageous. On the other hand, the rising bourgeoisie, the timid merchant-folk and city-dwellers, fresh from the oppressions and robberies of their rough-handed lords, seemed to possess an excess of fear, and to respond more readily to things fearsome. For this reason they greedily devoured Dickens's writings, for he was as peculiarly their spokesman as Scott was the spokesman of the old and dying nobility.

But since Dickens's day, if we may judge by the editorial attitude and by the dictum of the reading public, a change seems to have taken place. In Dickens's day, the bourgeoisie as a dominant class being but newly risen, had fear still strong upon it, much as a negro mammy, a couple of generations from Africa, stands in fear of the Voodoo. But today it would seem that this same bourgeoisie, firmly seated and triumphant, is ashamed of its old terror, which it remembers dimly, as it might a bad nightmare. When fear was strong upon it, it loved nothing better than fear-exciting things; but with fear far-removed, no longer menaced and harassed, it has become afraid of fear. By this is meant that the bourgeoisie has become self-conscious much in the same fashion that the black slave, freed and conscious of the stigma attached to "black," calls himself a colored gentleman, though in his heart of hearts he feels himself black nigger still. So the bourgeoisie may feel in a dim, mysterious way the stigma attached to the fear of its cowardly days, and, self-conscious, brands as improper all fear-exciting things, while deep down in its still secret being it delights in them still.

All this, of course, is by the way—a mere tentative attempt to account for a bit of contradictory psychology in the make-up of the reading public. But the facts of the case remain. The public is afraid of fear-exciting tales and hypocritically continues to enjoy them. W. W. Jacobs's recent collection of stories, *The Lady of the Barge,* contains his usual inimitable humorous yarns inter-sprinkled with several terror-tales. It was asked of a dozen friends as to which story had affected them the most forcibly, and the unanimous answer was "the 'Monkey's Paw.'" Now the "Monkey's Paw" is as perfect a terror-tale as any of its kind. Yet, without exception, after duly and properly shuddering and disclaiming all liking for such tales, they proceeded to discuss it with a warmth and knowledge which plainly advertised that, whatever strange sensations it had aroused, they were at any rate pleasurable sensations.

Long ago, Ambrose Bierce published his *Soldiers and Civilians,* a book crammed from cover to cover with unmitigated terror and horror. An editor who dared to publish one of these tales would be committing financial and professional suicide; and yet, year after year, people continue to talk about *Soldiers and Civilians,* while the innumerable sweet and wholesome, optimistic, and happy-ending books are forgotten as rapidly as they leave the press.

In the rashness of youth, before he became converted to soberer ways, Mr. Morrow was guilty of *The Ape, the Idiot, and Other People,* wherein are to be found some of the most horrible horror-stories in the English language. It made his instant reputation, whereupon he conceived higher notions of his art, forswore the terrible and the horrible, and wrote other and totally different books. But these other books are not remembered as readily as is his first one by the people who in the same breath say they do not like stories such as may be found in *The Ape, the Idiot, and Other People.*

Of two collections of tales recently published, each of which contained one terror-story, nine out of ten reviewers, in each instance, selected the terror-story as worthy of most praise, and, after they had praised, five out of the nine of them proceeded to damn it. Rider Haggard's *She,* which is filled with grewsome terror, had a long and popular vogue, while the *Strange Case of Dr. Jekyll and Mr. Hyde* achieved, if anything, a greater success and brought Stevenson to the front.

Putting the horror-story outside the pale, can any story be really great, the theme of which is anything but tragic or terrible? Can the sweet commonplaces of life be made into anything else than sweetly commonplace stories?

It would not seem so. The great short stories in the world's literary treasure-house seem all to depend upon the tragic and terrible for their strength and greatness. Not half of them deal with love at all; and when they do, they derive their greatness, not from the love itself, but from the tragic and terrible with which the love is involved.

In this class may be ranked "Without Benefit of Clergy," which is fairly typical. The love of John Holden and Ameera greatens because it is out of caste and precarious, and it is made memorable by the tragic deaths of Tota and Ameera, the utter obliteration of the facts that they have lived, and the return of John Holden to his kind. Stress and strain are required to sound the deeps of human nature, and there is neither stress nor strain in sweet, optimistic, and placidly happy events. Great things can be done only under great provocation, and there is nothing greatly provoking in the sweet and placid round of existence. Romeo and Juliet are not remembered because things slipped smoothly along, nor are Abélard and Heloise, Tristram and Iseult, Paolo and Francesca.

But the majority of the great short stories do not deal with love.

"A Lodging for the Night," for instance, one of the most rounded and perfect stories ever told, not only has no hint of love in it, but does not contain a hint of one character whom we would care to meet in life. Beginning with the murder of Thevenin, running through the fearful night in the streets and the robbing of the dead jade in the porch, and finishing with the old lord of Brisetout, who is not murdered because he possesses seven pieces of plate instead of ten, it contains nothing that is not terrible and repulsive. Yet it is the awfulness of it that makes it great. The play of words in the deserted house between Villon and the feeble lord of Brisetout, which is the story, would be no story at all were the stress and strain taken out of it and the two men placed *vis-à-vis* with a score of retainers at the old lord's back.

The *Fall of the House of Usher* depends upon all that is terrible for its greatness, and there is no more love in it than in Guy de Maupassant's "Necklace," or the "Piece of String," or in "The Man Who Was," and "Baa, Baa, Black Sheep," which last is the most pitiful of all tragedies, a child's.

The editors of the magazines have very good reasons for refusing admission to the terrible and tragic. Their readers say they do not like the terrible and tragic, and that is enough, without going farther. But either their readers prevaricate most shamelessly or delude themselves into believing they tell the truth, or else the people who read the magazines are not the people who continue to buy, say, the works of Poe.

In the circumstance, there being a proved demand for the terrible and tragic, is there not room in the otherwise crowded field for a magazine devoted primarily to the terrible and tragic? A magazine such as Poe dreamed of, about which there shall be nothing namby-pamby, yellowish, or emasculated, and which will print stories that are bids for place and permanence rather than for the largest circulation?

On the face of it two things appear certain: that enough of that portion of the reading public which cares for the tragic and terrible would be sufficiently honest to subscribe; and that the writers of the land would be capable of supplying the stories. The only reason why such stories are not being written today is that there is no magazine to buy them, and that the writer-folk are busy turning out the stuff, mainly ephemeral, which the magazines will buy. The pity of it is that the writer-folk are writing for bread first and glory after; and that their standard of living goes up as fast as their capacity for winning bread increases—so that they never get around to glory—the ephemeral flourishes, and the great stories remain unwritten.

THESE BONES SHALL RISE AGAIN

(The Reader, June, 1903)

⊕ ⊕ ⊕ ⊕ ⊕ ⊕ ⊕ ⊕ ⊕ ⊕ ⊕ ⊕

Jack London's devotion to Kipling has been the subject of considerable scholarly study. It is generally agreed that London misinterpreted Kipling's role as "hymner of the dominant bourgeosie," and conductor of the "war march of the white man around the world."

One recent writer on the subject says: "It is not surprising that writers like Jack London and Frank Norris, far better artists than critics, saw apparent glorification of brutality in the Anglo-Indian's work. If a reasoning critic like Lionel Trilling still feels the brutal Kipling so strongly, this same feeling is surely to be expected from two such passionate authors. Moreover, Norris's and London's delight in Kipling's seeming brutality is predictable in view of their commitment to the philosophies of Zola and Spencer. Far from being repelled, they were fascinated as the foremost literary exponents of these qualities. Of course, the two Americans were fortunate in never asking Kipling if he wanted to be so celebrated; his answer would obviously have been a vehement—if nonviolent—no."[*]

Andrew Sinclair observes starkly that London "demeaned Kipling by making him the mouthpiece of his own Anglo-Saxon racism," and writes that London's "These Bones Shall Rise Again" was "a generous and red-blooded defense of Kipling which revealed more of his own racial beliefs than the Englishman's."[**]

But there is ample evidence, undiscovered by Mr. Sinclair, that London effected a philosophical break with Kipling in 1911 with publication of London's superb parable, "The Strength of the Strong" (*Hampton's Magazine,* March, 1911). This story is an effective reply to Kipling's "The Mother Hive" (published in *Collier's Weekly* in 1908 as "The Adventures of Melissa").

This essay was originally collected in London's *Revolution and Other Essays* (1910).

⊕ ⊕ ⊕ ⊕ ⊕ ⊕ ⊕ ⊕ ⊕ ⊕ ⊕ ⊕

---

[*]James R. Giles, "Some Notes on the Red-Blooded Reading of Kipling by Jack London and Frank Norris," *Jack London Newsletter,* vol. 3, no. 2 (May–August, 1970), p. 62.

[**]Sinclair, p. 74.

Rudyard Kipling, "prophet of blood and vulgarity, prince of ephemerals and idol of the unelect"—as a Chicago critic chortles,—is dead. It is true. He is dead, dead and buried. And a fluttering, chirping host of men, little men and unseeing men, have heaped him over with the uncut leaves of "Kim," wrapped him in "Stalky & Co." for winding sheet, and for headstone reared his unconventional lines, "The Lesson." It was very easy. The simplest thing in the world. And the fluttering, chirping gentlemen are rubbing their hands in amazement and wondering why they did not do it long ago, it was so very, very simple.

But the centuries to come, of which the fluttering, chirping gentlemen are prone to talk largely, will have something to say in the matter. And when they, the future centuries, quest back to the nineteenth century to find what manner of century it was;—to find, not what the people of the nineteenth century thought they thought, but what they really thought, not what they thought they ought to do, but what they really did do, then a certain man, Kipling, will be read—and read with understanding. "They thought they read him with understanding, those people of the nineteenth century," the future centuries will say; "and then they thought there was no understanding in him, and after that they did not know what they thought."

But this is over-severe. It applies only to that class which serves a function somewhat similar to that served by the populace of old time in Rome. This is the unstable, mob-minded mass, which sits on the fence, ever ready to fall this side or that and indecorously clamber back again; which puts a Democratic administration into office one election, and a Republican the next; which discovers and lifts up a prophet to-day that it may stone him tomorrow; which clamors for the book everybody else is reading, for no reason under the sun save that everybody else is reading it. This is the class of whim and caprice, of fad and vogue, the unstable, incoherent, mob-mouthed, mob-minded mass, the "monkey-folk," if you please, of these latter days. Now it may be reading "The Eternal City." Yesterday it was reading "The Master-Christian," and some several days before that it was reading Kipling. Yes, almost to his shame be it, these folk were reading him. But it was not his fault. If he depended upon them he well deserves to be dead and buried and never to rise again. But to them, let us be thankful, he never lived. They thought he lived, but he was as dead then as he is now and as he always will be.

He could not help it because he became the vogue, and it is easily understood. When he lay ill, fighting in close grapples with death, those who knew him were grieved. They were many, and in many voices, to the rim of the Seven Seas, they spoke their grief. Whereupon, and with celerity, the mob-minded mass began to inquire as to this man whom so many mourned. If everybody else mourned, it were fit that they mourn too. So a vast wail went up. Each was a spur to the other's grief, and each began privately to read this man they had never read and publicly to proclaim this man they had always read. And straightaway next day they drowned their grief in a sea of historical romance and forgot all about him. The reaction was inevitable. Emerging from the sea into which they had plunged, they became aware that they had so soon forgotten him, and would have been ashamed, had not the fluttering, chirping men said, "Come, let us bury him." And they put him in a hole, quickly, out of their sight.

And when they have crept into their own little holes, and smugly laid themselves down in their last long sleep, the future centuries will roll the stone away and he will come forth again. *For be it known: That man of us is imperishable who makes his century imperishable.* That man of us who seizes upon the salient facts of our life, who tells what we thought, what we were, and for what we stood—that man shall be the mouthpiece to the centuries, and so long as they listen he shall endure.

We remember the caveman. We remember him because he made his century imperishable. But, unhappily, we remember him dimly, in a collective sort of way, because he memorialized his century dimly, in a collective sort of way. He had no written speech, so he left us rude scratchings of beasts and things, cracked marrow-bones, and weapons of stone. It was the best expression of which he was capable. Had he scratched his own particular name with the scratchings of beasts and things, stamped his cracked marrow-bones with his own particular seal, trade-marked his weapons of stone with his own particular device, that particular man would we remember. But he did the best he could, and we remember him as best we may.

Homer takes his place with Achilles and the Greek and Trojan heroes. Because we remember them, we remember him. Whether he be one or a dozen men, or a dozen generations of men, we remember him. And so long as the name of Greece is known on the lips of men, so long will the name of Homer be known. There are many such names, linked with their times, which have come down to us, many more which will yet go down; and to them, in token that we have lived, must we add some few of our own.

Dealing only with the artist, be it understood, only those artists will go down who have spoken true of us. Their truth must be the deepest and most significant, their voices clear and strong, definite and coherent. Half-truths and partial-truths will not do, nor will thin piping voices and quavering lays. There must be the cosmic quality in what they sing. They must seize upon and press into enduring art-forms the vital facts of our existence. They must tell why we have lived, for without any reason for living, depend upon it, in the time to come, it will be as though we had never lived. Nor are the things that were true of the people a thousand years or so ago true of us to-day. The romance of Homer's Greece is the romance of Homer's Greece. That is undeniable. It is not our romance. And he who in our time sings the romance of Homer's Greece cannot expect to sing it so well as Homer did, nor will he be singing about us or our romance at all. A machine age is something quite different from an heroic age. What is true of rapid-fire guns, stock-exchanges, and electric motors, cannot possibly be true of hand-flung javelins and whirring chariot wheels. Kipling knows this. He has been telling it to us all his life, living it all his life in the work he has done.

What the Anglo-Saxon has done, he has memorialized. And by Anglo-Saxon is not meant merely the people of that tight little island on the edge of the Western Ocean. Anglo-Saxon stands for the English-speaking people of all the world, who, in forms and institutions and traditions, are more peculiarly and definitely English than anything else. This people Kipling has sung. Their sweat and blood and toil have been the motives of his songs; but underlying all the motives of his songs is the motive of motives, the sum of them all and something more, which is one with what underlies all the Anglo-Saxon sweat and blood and toil; namely, the genius of the race. And this is the cosmic quality. Both that which is true of the race for all time, and that which is true of the race for all time applied to this particular time, he has caught up and pressed into his art-forms. He has caught the dominant note of the Anglo-Saxon and pressed it into wonderful rhythms which cannot be sung out in a day and which will not be sung out in a day.

The Anglo-Saxon is a pirate, a land robber and a sea robber. Underneath his thin coating of culture, he is what he was in Morgan's time, in Drake's time, in William's time, in Alfred's time. The blood and the tradition of Hengist and Horsa are in his veins. In battle he is subject to the blood lusts of the Berserkers of old. Plunder and booty fascinate him immeasurably. The schoolboy of today dreams the dream of Clive and Hastings. The Anglo-Saxon is strong of arm and heavy of hand, and he possesses a primitive brutality all his own. There is a discontent in his blood, an unsatisfaction that will not let him rest, but sends him adventuring over the sea and among the lands in the midst of the sea. He does not know when he is beaten, wherefore the term "bull-dog" is attached to him, so that all may know his unreasonableness. He has "some care as to the purity of his ways, does not wish to strange gods, nor juggle with intellectual phantasmagoria." He loves freedom, but is dictatorial to others, is self-willed, has boundless energy, and does things for himself. He is also a master of matter, an organizer of law, and an administrator of justice.

And in the nineteenth century he has lived up to his reputation. Being the nineteenth century and no other century, and in so far different from all other centuries, he has expressed himself differently. But blood will tell, and in the name of God, the Bible, and Democracy, he has gone out over the earth, possessing himself of broad lands and fat revenues, and conquering by virtue of his sheer pluck and enterprise and superior machinery.

Now the future centuries, seeking to find out what the nineteenth-century Anglo-Saxon was and what were his works, will have small concern with what he did not do and what he would have liked to do. These things he did do, and for these things will he be remembered. His claim on posterity will be that in the nineteenth century he mastered matter; his twentieth-century claim will be, in the highest probability, that he organized life—but that will be sung by the twentieth-century Kiplings or the twenty-first-century Kiplings. Rudyard Kipling of the nineteenth century has sung of "things as they are." He has seen life as it is, "taken it up squarely," in both his hands, and looked upon it. What better preachment upon the Anglo-Saxon and what he has done can be had than "The Bridge Builders"? what better appraisement than "The White Man's Burden"? As for faith and clean ideals—not of "children and gods, but men in a world of men"—who has preached them better than he?

Primarily, Kipling has stood for the doer as opposed to the dreamer— the doer, who lists not to idle songs of empty days, but who goes forth and does things, with bended back and sweated brow and work-hardened hands. The most characteristic thing about Kipling is his love of actuality, his intense practicality, his proper and necessary respect for the hard-headed, hard-fisted fact. And, above all, he has preached the gospel of work, and as potently as Carlyle ever preached. For he has preached it not only to those in high places, but to the common men, to the great sweating throng of common men who hear and understand yet stand agape at Carlyle's turgid utterance. Do the thing to your hand, and do it with all your might. Never mind what the thing is; so long as it is something. Do it. Do it and remember Tomlinson, sexless and soulless Tomlinson, who was denied at Heaven's gate.

The blundering centuries have perseveringly pottered and groped through the dark; but it remained for Kipling's century to roll in the sun, to formulate, in other words, the reign of law. And of the artists in Kipling's century, he of them all has driven the greater measure of law in the more consummate speech:—

> Keep ye the Law—be swift in all obedience.
> Clear the land of evil, drive the road and bridge the ford.
>   Make ye sure to each his own
>   That he reap what he hath sown;
> By the peace among Our peoples let men know we serve the Lord.

—And so it runs, from McAndrew's "Law, Order, Duty, and Restraint," to his last least line, whether of "The Vampire" or "The Recessional." And no prophet out of Israel has cried out more loudly the sins of the people, nor called them more awfully to repent.

"But he is vulgar, he stirs the puddle of life," object the fluttering, chirping gentlemen, the Tomlinsonian men. Well, and isn't life vulgar? Can you divorce the facts of life? Much of good is there, and much of ill; but who may draw aside his garment and say, "I am none of them"? Can you say that the part is greater than the whole? that the whole is more or less than the sum of the parts? As for the puddle of life, the stench is offensive to you? Well, and what then? Do you not live in it? Why do you not make it clean? Do you clamor for a filter to make clean only your own particular portion? And, made clean, are you wroth because Kipling has stirred it muddy again? At least he has stirred it healthily, with steady vigor and good-will. He has not brought to the surface merely its dregs, but its most significant values. He has told the centuries to come of our lyings and our lusts, but he has also told the centuries to come of the seriousness which is underneath our lyings and our lusts. And he has told us, too, and always has he told us, to be clean and strong and to walk upright and manlike.

"But he has no sympathy," the fluttering gentlemen chirp. "We admire his art and intellectual brilliancy, we all admire his art and intellectual brilliancy, his dazzling technique and rare rhythmical sense; but . . . he is totally devoid of sympathy." Dear! Dear! What is to be understood by this? Should he sprinkle his pages with sympathetic adjectives, so many to the paragraph, as the country compositor sprinkles commas? Surely not. The little gentlemen are not quite so infinitesimal as that. There have been many tellers of jokes, and the greater of them, it is recorded, never smiled at their own, not even in the crucial moment when the audience wavered between laughter and tears.

And so with Kipling. Take the "Vampire," for instance. It has been complained that there is no touch of pity in it for the man and his ruin, no sermon on the lesson of it, no compassion for the human weakness, no indignation at the heartlessness. But are we kindergarten children that the tale be told to us in words of one syllable? Or are we men and women, able to read between the lines what Kipling intended we should read between the lines? "For some of him lived, but the most of him died." Is there not here all the excitation in the world for our sorrow, our pity, our indignation? And what more is the function of art than to excite states of consciousness complementary to the thing portrayed? The color of tragedy is red. Must the artist also paint the watery tears and wan-faced grief? "For some of him lived, but the most of him died"— can the heartache of the situation be conveyed more achingly? Or were it better that the young man, some of him alive but most of him dead, should come out before the curtain and deliver a homily to the weeping audience?

The nineteenth century, so far as the Anglo-Saxon is concerned, was remarkable for two great developments: the mastery of matter and the expansion of the race. Three great forces operated in it: nationalism, commercialism, democracy—the marshalling of the races, the merciless, remorseless *laissez faire* of the dominant bourgeoisie, and the practical, actual working government of men within a very limited equality. The democracy of the nineteenth century is not the democracy of which the eighteenth century dreamed. It is not the democracy of the Declaration, but it is what we have practised and lived that reconciles it to the fact of the "lesser breeds without the Law."

It is of these developments and forces of the nineteenth century that Kipling has sung. And the romance of it he has sung, that which underlies and transcends objective endeavor, which deals with race impulses, race deeds, and race traditions. Even into the steam-leaden speech of his loco-motives has he breathed our life, our spirit, our significance. As he is our mouthpiece, so are they his mouthpieces. And the romance of the nineteenth-century man, as he has thus expressed himself in the nineteenth century, in shaft and wheel, in steel and steam, in far journeying and adventuring, Kipling has caught up in wondrous songs for the future centuries to sing.

If the nineteenth century is the century of the Hooligan, then is Kipling the voice of the Hooligan as surely as he is the voice of the nineteenth century. Who is more representative? Is "David Harum" more representative of the nineteenth century? Is Mary Johnston, Charles Major, or Winston Churchill? Is Bret Harte? William Dean Howells? Gilbert Parker? Who of them all is as essentially representative of nineteenth-century life? When Kipling is forgotten, will Robert Louis Stevenson be remembered for his "Dr. Jekyll and Mr. Hyde," his "Kidnapped," and his "David Balfour"? Not so. His "Treasure Island" will be a classic, to go down with "Robinson Crusoe," "Through the Looking-Glass," and "The Jungle Books." He will be remembered for his essays, for his letters, for his philosophy of life, for himself. He will be the well beloved, as he has been the well beloved. But his will be another claim upon posterity than what we are considering. For each epoch has its singer. As Scott sang the swan song of chivalry and Dickens the burgher-fear of the rising merchant class, so Kipling, as no one else, has sung the hymn of the dominant bourgeoisie, the war march of the white man round the world, the triumphant paean of commercialism and imperialism. For that will he be remembered.

Oakland, California,
October, 1901

STRANGER THAN FICTION
(*The Critic,* August, 1903)

"It is incontrovertible that one cannot do on the printed page what one can do in life," London writes in this piece on the mosquito in the Northland and other truths stranger than fiction.

⊕ ⊕ ⊕ ⊕ ⊕ ⊕ ⊕ ⊕ ⊕ ⊕ ⊕ ⊕

[An experience solemnly affirmed to be the truth, the whole truth, and nothing but the truth.]

I remember frying bacon at a noon halt on the Klondike Trail, some several years back, while I listened incredulously to a Yukon pioneer's tale of woe. There were tears in his voice and a querulous plaint, as he told me of all he had suffered from the mosquitoes. Before his recital reached a close he became angry at the little winged pests, the injuries they had done him waxed colossal, and he cursed them in terms the most uncompromisingly blasphemous I have ever heard.

He was a strong man. He had been seven years in the land. I knew, at that very moment, that he was resting from a tramp of fifty miles which he had covered in the last fifteen hours, and that he intended to cover twenty-five miles more before night came on.

As I say, I knew all this. The man was real. He had done things. He had a reputation. Yet I said to myself: *These mosquito-happenings are impossible things. They cannot be true. The man lies.*

Four months later, two comrades and I, three strong men of us, went down the Yukon two thousand miles in an open boat. Tears came into our voices and remained there, likewise the querulous plaint. We grew irritable and quarrelsome. Instead of talking like men we whined broken-spiritedly, and said that of mosquitoes the half had not been told. And I, for one, marvelled at the restraint and control of the man who had first told me of the mosquito at the noon halt on the Klondike Trail.

Since then, in civilization, I have attempted to tell the story of the mosquito. My friends have listened pityingly, or looked bored, or told me plainly that veracity was evidently not a Klondike product. These things I endured, striving to redeem myself with greater earnestness and detail; but, finally, when one fellow said, "That reminds me of a real mosquito story," I dropped the subject for good and all. Since then I have been most exemplary in my conduct and morals, and I still hope that before I totter into my grave I shall succeed in living down my reputation for untruthfulness.

I do not dare to tell the story of the mosquito here. I have merely hinted at it in this somewhat lengthy preamble in order to show that I understand and forgive the editorial mind when certain facts of mine, in fictional garb, are promptly returned to me. For be it known that truth is so much stranger than fiction that it is unreal to editors and readers.

For instance, I knew a girl. Our first meeting was typical. It was up in the rugged Sierras. In the cool of the day she came out of the dark pine woods, in short-skirted costume, her hair down her back, a shotgun across the hollow of her arm. She was hunting rabbits—for her, deer and a Winchester rifle would have been just as likely. She was quite unconventional, and she was straight. She could ride a horse better than the average broncho-buster. She could go down in a diving-bell, scratch off a magazine article (which would sell), or do a Highland fling on the vaudeville stage, for the fun of the thing. On the other hand, she had opened the books. I have at hand now a score of dainty poems by her. She was as close to culture as she was to the wild, free life of the open or of Bohemia. In a few words, she was a striking creature.

I toned her down and made a heroine of her. It was for the sake of veracity, and because I remembered the story of the mosquito, that I toned her down. I took away from her realness, diminished the living fact of her, in order that the reader might believe she was real and a living fact. The reviewers swiftly proved to me how signally I had failed. I quote at random: "One cannot believe in her, but one likes her and forgives her culture"; "a projection of the writer's ideal woman upon paper"; "a monster"; "a thing contrary to nature"; "remains at the end of the story utterly incredible and even inconceivable."

From time to time I have written short adventure-stories for a famous juvenile publication. My experience with these stories was practically uniform. Whenever I evolved out of my sheer inner consciousness some boyish adventure, it received the most flattering approval of the editors. Whenever my inner consciousness was not in working order, and I fell back on the facts of my life, wrote adventures I had actually gone through, things I had done with my own hands and head, the editors hummed and hawed. "It is not real," they said. "It is impossible. It could not have happened thus and so."

Once, when they commented in this fashion upon a cliff-climbing story of mine, a literal narrative of a thing I had done, as had thousands of others as well, I flew into rebellion. "I can readily comprehend," I wrote them, though I really didn't at the moment, so befuddled was my reason by my wrath, "I can readily comprehend that the state of consciousness you may achieve on the flat floor of your editorial sanctum concerning a man plastered against the frown of a cliff is a far different state of consciousness from that a man may achieve who is plastered against the frown of a cliff." They were very nice about it, taking my criticism in better part than I took theirs; and, for that matter, they could afford to, for they were in the right. It is incontrovertible that one cannot do on the printed page what one does in life.

I once wrote a story of a tramp. I intended it to be the first of a series of tramp stories, all of which were to relate the adventures of a single tramp character. I was well fitted to write this series, for two reasons. First, I had myself tramped ten thousand miles or so through the United States and Canada, begged for my food from door to door, and performed sentences for vagrancy in various jails. Second, my tramp character was a personal friend. Many a time he had shoved his legs under my table or turned into my bed with me. I knew him better than I did my brother. He was a remarkable man, college-educated, qualified to practice law in all the courts, spilling over with the minutest details of every world-philosophy from Zeno to Nietzsche, deeply versed in political economy and sociology, a brilliant lecturer—in short, a genius of extraordinary caliber.

To exploit in fiction this living fact, I not only toned him down, but actually used an experience of his for the *motif* of the first story. I make bold to say that it is one of the best stories I ever wrote, if it is not the best. When nobody is around I often sneak it out from the bottom of the box and read it with huge delight, hugging myself the while and feeling great sorrow for the world which is denied my joy.

I need hardly say that this story, to the editorial mind, was an unveracious thing. One editor, only, did it convince. And this is how it was. I knew a young writer in Southern California who tramped East for the experience. I shall call him Jones. Well, Jones met this particular editor in New York City and told him divers of his own tramp experiences. Shortly afterward, my tramp story was submitted to this editor. In this fashion he explained his rejection of it: "Had I not known Mr. Jones for some time, I should have said such a creation as your Tramp was absolutely and utterly impossible, and my reason for rejecting the MS. is that to other people who have not had the opportunity to really understand what a tramp may be, whence he may come, and into what he may be transformed, it might seem too great a tax upon credulity."

Tone down as I would, my Tramp was too real to be true. With the help of Mr. Jones he had convinced but one editor, who, in turn, said very truly that his readers, not having the advantage of Mr. Jones's acquaintance, would remain unconvinced. Suffice it to say, beyond the initial story, the series remains unwritten, and the world little recks of what it has lost.

I had a certain pastoral experience. The effect was cumulative. I had dealings with several hundred different people of all ages, sizes, and sexes, through a long period of time, so that the human traits and psychology involved were not extraordinary but merely average human traits and psychology. I sat down and brooded over this pastoral experience. Alas! said I to myself, it would make a bully story, but it is too real to be true.

I should have abandoned it altogether had not a new method of treating it come to me. I pulled up to my desk and started in. First I wrote the title. Underneath the title, in brackets, I wrote, "A True Narrative." Then I wrote the experience as it actually happened, using only the naked facts of it, bringing in for verities, and precisely labelled, my wife, my sister, my nephew, my maid-servant, myself, my house, and my post-office address.

Ah ha! chortled I, as I mailed it East; at last I have circumvented the editorial mind. But it came back. It continued to come back. The editors refused it with phrases complimentary and otherwise, and one and all thanked me for having allowed them the privilege of considering my *story* (!)

At last an editor looked kindly upon it, accepting it with qualifications. He wrote: "It is decidedly good . . . but I shy at the use of the ———. With the ordinary reader this would be considered carrying the matter too far, but I can believe it was necessary in reality." And after indicating the changes he would suggest, he wound up with: "For the *story* (!) I will then pay $———."

Oscar Wilde once proved with fair conclusiveness that Nature imitates Art. I have been forced to conclude that Fact, to be true, must imitate Fiction. The creative imagination is more veracious than the voice of life. Actual events are less true than logical conceits and whimsicalities. And the man who writes fiction had better leave fact alone.

I said to myself that the mosquito-man lied. By innumerable editorial rejections I have been informed that I have lied. And for all that I placed at the head of this narrative, in brackets, a solemn affirmation of its truthfulness I am confident that it will be believed by no one. It is too real to be true.

JACK LONDON TO THE "UNKNOWNS"
(*Ability*, April, 1905)

⊕ ⊕ ⊕ ⊕ ⊕ ⊕ ⊕ ⊕ ⊕ ⊕ ⊕ ⊕

This interesting letter was solicited of London by Gertrude F. Boyle, editor of the San Francisco magazine, *Ability*, which survived only a single issue.* London was asked for his "advice to unknown writers," and he gave it, somewhat caustically but truthfully. Yet it was a matter of "do what I say, not what I do," for London generously played the part of the literary bureau all his writing career, reading manuscripts from total strangers and writing long critiques of them for people often offended at his bluntness and seldom appreciative of his efforts in their behalf.

⊕ ⊕ ⊕ ⊕ ⊕ ⊕ ⊕ ⊕ ⊕ ⊕ ⊕ ⊕

Oakland, California
February 20, 1905

Dear Sir:

Every time a writer tells the truth about a manuscript (or book), to a friend-author, he loses that friend, or sees that friendship dim and fade away to a ghost of what it was formerly.

Every time a writer tells the truth about a manuscript (or book), to a stranger-author, he makes an enemy.

If the writer loves his friend and fears to lose him, he lies to his friend. But what's the good of straining himself to lie to strangers?

And, with like insistence, what's the good of making enemies anyway?

Furthermore, a known writer is overwhelmed by requests from strangers to read their work and pass judgment upon it. This is properly the work of a literary bureau. A writer is not a literary bureau. If he is foolish enough to become a literary bureau, he will cease to be a writer. He won't have time to write.

---

*The letter was reprinted as "London Explains Why He Refused to Become Critic" in the *Oakland Tribune*, November 28, 1932.

Also, as a charitable literary bureau, he will receive no pay. Wherefore he will soon go bankrupt and himself live upon the charity of friends (if he has not already made them all his enemies by telling them the truth), while he will behold his wife and children went their melancholy way to the poorhouse.

Sympathy for the struggling unknown is all very well. It is beautiful— but there are so many struggling unknowns, something like several millions of them. And sympathy can be worked too hard. Sympathy begins at home. The writer would far rather allow the multitudinous unknowns to remain unknown than to allow his near and dear ones to occupy pauper pallets and potters' fields.

Sincerely yours,
Jack London

REVIEW OF "THE LONG DAY"

(San Francisco *Examiner,* October 15, 1905)

⊕ ⊕ ⊕ ⊕ ⊕ ⊕ ⊕ ⊕ ⊕ ⊕ ⊕ ⊕

Published anonymously by the Century Company in 1905, the complete title of this book was *The Long Day: The True Story of a New York Working Girl as Told by Herself.* The author was Dorothy Richardson. London's passionate endorsement of the book suggests that *The Long Day* met his requirements for an indictment of American industrial society, a subject he knew intimately from his own early years as a "work beast" in the California Bay Area. The review also provided London an opportunity to restage the social, economic, and moral views he had presented in his indictment of Edwardian England's seamy side, *The People of the Abyss* (1903).

⊕ ⊕ ⊕ ⊕ ⊕ ⊕ ⊕ ⊕ ⊕ ⊕ ⊕ ⊕

Here is a true book. It is a human document. It should be read by every man, woman and child who cherishes the belief that he or she is not a selfish clod. It can be bought for $1.20 at any bookstore. For one who has not the price, it can be procured for nothing at any public library. The man who reads to the end of this review and then does not read the book, is a sneak. No, I refuse to take back the word. He is a sneak. He avoids his duty by shunning that which will teach him his duty. If he replies to this as Cain did to God, "Am I my brother's keeper?" then is that man a coward as well.

Every youth and maiden and every girl and boy whose heart is aught of goodness or desire for goodness should read this book. For here arises the cries of the many that are cast down and wounded, and here is work in the world to be done by every human creature that takes pride in the fact that he is human and not a beast. The work to be done is the righting of wrong, the alleviation of misery, and the destruction of injustice.

And now to the book. It contains the working out of a problem. Here is a young woman, clean and wholesome, thrown upon the world friendless in New York City. There is nobody to help her. She must depend upon herself. How will she keep that beautiful body of hers beautiful? How will she retain the color in her cheeks? the clearness and frankness in her eyes? How will she keep her springy step? her erect carriage? her delicate poise of head? the resilience of her muscles? How will she keep her flesh undegraded? her mind unsmirched? and, last but not least, how will she keep the strength in her loins, from which, strong or weak, must come the next generation of women and men?

What will this young woman do? How will she go about it? What will happen to her? This is the problem that was faced by the young woman who wrote *The Long Day*. Homesick and lonely, with only a small sum of money between her and destitution, she found herself in a cheap boarding-house. On every side were hands reaching out to rob her. The landlady wore a mask of good-nature and motherly solicitude, but beneath it was concealed "a shrewd, exacting, penny-for-penny and dollar-for-dollar business woman." One got nothing one did not pay for, and one paid right up to the notch.

The girl was eighteen years old, and practically penniless. There was nothing abstract about her problem, nothing difficult of comprehension. First, she must work or starve. Second, she must find the kind of work upon which she would not starve, for there were many working in New York City who starved at the same time.

In the ancient world, where men ran naked, killed with their hands and drank blood from their enemies' skulls, one worked for oneself. If he were hungry there was nothing between him and work. He went into the forest and killed his meat, caught his fish, picked his berries, or scratched the ground in spare moments and planted seed. But it is different in the modern world. The modern world is cultured and civilized and very complex. So complex is it that something interposes between work and the individual who wants to work. An individual wants to work because he is hungry. But work is done by machinery, and machines do not grow on bushes. Machines are owned, and before the hungry individual can go to work he must get permission from the owner of a machine.

This is what this eighteen-year-old girl had to do—work or starve, and, to work, get permission from the owner of a machine. In order to find this owner she read the advertisements in the daily papers. These advertisements were lies, but she did not know it until she had walked many, many, weary miles, worn out her shoes and her patience, and spent nearly her last cent in postage stamps and car fares.

Then she had to change her boarding-house. Five dollars per week was too lordly a manner of living for her depleted purse to stand. For a dollar a week she rented a room in a tenement with "light housekeeping" privileges thrown in. It was a vile den in which neither you nor I would be particularly glad to see a sister of ours live. Through the thin mattress of the bed she "could feel the slats, that seemed hard bands of pain across my tired body."

Outside her window women cursed each other and fought with their hands and nails like jungle beasts. Inside her head rang the eternal refrain, WORK OR STARVE! WORK OR STARVE! And she sought for work, for permission to work from some owner of a machine, cheered on the while by the landlady who told her of the terrible fate of the girl who had "gone wrong" on four dollars a week.

After all, the mere getting of work she did not find difficult. The trouble lay in getting work the wage of which would keep her alive. Two dollars and a half a week was the wage offered by the men who were willing to let her work on their machines. After she had paid a dollar for her room, this would leave her a dollar and a half with which to buy food, pay car fare, keep herself clothed, and have a good time.

So she tried to find a machine the owner of which paid a better wage. In order to make her last several dollars hold she began to ill-treat her body by starving it.

"Bread and butter and black coffee for breakfast, bread and butter for lunch, bread and butter for supper—this was my daily menu for the weeks that followed, varied on two occasions by the purchase of a half-pint of molasses."

Sleeping in a den, breathing the poisonous atmosphere of the slum, and living on such fare is not exactly the manner of living best fitted for the soul beautiful and the body beautiful.

WORK OR STARVE! WORK OR STARVE! Her condition was growing desperate. As a sample of the jobs she could have got, let the following be cited: That of "saleslady" at Lindbloom's store; wage $3.50 per week; hours from 7 in the morning till 9 at night, on Saturdays till midnight.

At last she was compelled to take what offered—$3 a week, while learning, in a paper-box factory. Having agreed to go to work next morning, she returned to her den to find it a heap of ashes in the midst of a curious crowd. Here was disaster. All she possessed in the world was a dollar and a half, the clothes on her back and the promise of a job at $3 per week. Night was coming on. She slept that night in a temporary shelter provided for the ones made homeless by the tenement fire.

In the morning she went to work. And here began the "Long Day." Only those that have experienced it know what the long day means— the age-long endless hours of unending toil.

"We worked steadily, and as the hours dragged on I began to grow dead tired. The awful noise and confusion, the terrific heat, the foul smell of the glue, and the agony of breaking ankles and blistered hands, seemed almost unendurable.''

At last it was 12 o'clock. The day was half done, and there was half an hour for lunch.

The author delineates well the psychology of the working girls among whom she found herself. The girls of the paper-box factory were great readers. They read such classics as *Woven on Fate's Loom; Little Rosebud's Love; A Coronet of Shame,* and, *Doris, or the Pride of Pemberton Mills,* or *Lost in a Fearful Fate's Abyss.* But they had never heard of Charles Dickens, nor *Gulliver's Travels,* nor *Little Women.* The author gave them a resume of *Little Women.* They listened intently; and when she was done, one, Mrs. Smith, said:

"Why, that's no story at all."

While another, Phoebe, declared: "I'll bet any money that lady that wrote it knew all about them boys and girls. They just sound like real live people. But I suppose farmer folks like them kind of stories. They ain't used to the same styles of anything that we city folks are."

The girls, after they had learned on $3 per week, became piece workers. They did not always do much better.

"I only made sixty cents yesterday, and I worked like a dog," says Henrietta.

There is an accident—a mere commonplace in the routine of factory work.

"One of the strippers is carried away, unconscious, with two bleeding finger-stumps. In an unguarded moment the fingers had been cut off in her machine. Although their work does not allow them to stop a moment, her companions were all loud in sympathy for this misfortune, which is not rare. Little Jennie, the unfortunate girl's turner-in and fellow worker for two years, wept bitterly as she wiped away the blood from the long, shining knife and prepared to take the place of her old superior with its increased wage of $3.50 a week. The little girl had only been making three dollars and a quarter, and so, as Henrietta remarked, 'It's a pretty bad accident that don't bring good to somebody.'"

So goes by the first long day, and thus the second long day:

"The last half of the weary day had begun. How my blistered hands ached now! How my swollen feet and ankles throbbed with pain! Every girl limped now as she crossed the floor . . . Each girl bent to her task with a fierce energy that was almost maddening in its intensity.

"Blind and dizzy with fatigue, I peered down the long dusty aisles of boxes toward the clock. It was only two. Every effort, human and mechanical, all over the great factory, was now strained almost to the breaking point. How long can this agony last? How long can this roar and the rush and the throbbing pain continue until that nameless and unknown something snaps like an overstrained fiddle-string and brings relief?. . . . The head foreman rushed through the aisles and bawled to us to 'hustle for all you're worth,' as the customers were demanding their goods.

"'My God! ain't we hustling?' angrily shouted Rosie Sweeny, a pretty girl at the next table. 'God Almighty! how I hate Easter and Christmas time! Oh, my legs is "most breaking,"' and with that the overwrought girl burst into a passionate tirade against everybody, the foreman included, and all the while she never ceased to work.

"There were not many girls in the factory like Rosie Sweeny. Hers were the quickest fingers, the sharpest tongue, the prettiest face.

"'That Rosie Sweeny'll go to the bad yet, you mark my words,' is Annie Kinzer's prophecy."

That night the author went home with Henrietta. They had figured that they could "bach" it together for a dollar and a half a week. But that night the author was surprised to see how little Henrietta ate, and Henrietta was surprised to see how much the author ate.

"Maybe you won't eat so much after a while," Henrietta said hopefully. "If I eat as much as you I'd be likely to starve to death. . . . But after a while you get used to being hungry for so long you couldn't eat if you had it to eat."

But the author did not remain to "bach" it with Henrietta. That same night she walked through horror, and fled to the streets after midnight to consort with homeless old hags and wait for morning.

It was Easter Sunday. She was without money, and that night she slept in a police station. It was during this period that she learned what was to her the "quintessence of poverty—the absolute impossibility of personal cleanliness and of decent raiment." For remember, soft and tender reader, there are single blocks in New York City in which live five hundred babies, to say nothing of men and women, and in which there is not a single bath-tub. And remember that dirt is degradation and a sin against the flesh.

The author went to live in a horror called a Working Girls' Home, where beds were ten cents a night. At 6 a.m. all lodgers were turned out of their beds, and they were not allowed to return to their beds until bedtime, which was 10 p.m. Also, each morning, when they left the lodging, they were searched to make sure that they had not stolen anything.

For sufficient reasons the author did not return to the paper-box factory. She got a job making artificial flowers at $3.50 per week. Here she worked a month, and here the long day ran on into the night:

"At night the work was harder, as the room grew terribly hot from the gas jets and from the stoves where the rosemakers heated their tools. The faces grew tired and pale and the girls sang to keep themselves awake."

Here is a description of a rosemaker's hand, twisted out of all beauty and shapeliness: "Calloused and hard as a piece of tortoise shell, ridged with innumerable corrugations, and hopelessly discolored, with the thumb and forefinger flattened like miniature spades, her right hand had long ago lost all semblance to the other."

But times grew slack and the girls were laid off by the weeping forewoman who knew the tragedy of it. The author's third job was running a "power Singer" in a great room that was "a very inferno of sound, a great, yawning chaos of terrific noise. The girls, who sat in long rows, did not raise their eyes. . . . Every pair of eyes seemed to be held in fascination upon the flying and endless strip of white that raced through a pair of hands to feed itself into the insatiable maw of the electric sewing machine. Every face, tense and stony, bespoke a superb effort to concentrate mind and body, and soul itself, literally, upon the point of a needle. Every form was crouched in the effort to guide the seam through the pressure-foot. And piled between the opposing phalanxes of set faces were billows upon billows of foamy white muslin and lace—the finished garments wrought by the so-many dozen per hour, for the so-many cents per day—and wrought, too, in this terrific, nerve-wracking noise."

But it was piece-work, the author was destitute, and she would have starved to death before she could have succeeded in learning the trade. Nay, more than mere training was necessary, if Rachel, the expert, was to be trusted. Rachel, who worked with the frenzy of a wild beast struggling for life, who, when the power broke down, "watched the clock impatiently and crouched sullenly over her machine," who claimed that one had to be born to work on muslin, and who imparted the information, "My mother was working on shirts for a straight ten months before I was born."

The the author got work in a steam laundry, shaking out the napkins and garments as they came from the steam wringer. Her wage was $3.50 per week while learning, $4 when she had learned.

"Ever worked at this before?" she asked another girl waiting for a job at pushing the heavy trucks of wet clothes.

The reply was a sharp laugh, and the girl, flinging back her sleeve, "thrust out the stump of a wrist."

"It happens every once in a while, when you are running the mangles and was tired. That's the way it was with me. I was clean done out, one Saturday night, and I just couldn't see no more; and the first thing I know—wo-o-w! and that hand went right straight, clean into the roller. And I was just tired, that's all!"

And here, too, in the steam laundry, was the long day.

"'You won't last long, mind ye; you young 'uns never do,' said old Mrs. Mooney. 'If you ain't strong as an ox it gits in your back and off you go to the 'orspital. And if you're not able to stand the drivin', and thinks you're good-lookin', off you goes to the bad sooner'n stay here.'"

Here the foreman advised the workers to stand "slack-like" and droop their shoulders in order to get easement of the pain from which all of them suffered. Here, toiling half-naked in an inferno of heat and steam, "there were not only aching backs and arms and legs, but feet parboiled to a blister on the burning floor. The air was rent with lamentations."

And still the long day dragged on. By 4 o'clock everybody had sunk into a state of apathetic quiet.

"'We're two days behind with them hospital sheets,' screamed the forewoman. 'S--- Hotel barber shop got to go out tonight!'

"'Mother of God!' groaned old Mrs. Mooney, 'Sure, and that means 9 o'clock tonight.'

"'Aren't we going to get out at 6?' asked the one-eyed girl (who had just gone to work that day).

"'God love ye, dearie, no,' replied Mrs. Mooney. 'Ye'll never get outside this shop at 6 any night, unless ye're carried out dead.'

"'Every night?'

"'Sure, every night exceptin' Saturday, and then it's twelve to half-past one.'"

It was at this stage of the afternoon that the author passed into that condition which is familiar to all who toil like beasts—the work trance. That night she came to herself walking along the sidewalk. "I realized that I had just passed out of a trance—a trance superinduced by physical misery—a merciful sub-conscious condition of apathy, in which my soul as well as my body had taken refuge when torture grew unbearable."

And all this for $3.50 per week, $4 when she had become a skilled hand!

She left the laundry, abruptly, in tragedy—the tragedy of the good-looking woman working for $3.50 per week and surrounded by human wolves. The wolf in this particular case was the proprietor of the laundry. He cast his eyes upon her and promptly promoted her. Then the foreman, who was a kindly man, smuggled a note into her hand. The first two sentences and the postscript tell sufficient of the story:

"'You'd better give up this job. It is no place for a girl who wants to do right.'

"'P.S.–Please don't show this or I lose my job.'"

And here ends *The Long Day*. It is a record of conditions of which we Americans can scarcely be proud. It is a record to be read by the ten thousand millionaires who live in New York City. It is a record to be read by every patriotic American who sings "My Country, 'tis of Thee, Sweet Land of Liberty," and who thinks that the United States cannot be improved upon. And it is a record to be read by every person who is not a coward and who is unafraid to face the truth.

And having read the book, let every one ponder upon this: There is now, today, being utilized in the United States, 30,000,000 horse-power. Engineers compute each horse-power as equivalent to the work of eight men. Here is energy eight times greater than that possessed by the naked savage. Who will dare to say that the working girls of New York City, tens of thousands of them, are eight times more comfortable and happy than the naked savage? And who will dare to say that at least they are as comfortable as the naked savage?

WHAT LIFE MEANS TO ME
(*Cosmopolitan*, March, 1906)

⊕ ⊕ ⊕ ⊕ ⊕ ⊕ ⊕ ⊕ ⊕ ⊕ ⊕ ⊕

This essay derived from a challenge by *Cosmopolitan* to a number of prominent American writers to contribute articles on the theme in the title. In a conversation with poet Edwin Markham, London outlined his socialist approach to the subject. Markham was sympathetic but doubted the expediency of the approach for William Randolph Hearst's *Cosmopolitan*.

Despite this caution, the article was published as London wrote it. "Writers for Hearst, special writers like myself," Jack said, "are paid well for expanding their own untrammeled views."

Charmian London wrote that in the essay "one reads what is perhaps his most impassioned committal of himself as a rebel toward the shames and uncleanness of the capitalist system. . . . His challenge is flung to that thin and cracking upper crust as he saw it: 'with all its rotten life and unburied dead, its monstrous selfishness and sodden materialism.'"*

The article was included in London's *Revolution & Other Essays* (New York: The Macmillan Co., 1910).

⊕ ⊕ ⊕ ⊕ ⊕ ⊕ ⊕ ⊕ ⊕ ⊕ ⊕ ⊕

I was born in the working-class. Early I discovered enthusiasm, ambition, and ideals; and to satisfy these became the problem of my child-life. My environment was crude and rough and raw. I had no outlook, but an uplook rather. My place in society was at the bottom. Here life offered nothing but sordidness and wretchedness, both of the flesh and the spirit; for here flesh and spirit were alike starved and tormented.

Above me towered the colossal edifice of society, and to my mind the only way out was up. Into this edifice I early resolved to climb.

---

*Charmian K. London, vol. 2, p. 106.

Up above, men wore black clothes and boiled shirts, and women dressed in beautiful gowns. Also, there were good things to eat, and there was plenty to eat. This much for the flesh. Then there were the things of the spirit. Up above me, I knew, were unselfishnesses of the spirit, clean and noble thinking, keen intellectual living. I knew all this because I read "Seaside Library" novels, in which, with the exception of the villains and adventuresses, all men and women thought beautiful thoughts, spoke a beautiful tongue, and performed glorious deeds. In short, as I accepted the rising of the sun, I accepted that up above me was all that was fine and noble and gracious, all that gave decency and dignity to life, all that made life worth living and that remunerated one for his travail and misery.

But it is not particularly easy for one to climb up out of the working-class—especially if he is handicapped by the possession of ideals and illusions. I lived on a ranch in California, and I was hard put to find the ladder whereby to climb. I early inquired the rate of interest on invested money, and worried my child's brain into an understanding of the virtues and excellencies of that remarkable invention of man, compound interest. Further, I ascertained the current rates of wages for workers of all ages, and the cost of living. From all this data I concluded that if I began immediately and worked and saved until I was fifty years of age, I could then stop working and enter into participation in a fair portion of the delights and goodnesses that would then be open to me higher up in society. Of course, I resolutely determined not to marry, while I quite forgot to consider at all that great rock of disaster in the working-class world—sickness.

But the life that was in me demanded more than a meagre existence of scraping and scrimping. Also, at ten years of age, I became a newsboy on the streets of a city, and found myself with a changed uplook. All about me were still the same sordidness and wretchedness, and up above me was still the same paradise waiting to be gained; but the ladder whereby to climb was a different one. It was now the ladder of business. Why save my earnings and invest in government bonds, when, by buying two newspapers for five cents, with a turn of the wrist I could sell them for ten cents and double my capital? The business ladder was the ladder for me, and I had a vision of myself becoming a baldheaded and successful merchant prince.

Alas for visions! When I was sixteen I had already earned the title of "prince." But this title was given me by a gang of cut-throats and thieves, by whom I was called "The Prince of the Oyster Pirates." And at that time I had climbed the first rung of the business ladder. I was a capitalist. I owned a boat and a complete oyster-pirating outfit. I had begun to exploit my fellow-creatures. I had a crew of one man. As captain and owner I took two-thirds of the spoils, and gave the crew one-third, though the crew worked just as hard as I did and risked just as much his life and liberty.

This one rung was the height I climbed up the business ladder. One night I went on a raid amongst the Chinese fishermen. Ropes and nets were worth dollars and cents. It was robbery, I grant, but it was precisely the spirit of capitalism. The capitalist takes away the possessions of his fellow-creatures by means of a rebate, or of a betrayal of trust, or by the purchase of senators and supreme-court judges. I was merely crude. That was the only difference. I used a gun.

But my crew that night was one of those inefficients against whom the capitalist is wont to fulminate, because, forsooth, such inefficients increase expenses and reduce dividends. My crew did both. What of his carelessness he set fire to the big mainsail and totally destroyed it. There weren't any dividends that night, and the Chinese fishermen were richer by the nets and ropes we did not get. I was bankrupt, unable just then to pay sixty-five dollars for a new mainsail. I left my boat at anchor and went off on a bay-pirate boat on a raid up the Sacramento River. While away on this trip, another gang of bay pirates raided my boat. They stole everything, even the anchors; and later on, when I recovered the drifting hulk, I sold it for twenty dollars. I slipped back the one rung I had climbed, and never again did I attempt the business ladder.

From then on I was mercilessly exploited by other capitalists. I had the muscle, and they made money out of it while I made but a very indifferent living out of it. I was a sailor before the mast, a longshoreman, a roustabout; I worked in canneries, and factories, and laundries; I mowed lawns, and cleaned carpets, and washed windows. And I never got the full product of my toil. I looked at the daughter of the cannery owner, in her carriage, and knew that it was my muscle, in part, that helped drag along that carriage on its rubber tires. I looked at the son of the factory owner, going to college, and knew that it was my muscle that helped, in part, to pay for the wine and good fellowship he enjoyed.

But I did not resent this. It was all in the game. They were the strong. Very well, I was strong, I would carve my way to a place amongst them and make money out of the muscles of other men. I was not afraid of work. I loved hard work. I would pitch in and work harder than ever and eventually become a pillar of society.

And just then, as luck would have it, I found an employer that was of the same mind. I was willing to work, and he was more than willing that I should work. I thought I was learning a trade. In reality, I had displaced two men. I thought he was making an electrician out of me; as a matter of fact, he was making fifty dollars per month out of me.

The two men I had displaced had received forty dollars each per month; I was doing the work of both for thirty dollars per month.

This employer worked me nearly to death. A man may love oysters, but too many oysters will disincline him toward that particular diet. And so with me. Too much work sickened me. I did not wish ever to see work again. I fled from work. I became a tramp, begging my way from door to door, wandering over the United States and sweating bloody sweats in slums and prisons.

I had been born in the working-class, and I was now, at the age of eighteen, beneath the point at which I had started. I was down in the cellar of society, down in the subterranean depths of misery about which it is neither nice nor proper to speak. I was in the pit, the abyss, the human cesspool, the shambles and the charnel-house of our civilization. This is the part of the edifice of society that society chooses to ignore. Lack of space compels me here to ignore it, and I shall say only that the things I there saw gave me a terrible scare.

I was scared into thinking. I saw the naked simplicities of the complicated civilization in which I lived. Life was a matter of food and shelter. In order to eat food and shelter men sold things. The merchant sold shoes, the politician sold his manhood, and the representative of the people, with exceptions, of course, sold his trust; while nearly all sold their honor. Women, too, whether on the street or in the holy bond of wedlock, were prone to sell their flesh. All things were commodities, all people bought and sold. The one commodity that labor had to sell was muscle. The honor of labor had no price in the market-place. Labor had muscle, and muscle alone, to sell.

But there was a difference, a vital difference. Shoes and trust and honor had a way of renewing themselves. They were imperishable stocks. Muscle, on the other hand, did not renew. As the show merchant sold shoes, he continued to replenish his stock. But there was no way of replenishing the laborer's stock of muscle. The more he sold of his muscle, the less of it remained to him. It was his one commodity, and each day his stock of it diminished. In the end, if he did not die before, he sold out and put up his shutters. He was a muscle bankrupt, and nothing remained to him but to go down into the cellar of society and perish miserably.

I learned, further, that brain was likewise a commodity. It, too, was different from muscle. A brain seller was only at his prime when he was fifty or sixty years old, and his wares were fetching higher prices than ever. But a laborer was worked out or broken down at forty-five or fifty. I had been in the cellar of society, and I did not like the place as a habitation. The pipes and drains were unsanitary, and the air was bad to breathe.

If I could not live on the parlor floor of society, I could, at any rate, have a try at the attic. It was true, the diet there was slim, but the air at least was pure. So I resolved to sell no more muscle, and to become a vender of brains.

Then began a frantic pursuit of knowledge. I returned to California and opened the books. While thus equipping myself to become a brain merchant, it was inevitable that I should delve into sociology. There I found, in a certain class of books, scientifically formulated, the simple sociological concepts I had already worked out for myself. Other and greater minds, before I was born, had worked out all that I had thought and a vast deal more. I discovered that I was a socialist.

The socialists were revolutionists, inasmuch as they struggled to overthrow the society of the present, and out of the material to build the society of the future. I, too, was a socialist and a revolutionist. I joined the groups of working-class and intellectual revolutionists, and for the first time came into intellectual living. Here I found keen-flashing intellects and brilliant wits; for here I met strong and alert-brained, withal horny-handed, members of the working-class; unfrocked preachers too wide in their Christianity for any congregation of Mammon-worshippers; professors broken on the wheel of university subserviance to the ruling class and flung out because they were quick with knowledge which they strove to apply to the affairs of mankind.

Here I found, also, warm faith in the human, glowing idealism, sweetnesses of unselfishness, renunciation, and martyrdom—all the splendid, stinging things of the spirit. Here life was clean, noble, and alive. Here life rehabilitated itself, became wonderful and glorious; and I was glad to be alive. I was in touch with great souls who exalted flesh and spirit over dollars and cents, and to whom the thin wail of the starved slum child meant more than all the pomp and circumstance of commercial expansion and world empire. All about me were nobleness of purpose and heroism of effort, and my days and nights were sunshine and starshine, all fire and dew, with before my eyes, ever burning and blazing, the Holy Grail, Christ's own Grail, the warm human, long-suffering and maltreated, but to be rescued and saved at the last.

And I, poor foolish I, deemed all this to be a mere fore-taste of the delights of living I should find higher above me in society. I had lost many illusions since the day I read "Seaside Library" novels on the California ranch. I was destined to lose many of the illusions I still retained.

As a brain merchant I was a success. Society opened its portals to me. I entered right in on the parlor floor, and my disillusionment proceeded rapidly. I sat down to dinner with the masters of society, and with the wives and daughters of the masters of society. The women were gowned beautifully, I admit; but to my naive surprise I discovered that they were of the same clay as all the rest of the women I had known down below in the cellar. "The colonel's lady and Judy O'Grady were sisters under their skins"—and gowns.

It was not this, however, so much as their materialism, that shocked me. It is true, these beautifully gowned, beautiful women prattled sweet little ideals and dear little moralities; but in spite of their prattle the dominant key of the life they lived was materialistic. And they were so sentimentally selfish! They assisted in all kinds of sweet little charities, and informed one of the fact, while all the time the food they ate and the beautiful clothes they wore were bought out of dividends stained with the blood of child labor, and sweated labor, and of prostitution itself. When I mentioned such facts, expecting in my innocence that these sisters of Judy O'Grady would at once strip off their blood-dyed silks and jewels, they became excited and angry, and read me preachments about the lack of thrift, the drink, and the innate depravity that caused all the misery in society's cellar. When I mentioned that I couldn't quite see that it was the lack of thrift, the intemperance, and the depravity of a half-started child of six that made it work twelve hours every night in a Southern cotton mill, these sisters of Judy O'Grady attacked my private life and called me an "agitator"—as though that, forsooth, settled the argument.

Nor did I fare better with the masters themselves. I had expected to find men who were clean, noble, and alive, whose ideals were clean, noble, and alive. I went about amongst the men who sat in the high places—the preachers, the politicians, the business men, the professors, and the editors. I ate meat with them, drank wine with them, automobiled with them, and studied them. It is true, I found many that were clean and noble; but with rare exceptions, they were not *alive*. I do verily believe I could count the exceptions on the fingers of my two hands. Where they were not alive with rottenness, quick with unclean life, they were merely the unburied dead—clean and noble, like well-preserved mummies, but not alive. In this connection I may especially mention the professors I met, the men who live up to that decadent university ideal, "the passionless pursuit of passionless intelligence."

I met men who invoked the name of the Prince of Peace in their diatribes against war, and who put rifles in the hands of Pinkertons with which to shoot down strikers in their own factories. I met men incoherent with indignation at the brutality of prize-fighting, and who, at the same time, were parties to the adulteration of food that killed each year more babies than even red-handed Herod had killed.

I talked in hotels and clubs and homes and Pullmans and steamer-chairs with captains of industry, and marvelled at how little travelled they were in the realm of intellect. On the other hand, I discovered that their intellect, in the business sense, was abnormally developed. Also, I discovered that their morality, where business was concerned, was nil.

This delicate, aristocratic-featured gentleman, was a dummy director and a tool of corporations that secretly robbed widows and orphans. This gentleman, who collected fine editions and was an especial patron of literature, paid blackmail to a heavy-jowled, black-browed boss of a municipal machine. This editor, who published patent medicine advertisements and did not dare print the truth in his paper about said patent medicines for fear of losing the advertising, called me a scoundrelly demagogue because I told him that his political economy was antiquated and that his biology was contemporaneous with Pliny.

This senator was the tool and the slave, the little puppet of a gross, uneducated machine boss; so was this governor and this supreme court judge; and all three rode on railroad passes. This man, talking soberly and earnestly about the beauties of idealism and the goodness of God, had just betrayed his comrades in a business deal. This man, a pillar of the church and heavy contributor to foreign missions, worked his shop girls ten hours a day on a starvation wage and thereby directly encouraged prostitution. This man, who endowed chairs in universities, perjured himself in courts of law over a matter of dollars and cents. And this railroad magnate broke his word as a gentleman and a Christian when he granted a secret rebate to one of two captains of industry locked together in a struggle to the death.

It was the same everywhere, crime and betrayal, betrayal and crime— men who were alive, but who were neither clean nor noble, men who were clean and noble but who were not alive. Then there was a great, hopeless mass, neither noble nor alive, but merely clean. It did not sin positively nor deliberately; but it did sin passively and ignorantly by acquiescing in the current immorality and profiting by it. Had it been noble and alive it would not have been ignorant, and it would have refused to share in the profits of betrayal and crime.

I discovered that I did not like to live on the parlor floor of society. Intellectually I was bored. Morally and spiritually I was sickened. I remembered my intellectuals and idealists, my unfrocked preachers, broken professors, and clean-minded, class-conscious workingmen. I remembered my days and nights of sunshine and starshine, where life was all a wild sweet wonder, a spiritual paradise of unselfish adventure and ethical romance. And I saw before me, ever blazing and burning, the Holy Grail.

So I went back to the working-class, in which I had been born and where I belonged. I care no longer to climb. The imposing edifice of society above my head holds no delights for me. It is the foundation of the edifice that interests me. There I am content to labor, crowbar in hand, shoulder to shoulder with intellectuals, idealists, and class-conscious workingmen, getting a solid pry now and again and setting the whole edifice rocking. Some day, when we get a few more hands and crowbars to work, we'll topple it over, along with all its rotten life and unburied dead, its monstrous selfishness and sodden materialism. Then we'll cleanse the cellar and build a new habitation for mankind, in which there will be no parlor floor, in which all the rooms will be bright and airy, and where the air that is breathed will be clean, noble, and alive.

Such is my outlook. I look forward to a time when man shall progress upon something worthier and higher than his stomach, when there will be a finer incentive to impel men to action than the incentive of today, which is the incentive of the stomach. I retain my belief in the nobility and excellence of the human. I believe that spiritual sweetness and unselfishness will conquer the gross gluttony of today. And last of all, my faith is in the working-class. As some Frenchman has said, "The stairway of time is ever echoing with the wooden shoe going up, the polished boot descending."

Newton, Iowa,
November, 1905

LETTER TO "THE BOOKMAN"
(April 10, 1906)

⊕ ⊕ ⊕ ⊕ ⊕ ⊕ ⊕ ⊕ ⊕ ⊕ ⊕ ⊕

"Love of Life" is one of Jack London's supreme achievements in the short story. It appeared in *McClure's Magazine* in December, 1905 (simultaneously in *Blackwood's Magazine* in Edinburgh), and was the title story of a 1907 London collection. The tale was a favorite of Lenin's and it was one of the things read to him by his wife Krupskaya as he lay on his death bed.

"Love of Life" generated plagiarism charges against London in 1906 when the *New York World,* using the familiar "deadly parallel column," showed the similarities in London's story to an article, "Lost in the Land of the Midnight Sun," which had appeared in *McClure's* in December, 1901. The article had been written by two journalists who had interviewed one Charles Bunn, a member of a small expedition exploring for minerals in the Canadian Barrens.*

⊕ ⊕ ⊕ ⊕ ⊕ ⊕ ⊕ ⊕ ⊕ ⊕ ⊕ ⊕

April 10, 1906

In reply to yours of April 3. Life is so short and people so silly, that from the very beginning of my career, when I first began to get newspaper notoriety because of my youthful socialism, I made a point to deny nothing charged against me in the newspapers. On the other hand, I have made it a courtesy to deny such things when requested to do so by my friends. Wherefore, because of your request, I am now making this explanation of the similarity between my "Love and Life" and Augustus Bridle's and J. K. MacDonald's "Lost in the Land of the Midnight Sun."

It is a common practice of authors to draw material for their stories from the newspapers. Here are facts of life reported in journalistic style,

---

*An excellent account of the controversy appears in Franklin Walker, pp. 245–54.

waiting to be made into literature. So common is this practice that often amusing consequences are caused by several writers utilizing the same material. Some years ago, while I was in England, a story of mine was published in the *San Francisco Argonaut*. In the *Century* of the same date was published a story by Frank Norris. While these two stories were quite different in manner of treatment, they were patently the same in foundation and motive. At once the newspapers paralleled our stories. The explanation was simple: Norris and I had read the same newspaper account, and proceeded to exploit it. But the fun did not stop there. Somebody dug up a *Black Cat* published a year previous, in which was a similar story by another man who used the same foundation and motive. Then Chicago hustled around and resurrected a story that had been published some months before the *Black Cat* story, and that was the same in foundation and motive. Of course, all these different writers had chanced upon the same newspaper article.

So common is this practice of authors, that it is recommended by all the instructors in the art of the short story, to read the newspapers and magazines in order to get material. Charles Reade swore by this practice. I might name a lengthy list of the great writers who have advised this practice.

All the foregoing merely to show that this practice exists and is generally employed by story-writers. Now to the "Love of Life," which the New York *World* so generously paralleled with "Lost in the Land of the Midnight Sun." "Lost in the Land of the Midnight Sun" is not a story. It is a narrative of fact. It was published in *McClure's Magazine*. It tells the actual sufferings of a man with a sprained ankle in the country of the Coppermine River. It is not fiction, and it is not literature. I took the facts of life contained in it, added to them many other facts of life gained from other sources, and made, or attempted to make, a piece of literature out of them. There was another narrative of suffering that I used quite as extensively as I did "Lost in the Land of the Midnight Sun." This older narrative was a newspaper account of a lost and wandering prospector near Nome, Alaska. On top of this, I drew upon all my own personal experience of hardship and suffering and starvation, and upon the whole fund of knowledge I had of the hardship and suffering and starvation of hundreds of thousands of other men.

If you will turn to the end of my "Love of Life," you will find that my rescued hero becomes suddenly fat. This abrupt obesity was caused by his stuffing under his shirt all the spare hardtack he could beg from the sailors. Now I did not invent this. It is a fact of life. You will find it in in Lieutenant Greely's narrative of the Greely Polar Expedition. I scarcely see how I could be charged with plagiarism from Lieutenant

Greely; and yet if I plagiarized from Augustus Bridle and J. K. Macdonald for some of my material, I must have plagiarized from the newspaper correspondent who described the wanderings of the Nome prospector— and I must have plagiarized from the experiences of scores and scores of Alaskan prospectors whose accounts I heard from their own lips.

The *World,* however, did not charge me with plagiarism. It charged me with identity of time and situation. Certainly the *World* is right. I plead guilty, and I am glad that the *World* was intelligent enough not to charge me with identity of language.

But little remains to be said. It might be well to explain why that half-page of deadly parallel was published in the *World.* In the first place, sensation. Sensation is the goods demanded by a newspaper of its space-writers. The suggestion of plagiarism is always sensational. When a half-page of deadly parallel is run in a newspaper, plagiarism is certainly suggested. The loose meaning of words in the average mind would make ninety per cent of the readers of such a parallel infer that plagiarism had been charged.

Secondly, the space-writer writes for a living. I hope for his own soul's sake that this particular space-writer also writes for his living. His newspaper wanted the goods of sensation, and by refusing to charge plagiarism, while leaving the inference of plagiarism to the reader, this space-writer sold half a page to the *World.*

In conclusion, I, in the course of making my living by turning journalism into literature, used material from various sources which had been collected and narrated by men who made their living by turning the facts of life into journalism. Along comes the space-writer of the *World* who makes his living by turning the doings of other men into sensation. Well, all three of us made our living; and who's got any kick coming?

Sincerely yours,
Jack London

THE JUNGLE
(New York Evening Journal, August 8, 1906)

⊕ ⊕ ⊕ ⊕ ⊕ ⊕ ⊕ ⊕ ⊕ ⊕ ⊕ ⊕

Upton Sinclair (1878-1968) wrote *The Jungle* in 1906—"it aimed at the people's heart and hit their stomach," he said. He had written six unsuccessful novels in the period 1901-06 and would write many successful ones in his long career, including *Dragon's Teeth* (1942), for which he won a Pulitzer Prize, and several books in which Jack London played a significant role: *Mammonart* (1925), *Money Writes* (1927), and *The Cup of Fury* (1956),* the latter a tract against alcohol.

⊕ ⊕ ⊕ ⊕ ⊕ ⊕ ⊕ ⊕ ⊕ ⊕ ⊕ ⊕

> At first, this Earth, a stage so gloomed with woe
> You all but sicken at the shifting of the scenes.
> And yet be patient, Our Playwright may show
> In some fifth Act what this Wild Drama means.

When John Burns, the great English labor leader and present member of the Cabinet, visited Chicago, he was asked by a reporter for his opinion of that city. "Chicago," he answered, "is a pocket edition of hell." Some time later, when Burns was going aboard his steamer to sail to England, he was approached by another reporter, who wanted to know if he had yet changed his opinion of Chicago. "Yes, I have," was the prompt reply. "My present opinion is that hell is a pocket edition of Chicago."

Possibly Upton Sinclair was of the same opinion when he selected Chicago for the scene of his novel of industry, *The Jungle.* At any rate, he selected the greatest industrial city in the country, the one city of the country that is ripest industrially, that is the most perfect specimen of jungle-civilization to be found. One cannot question the wisdom of the

---

*Sherman lists fourteen works by Sinclair, large and small, on Jack London, in the period 1906-72.

the author's choice, for Chicago certainly is industrialism incarnate, the storm-center of the conflict between capital and labor, a city of street battles and blood, with a class-conscious capitalist organization and a class-conscious workman organization, where the school teachers are formed into labor unions and are affiliated with the hod carriers and bricklayers of the American Federation of Labor, where the very office clerks rain office furniture out of the windows of the sky-scrapers upon the heads of the police who are trying to deliver scab meat in a beef strike, and where practically as many policemen as strikers are carried away in the ambulances.

This, then, is the scene of Upton Sinclair's novel, Chicago, the industrial jungle of twentieth century civilization. And right here it may be just as well to forestall the legions who will rise up and say that the book is untrue. In the first place, Upton Sinclair himself says: "The book is a true book, true in substance and in detail, an exact and faithful picture of life with which it deals."

Nevertheless, and in spite of the intrinsic evidence of truth, there will be many who will call *The Jungle* a tissue of lies, and first among them may be expected the Chicago newspapers. They are quick to resent the bald truth about their beloved city. Not more than three months ago, a public speaker, in New York City, instancing extreme cases of the smallness of wage in the Chicago sweat shops, spoke of women receiving ninety cents per week. He was promptly called a liar by the Chicago newspapers—all except one paper, that really investigated, and that found not only many who were receiving no more than ninety cents per week, but found some receiving as low as fifty cents per week.

For that matter, when the New York publishers of *The Jungle* first read it, they sent it on to the editor of one of the largest Chicago newspapers, and that gentlemen's written opinion was that Upton Sinclair was "the damndest liar in the United States." Then the publishers called Upton Sinclair upon the carpet. He gave his authorities. The publishers were still dubious—no doubt worried by visions of bankrupting libel suits. They wanted to make sure. They sent a lawyer to Chicago to investigate. And after a week or so the lawyer's report came back to the effect that Sinclair had left the worst untold.

Then the book was published, and here it is, a story of human destruction, of poor broken cogs in the remorseless grind of the industrial machine. It is essentially a book of today. It is alive and warm. It is brutal with life. It is written of sweat and blood, and groans and tears. It depicts, not what man ought to be, but what man is compelled to be in this, our world, in the twentieth century. It depicts, not what our country ought to be, nor what our country seems to be to those who live in softness and comfort far from the labor-ghetto, but it depicts what our country really is, the home of oppression and injustice, a nightmare of misery, an inferno of suffering, a jungle wherein wild beasts eat and are eaten. For a hero, Upton Sinclair did not select an American-born man, who through the mists of Fourth of July oratory and campaign spellbinding, sees clearly in a way the ferocious facts of the American workingman's life. Upton Sinclair made no such mistake. He selected a foreigner, a Lithuanian, fleeing from the oppression and injustice of Europe, and dreaming of liberty and freedom and equal rights with all men in the pursuit of happiness.

This Lithuanian was one Jurgis (pronounced Yoorghis), a young giant, broad of back, spilling over with vigor, passionately enamored of work, ambitious, a workingman in a thousand. He was the sort of a man that can set a work-pace that is heart-breaking and soul-killing to the men who work beside him and who must keep his pace despite the fact that they are weaklings compared with him.

In short, Jurgis was "the sort the bosses like to get hold of, the sort they make it a grievance they cannot get hold of." Jurgis was indomitable. This was because of his mighty muscles and superb health. No matter what the latest misfortune that fell upon him, he squared his shoulders and said, "Never mind, I will work harder!" That was his clarion cry, his Excelsior! "Never mind, I will work harder!" He had no thought of the time to come when his muscles would not be so mighty, nor his health so superb, and when he would not be able to work harder.

On his second day in Chicago he stood in the crowd at the gates of the packing-houses. "All day long these gates were besieged by starving and penniless men; they came, literally, by the thousands every single morning, fighting with each other for a chance for life. Blizzards and cold made no difference to them, they were always on hand two hours before the sun rose, an hour before the work began. Sometimes their faces froze, sometimes their feet and their hands—but still they came, for they had no other place to go."

But Jurgis stood only half an hour in this crowd. His huge shoulders, his youth and health and unsullied strength marked him out in the crowd like a virgin in the midst of many hags. For he was a labor-virgin, his magnificent body yet unbroken by toil, and he was quickly picked out by a boss and set to work. Jurgis was the one workingman in a thousand. There were men in that crowd who had stood there every day for a month. They were of the nine hundred and ninety-nine.

Jurgis was prosperous. He was getting seventeen and one-half cents per hour, and just then it happened that he worked many hours. The next thing he did needed no urging from President Roosevelt. With the joy of youth in his blood and the cornucopia of prosperity spilling over him, he got married. "It was the supreme hour of ecstasy in the life of one of God's gentlest creatures, the wedding feast and the joy transfiguration of the little Ona Lukozaite."

Jurgis worked on the killing floor, wading through the steaming blood that flowed upon the floor, with a street sweeper's broom sweeping the smoking entrails into a trap as fast as they were drawn from the carcasses of the steers. But he did not mind. He was wildly happy. He proceeded to buy a house—on the installment plan.

Why pay rent when one could buy a house for less? That was what the advertisement asked. "And why, indeed?" was what Jurgis asked. There was quite a number in the combined families of Jurgis and Ona, and they studied the house proposition long and carefully, and then paid all their old country savings (three hundred dollars) down, agreeing to pay twelve dollars per month until the balance of twelve hundred was paid. Then the house would be theirs. Until such time, according to the contract that was foisted on them, they would be renters. Failure to pay an installment would lose for them all they had already paid. And in the end they lost the three hundred dollars, and the rent and interest they had paid, because the house was built, not as a home, but as a gamble on misfortune, and resold many times to just such simple folk as they.

In the meantime Jurgis worked and learned. He began to see things and to understand. He saw "How there were portions of the work which determined the pace of the rest, and for these they had picked out men whom they paid high wages, and whom they changed frequently. This was called 'speeding up the gang,' and if any man could not keep up with the pace, there were hundreds outside begging to try.

"He saw that the bosses grafted off the men, and they grafted off each other, while the superintendents grafted off the bosses. Here was Durham's, owned by a man who was trying to make as much money of it as he could, and did not care in the least how he did it; and underneath, ranged in ranks and grades like an army, were managers, superintendents and foremen, each man driving the man next below him and trying to squeeze out of him as much work as possible. And all the men of the same rank were pitted against each other; the accounts of each were kept separately, and every man lived in terror of losing his job if another made a better record than he. There was no loyalty or decency anywhere about it, there was no place in it where a man counted for anything against a dollar. The man who told tales and spied upon his fellow creatures would rise; but the man who minded his own business and did his work—why, they would 'speed him up' till they had worn him out, and then they would throw him into the gutter."

And why should the bosses have any care for the men. There were always plenty more. "One day Durham advertised in the paper for two hundred men to cut ice; and all that day the homeless and starving of the city came trudging through the snow from all of its two hundred square miles. That night forty score of them crowded into the station house of the stockyards district—they filled the rooms, sleeping on each other's laps, toboggan fashion, and they piled on top of one another in the corridors, till the police shut the doors and left some to freeze outside. On the morrow, before daybreak, there were three thousand at Durham's, and the police reserves had to be sent for to quell the riot. Then Durham's bosses picked out twenty of the biggest," and set them to work.

And the accident began to loom big to Jurgis. He began to live in fear of the accident. The thing, terrible as death, that was liable to happen any time. One of his friends, Mikolas, a beef-boner, had been laid up at home twice in three years with blood poisoning, once for three months and once for seven months.

Also, Jurgis saw how the "speeding up" made the accident more imminent. "In the winter time, in the killing floor, one was apt to be covered with blood, and it would freeze solid. The men would tie up their feet in newspapers and old sacks, and these would be soaked in blood and frozen. All of them that used knives were unable to wear gloves, and their arms would be white with frost, and their hands would grow numb, and then of course there would be accidents." Now and then, when the bosses were not looking, the men, for very relief from the cold, would plunge their feet and ankles into the steaming carcasses of the fresh-killed steers.

Another thing that Jurgis saw, and gathered from what was told him, was the procession of the nationalities. At one time "the workers had all been Germans. Afterwards, as cheaper labor came, these Germans had moved away. The next had been the Irish. The Bohemians had come then, and after them the Poles. The people had come in hordes; and old Durham had squeezed them tighter and tighter, speeding them up and grinding them to pieces. The Poles had been driven to the wall by the Lithuanians, and now the Lithuanians were giving way to the Slovaks. Who there was poorer and more miserable than the Slovaks, there was no telling; but the packers would find them, never fear. It was easy to bring them, for wages were really much higher, and it was only when it was too late that the poor people found out that everything else was higher, too."

Then there was the lie of society, or the countless lies, for Jurgis to learn. The food was adulterated, the milk for the children was doctored, the very insect-powder for which Jurgis paid twenty-five cents was adulterated and harmless to insects. Under his house was a cesspool containing the sewage of fifteen years. "Jurgis went about with his soul full of suspicion; he understood that he was environed by hostile powers that were trying to get his money. The storekeepers plastered up their windows with all sorts of lies to entice him, the very fences by the wayside, the lampposts and telegraph poles were pasted over with lies. The great corporation that employed him lied to him and lied to the whole country—from top to bottom it was nothing but one gigantic lie."

Work became slack, and Jurgis worked part time and learned what the munificent pay of seventeen and one-half cents per hour really meant. There were days when he worked no more than two hours, and days when there was no work at all. But he managed to average nearly six hours a day, which meant six dollars per week.

Then came to Jurgis that haunting thing of the labor world, the accident. It was only an injured ankle. He worked on it till he fainted. After that he spent three weeks in bed, went to work on it again too soon, and went back to bed for two months. By that time everybody in the combined families had to get to work. The children sold papers on the streets. Ona sawed hams all day long, and her cousin, Marija, painted cans. And little Stanislovas worked on a marvelous machine that almost did all the work. All Stanislovas had to do was to place an empty lard-can every time the arm of the machine reached out to him.

"And so was decided the place in the universe for little Stanislovas, and his destiny till the end of his days. Hour after hour, day after day, year after year, it was fated that he should stand on a certain square-foot of floor from seven in the morning until noon, and again from half-past twelve to half-past five, making never a motion and thinking never a thought, save for the settling of lard-cans." And for this he received something like three dollars per week, which was his proper share of the total earnings of the million and three-quarters of child laborers in the United States. And his wages a little more than paid the interest on the house.

And Jurgis lay on his back, helpless, starving, in order that the payments and interest on the house should be met. Because of this, when he got on his feet again he was no longer the finest-looking man in the crowd. He was thin and haggard, and he looked miserable. His old job was gone, and he joined the crowd at the gate, morning after morning, striving to keep to the front and to look eager.

"The peculiar bitterness of all this was that Jurgis saw so plainly the meaning of it. In the beginning he had been fresh and strong, and he had gotten a job the first day; but now he was second-hand, a damaged article, so to speak, and they did not want him. They had got the best out of him—they had worn him out, with their speeding up and their carelessness, and now they had thrown him away."

The situation was now desperate. Several of the family lost their jobs, and Jurgis, as a last resort, descended into the inferno of the fertilizer-works and went to work. And then came another accident, of a different sort. Ona, his wife, was vilely treated by her foreman (too vilely treated for narration here), and Jurgis thrashed the foreman and was sent to jail. Both he and Ona lost their jobs.

In the working-class world, disasters do not come singly. The loss of the house followed the loss of the jobs. Because Jurgis had struck a boss he was blacklisted in all the packing-houses and could not even get back his job in the fertilizer-works. The family was broken up, and its members went their various ways to living hell. The lucky ones died, such as Jurgis's father, who died of blood-poisoning, contracted by working in chemicals, and Jurgis's little son, Antanas, who was drowned in the street. (And in this connection I wish to say that this last is a fact. I have personally talked with a man in Chicago, a charity-worker, who buried the child drowned in the streets of Packingtown.)

And Jurgis, under the ban of the blacklist, mused thus: "There was no justice, there was no right, anywhere in it—it was only force, it was tyranny, the will and the power, reckless and unrestrained. They had ground him beneath their heel, they had devoured all his substance, they had murdered his old father, they had broken and wrecked his wife, they had crushed and cowed his whole family. And now they were through with him. They had no further use for him."

"Then men gazed on him with pitying eyes—poor devil, he was black-listed. He stood as much chance of getting a job in Packingtown as of being chosen Mayor of Chicago. They had his name on a secret list in every office, big and little, in the place. They had his name in St. Louis and New York, in Omaha and Boston, in Kansas City and St. Joseph. He was condemned and sentenced without trial and without appeal; he could never work for the packers again."

Nor does *The Jungle* end here. Jurgis lives to get on the inside of the rottenness and corruption of the industrial and political machinery; and of all that he sees and learns nothing less than the book itself can tell.

It is a book well worth the reading, and it is a book that may well make history, as *Uncle Tom's Cabin* made history. For that matter, there are large chances that it may prove to be the *Uncle Tom's Cabin* of wage slavery. It is dedicated, not to a Huntington nor to a Carnegie, but to the Workingmen of America. It has truth and power, and it has behind it in the United States over four hundred thousand men and women who are striving to give it a wider hearing than any book has been given in fifty years. Not only may it become one of the "great sellers," but it is very likely to become the greatest seller. And yet, such is the strangeness of modern life, *The Jungle* may be read by the hundreds of thousands and by the millions of copies and yet not be listed as a "best seller" in the magazines. The reason for this will be that it will be read by the working-class, as it has already been read by hundreds of thousands of the working class. Dear masters, would it not be wise to read for once the literature that all your working-class is reading?

⊕ ⊕ ⊕ ⊕ ⊕ ⊕ ⊕ ⊕ ⊕ ⊕ ⊕ ⊕

This letter appeared in an article in *The Independent* of February 14, 1907, entitled "Is Jack London a Plagiarist?" One L. A. M. Bosworth, writing from Eureka, Kansas, and using the "deadly parallel column," compared portions of London's *The Call of the Wild* (1903) to portions of *My Dogs in the Northland* (1902) by Egerton R. Young, a missionary to the Indians in the Lake Winnipeg region of Canada.

Bosworth saw the similarities as "startling" and "striking" and the *Independent* editors reminded their readers that London had only recently been enmeshed in charges of plagiarism stemming from the similarities between his novel *Before Adam* (1907) and Stanley Waterloo's *The Story of Ab, the Cave-Man* (1897).

⊕ ⊕ ⊕ ⊕ ⊕ ⊕ ⊕ ⊕ ⊕ ⊕ ⊕ ⊕

To the Editor of *The Independent:*

In reply to yours of January 16. By all means go ahead and publish that article that accuses me of plagiarism of many passages in *The Call of the Wild.* So far as concerns the source of much of my material in *The Call of the Wild* being Egerton R. Young's *My Dogs in the Northland,* I plead guilty. A couple of years ago, in the course of writing to Mr. Young, I mentioned the same fact, and thanked him for the use his book had been to me.

I wish, however, that you would get the writer of the said article to include in it a definition of what constitutes plagiarism.

Mr. Young's book, *My Dogs in the Northland,* was a narrative of fact, giving many interesting true details of his experiences with dogs in the Northland. Fiction-writers have always considered actual experiences of life to be a lawful field for exploitation—in fact, every historical novel is a sample of fictional exploitation of published narratives of fact.

Take an instance from the article accusing me of plagiarism, now in your hands—that of the dog that lay down on its back with its paws in the air and begged for moccasins. This happened to one of Mr. Young's dogs and I exploited it in my story. But suppose that I am in the Klondike. Suppose this incident occurs with one of my dogs. I can utilize this material in a story, can I not? Agreed. Now suppose it doesn't happen with my dog, but with some one else's dog, but that I happen to see the incident. May I use it? Agreed again. Now, however, I do not see the incident, but the man with whose dog it occurred tells me about it. May I use it? Again agreed. A step further, instead of telling about it, a man writes the incident, not in a story, but in a plain narrative of incidents. May I use it in my story? And if not, why not?

Another instance. In the course of writing my *Sea-Wolf*, I wanted to exploit a tumor and its ravages on the brain of a man. I asked my family physician for data. It happened that he was the author of a brochure upon tumors on the brain. He turned this brochure over to me. In it was everything all written out. I used the material. Was it plagiarism? His brochure was not fiction. It was a compilation of facts and real happenings in a non-fiction form.

And so it was with Mr. Young's *My Dogs in the Northland*. Really, to charge plagiarism in such a case is to misuse the English language. To be correct, "sources of materials used in *The Call of the Wild*" should be substituted for "Plagiarism."

Jack London
Oakland, Cal.

THE OTHER ANIMALS
(*Collier's*, September, 1908)

⊕ ⊕ ⊕ ⊕ ⊕ ⊕ ⊕ ⊕ ⊕ ⊕ ⊕ ⊕

In an interview published in *Everybody's Magazine* in June, 1907, President Theodore Roosevelt berated certain episodes in London's *White Fang* (1906). Of a fight between Fang, a northern wolf, and a bulldog, the President said: "This thing is a very sublimity of absurdity.... This kind of realism is a closet product." TR also sneered at London's writing, in the same novel, of "a great dog wolf being torn to pieces by a lucivee, a northern lynx. This is about as sensible as to describe a tom cat tearing to pieces a thirty-pound fighting bull-terrier." He ended the interview by observing, "Men who have visited the haunts of the wild beasts, who have seen them, and have learned at least something of their ways, resent such gross falsifying of nature's records."*

The President was vulnerable in his attack: He had misread the wolf-lynx episode. London's wolf killed the lynx, not vice-versa.

In this splendid rebuttal, London tackles both the President and TR's ideal naturalist, John Burroughs. The article was written during the *Snark* voyage ("Jack had much fun over the charge of 'nature-faking,'" wrote Charmian London**) and when *Collier's* published it, a caption ran with the piece saying London was "locating the President in the Ananias Club" —saying, in other words, the President was a liar. London, of course, had nothing to do with the caption, and the rebuttal, while devastating, is respectful and mild. And, London subsequently admitted to the editor of *Collier's,* "I confess that my field observations, so far as the text of my own book is concerned, are rotten."***

London was the focus of several literary feuds and controversies during his writing career but perhaps none had so great an adversary as this:

---

*The article is reprinted as "Men Who Misinterpret Nature" in *The Works of Theodore Roosevelt*, vol. 6, New York: Scribner's, 1924.
**Charmian K. London, vol. 2, 171.
***Hendricks, **Letters,** p. 275.

Theodore Roosevelt, not only President of the United States but a considerable literary force in his own right.

"The Other Animals" was included in London's *Revolution & Other Essays* (1910).

⊕ ⊕ ⊕ ⊕ ⊕ ⊕ ⊕ ⊕ ⊕ ⊕ ⊕ ⊕

American journalism has its moments of fantastic hysteria, and when it is on the rampage the only thing for a rational man to do is to climb a tree and let the cataclysm go by. And so, some time ago, when the word *nature-faker* was coined, I, for one, climbed into my tree and stayed there. I happened to be in Hawaii at the time, and a Honolulu reporter elicited the sentiment from me that I thanked God I was not an authority on anything. This sentiment was promptly cabled to America in an Associated Press despatch, whereupon the American press (possibly annoyed because I had not climbed down out of my tree) charged me with paying for advertising by cable at a dollar per word—the very human way of the American press, which, when a man refuses to come down and be licked, makes faces at him.

But now that the storm is over, let us come and reason together. I have been guilty of writing two animal-stories—two books about dogs. The writing of these two stories, on my part, was in truth a protest against the "humanizing" of animals, of which it seemed to me several "animal writers" had been profoundly guilty. Time and again, and many times, in my narratives, I wrote, speaking of my dog-heroes: "He did not think these things; he merely did them," etc. And I did this repeatedly, to the clogging of my narrative and in violation of my artistic canons; and I did it in order to hammer into the average human understanding that these dog-heroes of mine were not directed by abstract reasoning, but by instinct, sensation, and emotion, and by simple reasoning. Also, I endeavored to make my stories in line with the facts of evolution; I hewed them to the mark set by scientific research, and awoke, one day, to find myself bundled neck and crop into the camp of the nature-fakers.

President Roosevelt was responsible for this, and he tried and condemned me on two counts. (1) I was guilty of having a big, fighting bull-dog whip a wolf-dog. (2) I was guilty of allowing a lynx to kill a wolf-dog in a pitched battle. Regarding the second count, President Roosevelt was wrong in his field observations taken while reading my book. He must have read it hastily, for in my story I had the wolf-dog kill the lynx. Not only did I have my wolf-dog kill the lynx, but I made him eat the body of the lynx as well. Remains only the first count on which to convict me of nature-faking, and the first count does not charge me with diverging from ascertained facts. It is merely a statement of a difference of opinion. President Roosevelt does not think a bull-dog can lick a wolf-dog. I think a bull-dog can lick a wolf-dog. And there we are. Difference of opinion may make, and does make, horse-racing. I can understand that difference of opinion can make dog-fighting. But what gets me is how difference of opinion regarding the relative fighting merits of a bull-dog and a wolf-dog makes me a nature-faker and President Roosevelt a vindicated and triumphant scientist.

Then entered John Burroughs to clinch President Roosevelt's judgments. In this alliance there is no difference of opinion. That Roosevelt can do no wrong is Burroughs's opinion; and that Burroughs is always right is Roosevelt's opinion. Both are agreed that animals do not reason. They assert that all animals below man are automatons and perform actions only of two sorts—mechanical and reflex—and that in such actions no reasoning enters at all. They believe that man is the only animal capable of reasoning and that ever does reason. This is a view that makes the twentieth-century scientist smile. It is not modern at all. It is distinctly mediaeval. President Roosevelt and John Burroughs, in advancing such a view, are homocentric in the same fashion that the scholastics of earlier and darker centuries were homocentric. Had the world not been discovered to be round until after the births of President Roosevelt and John Burroughs, they would have been geocentric as well in their theories of the Cosmos. They could not have believed otherwise. The stuff of their minds is so conditioned. They talk the argot of evolution, while they no more understand the essence and the import of evolution than does a South Sea Islander or Sir Oliver Lodge understands the noumena of radioactivity.

Now, President Roosevelt is an amateur. He may know something of statecraft and of big-game shooting; he may be able to kill a deer when he sees it and to measure it and weigh it after he has shot it; he may be able to observe carefully and accurately the actions and antics of tom-tits and snipe, and, after he has observed it, definitely and coherently to convey the information of when the first chipmunk, in a certain year and a certain latitude and longitude, came out in the spring and chattered and gambolled—but that he should be able, as an individual observer, to analyze all animal life and to synthesize and develop all that is known of the method and significance of evolution, would require a vaster credulity for you or me to believe than is required for us to believe the biggest whopper ever told by an unmitigated nature-faker. No, President Roosevelt does not understand evolution, and he does not seem to have made much of an attempt to understand evolution.

Remains John Burroughs, who claims to be a thoroughgoing evolutionist. Now, it is rather hard for a young man to tackle an old man. It is the nature of young men to be more controlled in such matters, and it is the nature of old men, presuming upon the wisdom that is very often erroneously associated with age, to do the tackling. In this present question of nature-faking, the old men did the tackling, while I, as one young man, kept quiet a long time. But here goes at last. And first of all let Mr. Burroughs's position be stated, and stated in his words.

"Why impute reason to an animal if its behavior can be explained of the theory of instinct?" Remember these words, for they will be referred to later, "A goodly number of persons seems to have persuaded themselves that animals do reason." "But instinct suffices for the animals . . . they get along very well without reason." "Darwin tried hard to convince himself that animals do at times reason in a rudimentary way; but Darwin was also a much greater naturalist than psychologist." The preceding quotation is tantamount, on Mr. Burroughs's part, to a flat denial that animals reason even in a rudimentary way. And when Mr. Burroughs denies that animals reason even in a rudimentary way, it is equivalent to affirming, in accord with the first quotation in this paragraph, that instinct will explain every animal act that might be confounded with reason by the unskilled or careless observer.

Having bitten off this large mouthful, Mr. Burroughs proceeds with serene and beautiful satisfaction to masticate it in the following fashion. He cites a large number of instances of purely instinctive actions on the parts of animals, and triumphantly demands if they are acts of reason. He tells of the robin that fought day after day its reflected image in a window-pane; of the birds in South America that were guilty of drilling clear through a mud wall, which they mistook for a solid clay bank; of the beaver that cut down a tree four times because it was held at the top by the branches of other trees; of the cow that licked the skin of her stuffed calf so affectionately that it came apart, whereupon she proceeded to eat the hay with which it was stuffed. He tells of the phoebe-bird that betrays her nest on the porch by trying to hide it with moss in similar fashion to the way all phoebe-birds hide their nests when they are built among rocks. He tells of the highhole that repeatedly drills through the clapboards of an empty house in a vain attempt to find a thickness of wood deep enough in which to build its nest. He tells of the migrating lemmings of Norway that plunge into the sea and drown in vast numbers because of their instinct to swim lakes and rivers in the course of their migrations. And, having told a few more instances of like kidney, he triumphantly demands: Where now is your much-vaunted reasoning of the lower animals?

No schoolboy in a class debate could be guilty of unfairer argument.

It is equivalent to replying to the assertion that $2 + 2 = 4$, by saying: "No; because $12 \div 4 = 3$; I have demonstrated my honorable opponent's error." When a man attacks your ability as a foot-racer, promptly prove to him that he was drunk the week before last, and the average man in the crowd of gaping listeners will believe that you have convincingly refuted the slander on your fleetness of foot. On my honor, it will work. Try it sometime. It is done every day. Mr. Burroughs has done it himself, and, I doubt not, pulled the sophistical wool over a great many pairs of eyes. No, no, Mr. Burroughs; you can't disprove that animals reason by proving that they possess instincts. But the worst of it is that you have at the same time pulled the wool over your own eyes. You have set up a straw man and knocked the stuffing out of him in the complacent belief that it was the reasoning of lower animals you were knocking out of the minds of those who disagreed with you. When the highhole perforated the ice-house and let out the sawdust, you called him a lunatic. . . .

But let us be charitable—and serious. What Mr. Burroughs instances as acts of instinct certainly are acts of instinct. By the same method of logic one could easily adduce a multitude of instinctive acts on the part of man and thereby prove that man is an unreasoning animal. But man performs actions of both sorts. Between man and the lower animals Mr. Burroughs finds a vast gulf. This gulf divides man from the rest of his kin by virtue of the power of reason that he alone possesses. Man is a voluntary agent. Animals are automatons. The robin fights its reflection in the window-pane because it is his instinct to fight and because he cannot reason out the physical laws that make his reflection appear real. An animal is a mechanism that operates according to fore-ordained rules. Wrapped up in its heredity, and determined long before it was born, is a certain limited capacity of ganglionic response to external stimuli. These responses have been fixed in the species through adaptation to environment. Natural selection has compelled the animal automatically to respond in a fixed manner and a certain way to all the usual external stimuli it encounters in the course of a usual life. Thus, under usual circumstances, it does the usual thing. Under unusual circumstances it still does the usual thing, wherefore the highhole perforating the ice-house is guilty of lunacy—of unreason, in short. To do the unusual thing under unusual circumstances, successfully to adjust to a strange environment for which his heredity has not automatically fitted an adjustment, Mr. Burroughs says is impossible. He says it is impossible because it would be a non-instinctive act, and, as is well known, animals act only through instinct. And right here we catch a glimpse of Mr. Burroughs's cart standing before his horse. He has a thesis, and though the heavens fall he will fit the facts to the thesis. Agassiz, in his opposition to evolution, had a similar thesis, though neither did he fit the facts to it nor did the heavens fall. Facts are very disagreeable at times. But let us see. Let us test Mr. Burroughs's test of reason and instinct. When I was a small boy I had a dog named Rollo. According to Mr. Burroughs, Rollo was an automaton, responding to external stimuli mechanically as directed by his instincts. Now, as is well known, the development of instinct in animals is a dreadfully slow process. There is no known case of the development of a single instinct·in domestic animals in all the history of their domestication. Whatever instincts they possess they brought with them from the wild thousands of years ago. Therefore, all Rollo's actions were ganglionic discharges mechanically determined by the instincts that had been developed and fixed in the species thousands of years ago. Very well. It is clear, therefore, that in all his play with me he would act in old-fashioned ways, adjusting himself to the physical and psychical factors in his environment according to the rules of adjustment which he had obtained in the wild and which had become part of his heredity.

Rollo and I did a great deal of rough romping. He chased me and I chased him. He nipped my legs, arms, and hands, often so hard that I yelled, while I rolled him and tumbled him and dragged him about, often so strenuously as to make him yelp. In the course of the play many variations arose. I would make believe to sit down and cry. All repentance and anxiety, he would wag his tail and lick my face, whereupon I would give him the laugh. He hated to be laughed at, and promptly he would spring for me with good-natured, menacing jaws, and the wild romp would go on. I had scored a point. Then he hit upon a trick. Pursuing him into the woodshed, I would find him in a far corner, pretending to sulk. Now, he dearly loved to play, and never got enough of it. But at first he fooled me. I thought I had somehow hurt his feelings and I came and knelt before him, petting him and speaking lovingly. Promptly, in a wild outburst, he was up and away, tumbling me over on the floor as he dashed out in a mad scurry around the yard. He had scored a point.

After a time, it became largely a game of wits. I reasoned my acts, of course, while his were instinctive. One day, as he pretended to sulk in the corner, I glanced out of the woodshed doorway, simulated pleasure in face, voice, and language, and greeted one of my schoolboy friends. Immediately Rollo forgot to sulk, rushed out to see the newcomer, and saw empty space. The laugh was on him, and he knew it, and I gave it to him, too. I fooled him in this way two or three times; then he became wise. One day I worked a variation. Suddenly looking out the door, making believe that my eyes had been attracted by a moving form, I said coldly, as a child educated in turning away bill-collectors would say:

"No, my father is not at home." Like a shot, Rollo was out the door. He even ran down the alley to the front of the house in a vain attempt to find the man I had addressed. He came back sheepishly to endure the laugh and resume the game.

And now we come to the test. I fooled Rollo, but how was the fooling made possible? What precisely went on in that brain of his? According to Mr. Burroughs, who denies even rudimentary reasoning to the lower animals, Rollo acted instinctively, and since all instincts are very ancient, tracing back to the predomestication period, we can conclude only that Rollo's wild ancestors, at the time this particular instinct was fixed into the heredity of the species, must have been in close, long-continued, and vital contact with man, the voice of man, and the expressions on the face of man. But since the instinct must have been developed during the predomestication period, how under the sun could his wild, undomesticated ancestors have experienced the close, long-continued, and vital contact with man?

Mr. Burroughs says that "instinct suffices for the animals," and that "they get along very well without reason." But I say, what all the poor nature-fakers will say, that Rollo reasoned. He was born into the world a bundle of instincts and a pinch of brain-stuff, all wrapped around in a framework of bone, meat, and hide. As he adjusted to the environment he gained experiences. He remembered these experiences. He learned that he mustn't chase the cat, kill chickens, nor bite little girls' dresses. He learned that little boys had little boy playmates. He learned that men came into back yards. He learned that the animal man, on meeting with his own kind, was given to verbal and facial greeting. He learned that when a boy greeted a playmate he did it differently from the way he greeted a man. All these he learned and remembered. They were so many observations—so many propositions, if you please. Now what went on behind those brown eyes of his, inside that pinch of brain-stuff, when I turned suddenly to the door and greeted an imaginary person outside? Instantly, out of the thousands of observations stored in his brain, came to the front of his consciousness the particular observation connected with this particular situation. Next, he established a relation between these observations. This relation was his conclusion, achieved, as every psychologist will agree, by a definite cell-action of his gray matter. From the fact that his master turned suddenly toward the door, and from the fact that his master's voice, facial expression, and whole demeanor expressed surprise and delight, he concluded that a friend was outside. He established a relation between various things, and the act of establishing relations between things is an act of reason—of rudimentary reason, granted, but none the less of reason.

Of course Rollo was fooled. But that is no call for us to throw chests about it. How often has every last one of us been fooled in precisely similar fashion by another who turned and suddenly addressed an imaginary intruder? Here is a case in point that occurred in the West. A robber had held up a railroad train. He stood in the aisle between the seats, his revolver presented at the head of the conductor, who stood facing him. The conductor was at his mercy. But the conductor suddenly looked over the robber's shoulder, at the same time saying aloud to an imaginary person standing at the robber's back: "Don't shoot him." Like a flash the robber whirled about to confront this new danger, and like a flash the conductor shot him down. Show me, Mr. Burroughs, where the mental process in the robber's brain was a shade different from the mental process in Rollo's brain, and I'll quit nature-faking and join the Trappists. Surely, when a man's mental process and a dog's mental process are precisely similar, the much-vaunted gulf of Mr. Burroughs's fancy has been bridged.

I had a dog in Oakland. His name was Glen. His father was Brown, a wolf-dog that had been brought down from Alaska, and his mother was a half-wild mountain shepherd dog. Neither father nor mother had any experience with automobiles. Glen came from the country, a half-grown puppy, to live in Oakland. Immediately he became infatuated with an automobile. He reached the culmination of happiness when he was permitted to sit up in the front seat alongside the chauffeur. He would spend a whole day at a time on an automobile debauch, even going without food. Often the machine started directly from inside the barn, dashed out the driveway without stopping, and was gone. Glen got left behind several times. The custom was established that whoever was taking the machine out should toot the horn before starting. Glen learned the signal. No matter where he was nor what he was doing, when the horn tooted he was off for the barn and up into the front seat.

One morning, while Glen was on the back porch eating his breakfast of mush and milk, the chauffeur tooted. Glen rushed down the steps, into the barn, and took his front seat, the mush and milk dripping down his excited and happy chops. In passing, I may point out that in thus forsaking his breakfast for the automobile he was displaying what is called the power of choice—a peculiarly lordly attribute that, according to Mr. Burroughs, belongs to man alone. Yet Glen made his choice between food and fun.

It was not that Glen wanted his breakfast less, but that he wanted his ride more. The toot was only a joke. The automobile did not start. Glen waited and watched. Evidently he saw no signs of an immediate start, for finally he jumped out of the seat and went back to his breakfast.

He ate with indecent haste, like a man anxious to catch a train. Again the horn tooted, again he deserted his breakfast, and again he sat in the seat and waited vainly for the machine to go. They came close to spoiling Glen's breakfast for him, for he was kept on the jump between porch and barn. Then he grew wise. They tooted the horn loudly and insistently, but he stayed by his breakfast and finished it. Thus once more did he display power of choice, incidentally of control, for when the horn tooted it was all he could do to refrain from running for the barn.

The nature-faker would analyze what went on in Glen's brain somewhat in the following fashion. He had had, in his short life, experiences that not one of all his ancestors had ever had. He had learned that automobiles went fast, that once in motion it was impossible for him to get on board, that the toot of the horn was a noise that was peculiar to automobiles. These were so many propositions. Now reasoning can be defined as the act or process of the brain by which, from propositions known or assumed, new propositions are reached. Out of the propositions which I have shown were Glen's, and which had become his through the medium of his own observation of the phenomena of life, he made the new proposition that when the horn tooted it was time for him to get on board.

But on the morning I have described, the chauffeur fooled Glen. Somehow, and much to his own disgust, his reasoning was erroneous. The machine did not start after all. But to reason incorrectly is very human. The great trouble in all acts of reasoning is to include all the propositions in the problem. Glen had included every proposition but one, namely, the human proposition, the joke in the brain of the chauffeur. For a number of times Glen was fooled. Then he performed another mental act. In his problem he included the human proposition (the joke in the brain of the chauffeur), and he reached the new conclusion that when the horn tooted the automobile was *not* going to start. Basing his action on this conclusion, he remained on the porch and finished his breakfast. You and I, and even Mr. Burroughs, perform acts of reasoning precisely similar to this every day in our lives. How Mr. Burroughs will explain Glen's action by the instinctive theory is beyond me. In wildest fantasy, even, my brain refuses to follow Mr. Burroughs into the primeval forest, where Glen's dim ancestors, to the tooting of automobile horns, were fixing into the heredity of the breed the particular instinct that would enable Glen, a few thousand years later, capably to cope with automobiles.

Dr. C. J. Romanes tells of a female chimpanzee who was taught to count straws up to five. She held the straws in her hand, exposing the ends to the number requested. If she were asked for three, she held up three. If she were asked for four, she held up four. All this is a mere matter of training. But consider now, Mr. Burroughs, what follows. When she was asked for five straws and she had only four, she doubled one straw, exposing both its ends and thus making up the required number. She did not do this only once, and by accident. She did it whenever more straws were asked for than she possessed. Did she perform a distinctly reasoning act? or was her action the result of blind, mechanical instinct? If Mr. Burroughs cannot answer to his own satisfaction, he may call Dr. Romanes a nature-faker and dismiss the incident from his mind.

The foregoing is a trick of erroneous human reasoning that works very successfully in the United States these days. It is certainly a trick of Mr. Burroughs, of which he is guilty with distressing frequency. When a poor devil of a writer records what he has seen, and when what he has seen does not jibe with Mr. Burroughs's mediaeval theory, he calls said writer a nature-faker. When a man like Mr. Hornaday comes along, Mr. Burroughs works a variation of the trick on him. Mr. Hornaday has made a close study of the orang in captivity and of the orang in its native state. Also, he has studied closely many other of the higher animal types. Also, in the tropics, he has studied the lower types of man. Mr. Hornaday is a man of experience and reputation. When he was asked if animals reasoned, out of all his knowledge on the subject he replied that to ask him such a question was equivalent to asking him if fishes swim. Now Mr. Burroughs has not had much experience in studying the lower human types and the higher animal types. Living in a rural district in the state of New York, and studying principally birds in that limited habitat, he has been in contact neither with the higher animal types nor the lower human types. But Mr. Hornaday's reply is such a facer to him and his homocentric theory that he has to do something. And he does it. He retorts: "I suspect that Mr. Hornaday is a better naturalist than he is a comparative psychologist." Exit Mr. Hornaday. Who the devil is Mr. Hornaday, anyway? The sage of Slabsides has spoken. When Darwin concluded that animals were capable of reasoning in a rudimentary way, Mr. Burroughs laid him out in the same fashion by saying: "But Darwin was also a much greater naturalist than psychologist"—and this despite Darwin's long life of laborious research that was not wholly confined to a rural district such as Mr. Burroughs inhabits in New York. Mr. Burroughs's method of argument is beautiful. It reminds one of the man whose pronunciation was vile, but who said: "Damn the dictionary; ain't I here?"

And now we come to the mental processes of Mr. Burroughs—to the psychology of the ego, if you please. Mr. Burroughs has troubles of his own with the dictionary. He violates language from the standpoint both of logic and science. Language is a tool, and definitions embodied in language should agree with the facts and history of life. But Mr.

Burroughs's definitions do not so agree. This, in turn, is not the fault of his education, but of his ego. To him, despite his well-exploited and patronizing devotion to them, the lower animals are disgustingly low. To him, affinity and kinship with the other animals is a repugnant thing. He will have none of it. He is too glorious a personality not to have between him and the other animals a vast and impassable gulf. The cause of Mr. Burroughs's mediaeval view of the other animals is to be found, not in his knowledge of those other animals, but in the suggestion of his self-exalted ego. In short, Mr. Burroughs's homocentric theory has been developed out of his homocentric ego, and by the misuse of language he strives to make the facts of life jibe with his theory.

After the instances I have cited of actions of animals which are impossible of explanation as due to instinct, Mr. Burroughs may reply: "Your instances are easily explained by the simple law of association." To this I reply, first, then why did you deny rudimentary reason to animals? and why did you state flatly that "instinct suffices for the animals"? And, second, with great reluctance and with overwhelming humility, because of my youth, I suggest that you do not know exactly what you do mean by that phrase "the simple law of association." Your trouble, I repeat, is with definitions. You have grasped that man performs what is called *abstract* reasoning, you have made a definition of abstract reason, and, betrayed by that great maker of theories, the ego, you have come to think that all reasoning is abstract and that what is not abstract reason is not reason at all. This is your attitude toward rudimentary reason. Such a process, in one of the other animals, must be either abstract or it is not a reasoning process. Your intelligence tells you that such a process is not abstract reasoning, and your homocentric thesis compels you to conclude that it can be only a mechanical, instinctive process.

Definitions must agree, not with egos, but with life. Mr. Burroughs goes on the basis that a definition is something hard and fast, absolute and eternal. He forgets that all the universe is in flux; that definitions are arbitrary and ephemeral; that they fix, for a fleeting instant of time, things that in the past were not, that in the future will be not, that out of the past become, and that out of the present pass on to the future and become other things. Definitions cannot rule life. Definitions cannot be made to rule life. Life must rule definitions or else the definitions perish.

Mr. Burroughs forgets the evolution of reason. He makes a definition of reason without regard to its history, and that definition is of reason purely abstract. Human reason, as we know it today, is not a creation, but a growth. Its history goes back to the primordial slime that was quick with muddy life; its history goes back to the first vitalized inorganic.

And here are the steps of its ascent from the mud to man: simple reflex action, compound reflex action, memory, habit, rudimentary reason, and abstract reason. In the course of the climb, thanks to natural selection, instinct was evolved. Habit is a development of the individual. Instinct is a race-habit. Instinct is blind, unreasoning, mechanical. This was the dividing of the ways in the climb of aspiring life. The perfect culmination of instinct we find in the ant-heap and the beehive. Instinct proved a blind alley. But the other path, that of reason, led on and on even to Mr. Burroughs and you and me.

There are no impassable gulfs, unless one chooses, as Mr. Burroughs does, to ignore the lower human types and the higher animal types, and to compare human mind with bird mind. It was impossible for life to reason abstractly until speech was developed. Equipped with swords, with tools of thought, in short, the slow development of the power to reason in the abstract went on. The lowest human types do little or no reasoning in the abstract. With every word, with every increase in the complexity of thought, with every ascertained fact so gained, went on action and reaction in the gray matter of the speech discoverer, and slowly, step by step, through hundreds of thousands of years, developed the power of reason.

Place a honey-bee in a glass bottle. Turn the bottom of the bottle toward a lighted lamp so that the open mouth is away from the lamp. Vainly, ceaselessly, a thousand times, undeterred by the bafflement and the pain, the bee will hurl himself against the bottom of the bottle as he strives to win to the light. That is instinct. Place your dog in a back yard and go away. He is your dog. He loves you. He yearns toward you as the bee yearns toward the light. He listens to your departing footsteps. But the fence is too high. Then he turns his back upon the direction in which you are departing, and runs around the yard. He is frantic with affection and desire. But he is not blind. He is observant. He is looking for a hole under the fence, or through the fence, or for a place where the fence is not so high. He sees a dry-goods box standing against the fence. Presto! He leaps upon it, goes over the barrier, and tears down the street to overtake you. Is that instinct?

Here, in the household where I am writing this, is a little Tahitian "feeding-child." He believes firmly that a tiny dwarf resides in the box of my talking-machine and that it is the tiny dwarf who does the singing and talking. Not even Mr. Burroughs will affirm that the child has reached this conclusion by an instinctive process. Of course the child reasons the existence of the dwarf in the box. How else could the box talk and sing? In that child's limited experience it has never encountered a single instance where speech and song were produced otherwise than by direct human agency. I doubt not that the dog is considerably surprised when he hears his master's voice coming out of a box.

The adult savage, on his first introduction to a telephone, rushes around to the adjoining room to find the man who is talking through the partition. Is this act instinctive? No. Out of his limited experience, out of his limited knowledge of physics, he reasons that the only explanation possible is that a man is in the other room talking through the partition.

But that savage cannot be fooled by a hand-mirror. We must go lower down in the animal scale, to the monkey. The monkey swiftly learns that the monkey it sees is not in the glass, wherefore it reaches craftily behind the glass. Is this instinct? No. It is rudimentary reasoning. Lower than the monkey in the scale of brain is the robin, and the robin fights its reflection in the window-pane. Now climb with me for a space. From the robin to the monkey, where is the impassable gulf? and where is the impassable gulf between the monkey and the feeding child? between the feeding-child and the savage who seeks the man behind the partition? aye, and between the savage and the astute financiers Mrs. Chadwick fooled and the thousands who were fooled by the Keeley Motor swindle?

Let us be very humble. We who are so very human are very animal. Kinship with the other animals is no more repugnant to Mr. Burroughs than was the heliocentric theory to the priests who compelled Galileo to recant. Not correct human reason, not the evidence of the ascertained fact, but pride of ego, was responsible for the repugnance.

In his stiff-necked pride, Mr. Burroughs runs a hazard more humiliating to that pride than any amount of kinship with the other animals. When a dog exhibits choice, direction, control, and reason; when it is shown that certain mental processes in that dog's brain are precisely duplicated in the brain of man; and when Mr. Burroughs convincingly proves that every action of the dog is mechanical and automatic—then, by precisely the same argument, can it be proved that the similar actions of man are mechanical and automatic. No. Mr. Burroughs, though you stand on the top of the ladder of life, you must not kick out that ladder from under your feet. You must not deny your relatives, the other animals. Their history is your history, and if you kick them to the bottom of the abyss, to the bottom of the abyss you go yourself. By them you stand or fall. What you repudiate in them you repudiate in yourself—a pretty spectacle, truly, of an exalted animal striving to disown the stuff of life out of which it is made, striving by use of the very reason that was developed by evolution to deny the processes of evolution that developed it. This may be good egotism, but it is not good science.

Papeete, Tahiti
March, 1908

LETTER TO "VANITY FAIR"
(July 1, 1909)

⊕ ⊕ ⊕ ⊕ ⊕ ⊕ ⊕ ⊕ ⊕ ⊕ ⊕ ⊕

The controversy with Frank Harris began in the *Vanity Fair* issue of April 14, 1909, in an article by Harris entitled "How Mr. Jack London Writes a Novel." Using parallel columns, Harris demonstrated that a portion of his article, "The Bishop of London and Public Morality," which appeared in a British periodical, *The Candid Friend*, on May 25, 1901, had been used almost word-for-word by London in his 1908 novel, *The Iron Heel.*

London replied to the Harris charge in the letter that follows.*

⊕ ⊕ ⊕ ⊕ ⊕ ⊕ ⊕ ⊕ ⊕ ⊕ ⊕ ⊕

Canal Zone, Panama, July 1st, 1909
To the Editor of *Vanity Fair:*

Arriving at Panama from South America, after being four months away from newspapers and letters, I got in touch with my mail, and found the usual charge of plagiarism awaiting me. Mr. Frank Harris, using the deadly parallel column, has published in *Vanity Fair* an extract from an article written by him in 1901, and an extract from *The Iron Heel*, published by me in 1909. Line by line, and paragraph by paragraph, he proves conclusively that I have lifted from him bodily fully a thousand words of his own composition. On the fact of it I should be hanged. That is the way we used to have of dealing with horsethieves in the Wild West. Of course, occasional horsethieves were hanged on strong circumstantial evidence, and afterwards found to be not guilty. I do not know whether I am guilty or not, but I shall state my side of the case to the public, and let it judge.

Mr. Frank Harris says: "A great meeting was to be held at Westminster

---

*Reprinted from *Vanity Fair,* July 28, 1909.

Town Hall for the promotion of public morality. The Bishop of London presided. . . It occurred to me that it would be amusing to picture what would be the effect on the meeting if the Bishop of London had suddenly become a Christian. I wrote it all down."

Now, in 1901, I found Mr. Harris's composition published in an American paper. To it was affixed an introduction by an American journalist, in which he said that these quoted words of the Bishop of London had been taken from the one London publication that had had the courage to print what the Bishop of London had actually said. Now, I have never heard of Mr. Harris; I did not know that the unknown English journalist had perpetrated a canard; I don't think the American journalist knew that Mr. Harris had perpetrated a canard. He took Mr. Harris's article in good faith. And I certainly took it in good faith. I took what I saw in the newspaper as the quoted words of the Bishop of London uttered on a public platform. I thought I had a human document, and it made such a striking impression upon me that I filed it away for future use. Years afterwards, in writing *The Iron Heel,* I resurrected the clipping. And with glee I used it word for word, and again filed the clipping against the possibility of being charged in the future with having stretched realism and human probability. I smiled to myself at the thought that, when such a charge was laid at my door, I would bring forth the clipping—the human document containing the publicly-uttered words of the Bishop of London. And behold, it was a canard!

Mr. Harris made a canard that fooled an American journalist, and that, through the American journalist, fooled me. Mr. Harris baited his hook and caught me. I was what we call a sucker. But Mr. Harris, instead of gaily crying, "Sucker!" gravely cried "Thief!" I am afraid that Mr. Harris is a very precipitous and guileless young man, or else dreadfully desirous of getting free advertising. If somebody else who did not know all the ins and outs of the affair had called me a thief, then Mr. Harris could have enjoyed a further and hearty laugh at my expense. But Mr. Harris himself, the man who made the canard and who caught me with it, carried the joke to the further extent of calling me a thief, and in so doing, exceeded all decent limits of humor. Mr. Harris either has so sense of humor, or, I repeat, is a very guileless young man.

The laugh is on me. I confess to having been fooled by Mr. Harris's canard. And I have but one regret—namely, that Mr. Harris did not make sure of his ground before he made a sensational public charge. Mr. Harris came out of the affair all right. Thanks to me, he has managed to sell the same composition at space rates twice, and has received a lot of advertising. I do not come out of it so well! Not being content with having hooked me with his canard, Mr. Harris has publicly branded me as a thief, and has done so in a pert and patronizing way.

Jack London

LETTER TO "VANITY FAIR"
(August 16, 1909)

⊕ ⊕ ⊕ ⊕ ⊕ ⊕ ⊕ ⊕ ⊕ ⊕ ⊕ ⊕

Frank Harris had no patience with London's response to his charge and challenged London to produce the clipping and to pay him one-sixtieth of the royalties from *The Iron Heel,* maintaining that of the three hundred pages in the novel, five had been appropriated from Harris's article.

⊕ ⊕ ⊕ ⊕ ⊕ ⊕ ⊕ ⊕ ⊕ ⊕ ⊕ ⊕

August 16th, 1909
To the Editor of *Vanity Fair*

Dear Sir,—I have received through my clipping agency a clipping from *Vanity Fair,* under date of July 28th, 1909, in which Mr. Frank Harris is so incredibly stupid as to call me a liar and to insinuate that I do not possess the clipping I referred to in my letter to you of July 1st.

In my letter to you of July 1st, having been two years and a half away from the United States, and being then at the Panama Canal, on my way home from South America, I had to write wholly from memory. I told you, as nearly as I could remember, how I had read Mr. Harris's composition, published in an American paper, in which form it had affixed an introduction by an American journalist to the effect that only one London publication had had the courage to print what the Bishop of London had actually said. I told my story from memory, simply and sincerely. I never dreamed that my word would be doubted in the affair, as Mr. Harris had publicly doubted it.

Upon my return home to California, I went up to my ranch, and in the barn resurrected a large box labelled on the outside with "Iron Heel Clippings." Running through these clippings I found the one about which Mr. Harris said I lied when I stated I possessed it. Here is the clipping, with my marks on it and my notes made at the time when I utilized it for *The Iron Heel.*

But Mr. Frank Harris has proved himself so suspicious a man, so prone to impute evil to others, that he will doubtless aver that this clipping is not a clipping, but that I have had it privately printed at this late day. In a reply to any such anticipated move, I may as well say that if Mr. Harris be guilty of it, that he will render himself beneath my contempt and beyond my notice.

If, on the other hand, Mr. Frank Harris be honorable enough to accept this clipping as *bona fide,* and to take my explanation of July 1st as a true explanation, then there will be owing to me a sincere apology from Mr. Frank Harris. This apology, in the nature of the case, must be as public as has been his violent charges concerning my veracity, my honesty, and my sanity.

The rest of Mr. Harris's argument, published in your columns on July 28th, is so beside the question that I need not refer to it. I can only say regarding his treatment of me that his methods are unfair. He is a bully of the pen and the printed page. He is a yellow-journalist. But even a bully of the pen, with the taint of yellow in him, cannot override facts. I have presented my facts. First, my explanation contained in my letter of July 1st, and, second, the clipping referred to. It seems to me, as regards this clipping, that it should be published in your columns entire, including the remarks of the American journalist, which were appended to the quotation and not prefaced as was my faulty memory of it.

Very truly yours,
Jack London.

P.S.—Will you please see that this clipping is returned to me. Also, will you please mail to me a copy of *Vanity Fair* in which this letter is published? I can say, in addition, that I do not know where in the United States "The Socialist Spirit" was published, nor when, nor by whom. But if necessary, by writing to all the large cities, I am sure that I can discover all the facts concerning this now defunct publication.

LETTER TO FRANK HARRIS

(November 15, 1909)

⊕ ⊕ ⊕ ⊕ ⊕ ⊕ ⊕ ⊕ ⊕ ⊕ ⊕ ⊕

After his August 16 letter, Harris insisted, tongue-in-cheek, on payment for his work. London's response was a personal note to Harris. The editors of *Letters From Jack London,* from which this letter is reprinted, note that after London's death, Harris wrote a facetious letter to Charmian London insisting that he (Harris) was in the right in the controversy.

⊕ ⊕ ⊕ ⊕ ⊕ ⊕ ⊕ ⊕ ⊕ ⊕ ⊕ ⊕

Glen Ellen, Calif.
Nov. 15, 1909

Dear Mr. Harris:—

I have just received clipping from *Vanity Fair* of date of October 27. There seems nothing more to be said so far as the public discussion is concerned. The charge of knavish, idiotic and impudent plagiarism against me has been satisfactorily disproved. So this is just a letter to you. Believe me, throughout this correspondence I have been absolutely sincere, and all I cared for was that my sincerity should be accepted.

But, just good-naturedly of course, it seems to me that you have got yourself into several logical tangles. The first of these is your request that I should have apologized to you for having been deceived by an American journalist. (See second sentence in penultimate paragraph of your last article.)

While your demand that I should pay you for the portion of your work used by me was cleverly facetious in its origin in your mind, it seems that in the intervening time you have taken your own facetiousness seriously. Of course I have no objection to that, and merely mention it in order to lead up to another tangle of logic, namely, your refusal to apologize to me for having doubted my word (euphemism for liar), until I paid you your share of *The Iron Heel.* This is queer admixture of ethics, commercialism, and facetiousness.

But why go any further with the tangles! I think you realize by this time that I was innocent of deliberate plagiarism.

Sincerely yours,
Jack London

P.S. Are you the Frank Harris who wrote *The Bomb*—a book recently published in the United States? I haven't read it yet; but if you are the author, I shall. There! That shows you how good-natured I am.

Reprinted from *Letters From Jack London* (1965).

LETTER TO SINCLAIR LEWIS
(October 4, 1910)

⊕ ⊕ ⊕ ⊕ ⊕ ⊕ ⊕ ⊕ ⊕ ⊕ ⊕ ⊕

In a letter written on June 17, 1900—only two months following publication of his first book, London admitted, "Expression with me is far easier than invention. It is with the latter I have the greatest trouble, and work the hardest." (Quoted in Andrew Sinclair, *Jack,* p. 131.)

Between September, 1910, and November, 1911, London purchased a number of story plots from Sinclair Lewis.* (Mary Austin, among others, believed the arrangement a typical example of London's well-known generosity—trying to help the impecunious young "Red" Lewis without the stigma of an ordinary handout.) From the plots thus purchased, at prices ranging from five to fifteen dollars each, came the novelette, *The Abysmal Brute* (1913) and the stories "Winged Blackmail," "The Prodigal Father," and "When the World Was Young." Another novelette *The Assassination Bureau,* was left incomplete by London at his death; it was completed by renowned mystery writer Robert L. Fish and published in 1963.

⊕ ⊕ ⊕ ⊕ ⊕ ⊕ ⊕ ⊕ ⊕ ⊕ ⊕ ⊕

Glen Ellen, Calif.
Oct. 4, 1910

Dear Sinclair Lewis:

Your plots came in last night, and I have promptly taken nine (9) of them for which same, according to invoice, I am remitting you herewith check for $52.50.

---

*For details of this episode, see Franklin Walker, "Jack London's Use of Sinclair Lewis Plots Together With a Printing of Three of the Plots," *Huntington Library Quarterly* 17, no. 1 (November, 1953); King Hendricks and Irving Shepard, *Letters From Jack London,* pp. 483–89; and Mark Schorer, *Sinclair Lewis: An American Life* (New York: McGraw-Hill Co., 1961), pp. 166–67.

Some of the rejected ones were not suited to my temperament; others did not suit because I am too damn lazy to dig up requisite data or atmosphere.

I didn't care to tackle the World Police (which is a splendid series), because I am long on splendid novel-motifs of my own, which require only time and relaxed financial pressure for me to put through.

I'll let you know whenever one of your plots is published.

"Winged Blackmail" was published in Sept. number of *The Lever*, a monthly magazine issued in Chicago.

I have 20,000 words done on *The Assassination Bureau* and for the first time in my life am stuck and disgusted. I haven't done my best by it, and cannot make up my mind whether or not to go ahead with it.

Be sure to send me plots from time to time, with prices attached, and for heaven's sake, remember the ones I take, so that you won't make the mistake of writing them up yourself some time.

In a wild rush,

Sincerely yours,
Jack London

*Reprinted from *Letters From Jack London* (1965).

INTRODUCTION TO "THE RED HOT DOLLAR"
(1911)

⊕ ⊕ ⊕ ⊕ ⊕ ⊕ ⊕ ⊕ ⊕ ⊕ ⊕ ⊕

The forty dollars Jack London received from *The Black Cat* for his story "A Thousand Deaths" (published in the May, 1899, issue), saved him "literally and literarily," he said. Many times London paid tribute to the magazine (thinly disguised as "The White Mouse" in *Martin Eden*) and its editor, H. D. Umbstaetter. To help repay the debt he felt toward *The Black Cat* he wrote this introduction to *The Red Hot Dollar & Other Stories From the Black Cat* by H. D. Umbstaetter (Boston: L. C. Page & Co., 1911.)

⊕ ⊕ ⊕ ⊕ ⊕ ⊕ ⊕ ⊕ ⊕ ⊕ ⊕ ⊕

It is indeed a pleasure to write an introduction for a collection of tales by Mr. H. D. Umbstaetter. His stories are *Black Cat* stories, and by such designation is meant much. The field of the *Black Cat* is unique, and a *Black Cat* story is a story apart from all other short stories. While Mr. Umbstaetter may not have originated such a type of story, he made such a type possible, and many a writer possible. I know he made me possible. He saved my literary life, if he did not save my literal life. And I think he was guilty of this second crime, too.

For months, without the smallest particle of experience, I had been attempting to write something marketable. Everything I possessed was in pawn, and I did not have enough to eat. I was sick, mentally and physically, from lack of nourishment. I had once read in a Sunday supplement that the minimum rate paid by the magazines was ten dollars per thousand words. But during all the months devoted to storming the magazine field, I had received back only manuscripts. Still I believed implicitly what I had read in the Sunday supplement.

As I say, I was at the end of my tether, beaten out, starved, ready to go back to coal-shoveling or ahead to suicide. Being very sick in mind and body, the chance was in favor of my self-destruction. And then, one morning, I received a short, thin letter from a magazine. This magazine had a national reputation. It had been founded by Bret Harte. It sold for twenty-five cents a copy. It held a four-thousand-word story of mine, "To the Man on Trail." I was modest. As I tore the envelope across the end, I expected to find a check for no more than forty dollars. Instead, I was coldly informed (by the Assistant Sub-scissors, I imagine), that my story was "available" and that on publication I would be paid for it the sum of five dollars.

The end was in sight. The Sunday supplement had lied. I was finished —finished as only a very young, very sick, and very hungry young man could be. I planned—I was too miserable to plan anything save that I would never write again. And then, that same day, that very afternoon, the mail brought a short, thin letter from Mr. Umbstaetter of the *Black Cat.* He told me that the four-thousand-word story submitted to him was more lengthy than strengthy, but that if I would give permission to cut it in half, he would immediately send me a check for forty dollars.

Give permission! It was equivalent to twenty dollars per thousand, or double the minimum rate. Give permission! I told Mr. Umbstaetter he could cut it down two-halves if he'd only send the money along. He did, by return mail. And that is just precisely how and why I stayed by the writing game. Literally and literarily, I was saved by the *Black Cat* short story.

To many a writer with a national reputation, the *Black Cat* has been the stepping stone. The marvelous, unthinkable thing Mr. Umbstaetter did, was to judge a story on its merits and *to pay for it on its merits.* Also, and only a hungry writer can appreciate it, he paid immediately on acceptance.

Of the stories in this volume, let them speak for themselves. They are true *Black Cat* stories. Personally, I care far more for men than for the best stories ever hatched. Wherefore, this introduction has been devoted to Mr. Umbstaetter, the Man.

Jack London

Glen Ellen, California
March 25, 1911

LETTER TO "THE AMERICAN HEBREW"
(August 27, 1911)

⊕ ⊕ ⊕ ⊕ ⊕ ⊕ ⊕ ⊕ ⊕ ⊕ ⊕ ⊕

In the September 22, 1911, issue of *The American Hebrew,* the editors published letters from a number of prominent world authors (Thomas Nelson Page, Israel Zangwill, Maarten Maartens, William J. Locke, and Robert Hichens, among others) on the subject of how each author depicted the Jew in his works.

London displays an ignorance of the Jew in his response—writing of the Jewish "race" and later of the Jewish "nationality"—but his answer is otherwise pertinent and provocative. It is a brief for the writer's freedom to portray as he pleases—a far cry from today's prevailing attitude to be hypersensitive toward minorities and always on guard against offending them.

⊕ ⊕ ⊕ ⊕ ⊕ ⊕ ⊕ ⊕ ⊕ ⊕ ⊕ ⊕

I have made villains, scoundrels, weaklings, and degenerates of Cockneys, Scotchmen, Englishmen, Americans, Frenchmen and Irish, and I don't know what other nationalities. I have no recollection of having made a Jew serve a mean fictional function. But I see no reason why I should not, if the need and the setting of my story demanded it. I cannot reconcile myself to the attitude that in humor and fiction the Jew should be a favored race, and therefore be passed over, or used only for his exalted qualities.

I have myself, not as an American, but personally and with the name so little different from mine that it was not even a thin disguise, been exploited before Jewish audiences in the most despicable of characters. The only sensation I experienced was regret at not being able to be present to enjoy the fun.

Finally, I am a terrific admirer of the Jews; I have consorted more with Jews than with any other nationality; I have among the Jews some of my finest and noblest friends; and, being a Socialist, I subscribe to the Brotherhood of Man. In this connection, let me add that it is as unfair for a writer to make villains of all races except the Jews, as it is to make villains only of Jews. To ignore the Jew in the matter of villainy is so invidious an exception as to be unfair to the Jews.

Sincerely yours,
Jack London

LETTER TO MAURICE MAGNUS
(October 23, 1911)

⊕ ⊕ ⊕ ⊕ ⊕ ⊕ ⊕ ⊕ ⊕ ⊕ ⊕ ⊕

From a comment on the portrayal of the Jew in his fiction to one on the dearth of homosexual characters in his works . . .

Maurice Magnus, probably unknown to London, was as curious a figure as ever wrote him a letter. Magnus's career ranged from managing the business affairs of Isadora Duncan to desertion from the French Foreign Legion. He committed suicide on Malta in 1920 at the age of forty-four by swallowing prussic acid, while Maltese police were preparing to arrest him as a swindler and chronic debtor. A notorious homosexual, he was author of *Memoirs of the Foreign Legion* (New York: Alfred A. Knopf, 1925), posthumously edited and published through the efforts of D. H. Lawrence who was probably trying to recoup a loan he had made to Magnus.*

The letter forms one of the few statements London ever made on the subject of homosexuality and it discredits the theorizing of some recent "psychoanalytic" critics on London's alleged latent homosexuality.

⊕ ⊕ ⊕ ⊕ ⊕ ⊕ ⊕ ⊕ ⊕ ⊕ ⊕ ⊕

Glen Ellen, Calif.
Oct. 23, 1911

Dear Maurice Magnus:

In reply to yours of September 21, 1911, which has only just now come to hand, having been forwarded to me via various comrades in the Socialist movement.

Nay—but I have always imagined Wolf Larsen and Burning Daylight as "knowing" women—but I did not think it necessary explicitly to state in my writing.

---

*See Dale L. Walker, "Jack London and Maurice Magnus," *Jack London News-letter,* vol. 5, no. 3 (September–December, 1972).

You are certainly right. A certain definite percentage of men are so homosexual, or so nearly homosexual, that they can love another man more than they can love any woman. But then, I dare say, no homosexual is qualified to say whether a fictional woman is real or not to a normally sexed man. A man who is normal sexually conceives of women in ways repellant to a homosexual man.

Surely, I have studied the sex problem even in its "most curious ways." I, however, have drawn men-characters who were sexually normal. I have never dreamed of drawing a homosexual male character. Perhaps I am too prosaically normal myself, though I do know the whole literature and all the authorities of the "curious ways."

I think I know the problem you suggest, and I think I know it fairly thoroughly and scientifically. Unfortunately, those who figure vitally in that problem constitute too small a percentage of the human race to be an adequate book-buying inducement to a writer.

I think I get your point of view. Am I wrong? Do you get my point of view? Flatly, I am a lover of women.

Sincerely yours,
Jack London

Reprinted from *Letters From Jack London* (1965).

(*The Independent,* December 14, 1911)

⊕ ⊕ ⊕ ⊕ ⊕ ⊕ ⊕ ⊕ ⊕ ⊕ ⊕ ⊕

This introductory essay to Richard Henry Dana's *Two Years Before the Mast* was published less than three months before London, his wife, the manservant Nakata and the London's fox terrier "Possum" embarked from Baltimore around Cape Horn to Seattle on the four-masted barque *Dirigo*—a 148-day voyage.

Dana (1815-82) shipped before the mast as an ordinary seaman in August, 1834, on the brig *Pilgrim* around Cape Horn to California. He hoped to recover his health on the voyage and did so. His minute diary formed the basis for his 1840 classic of the sea, *Two Years Before the Mast.*

"A Classic of the Sea" was included in London's posthumous collection, *The Human Drift* (1917).

⊕ ⊕ ⊕ ⊕ ⊕ ⊕ ⊕ ⊕ ⊕ ⊕ ⊕ ⊕

Once in a hundred years is a book written that lives not alone for its own century but which becomes a document for the future centuries. Such a book is Dana's. When Marryat's and Cooper's sea novels are gone to dust, stimulating and joyful as they have been to generations of men, still will remain *Two Years Before the Mast.*

Paradoxical as it may seem, Dana's book is the classic of the sea, not because there was anything extraordinary about Dana, but for the precise contrary reason that he was just an ordinary, normal man, clear-seeing, hard-headed, controlled, fitted with adequate education to go about the work. He brought a trained mind to put down with untroubled vision what he saw of a certain phase of work-a-day life. There was nothing brilliant nor fly-away about him. He was not a genius. His heart never rode the head. He was neither overlorded by sentiment nor hag-ridden by imagination. Otherwise he might have been guilty of the beautiful exaggerations in Melville's *Typee* or the imaginative orgies in the latter's *Moby Dick.* It was Dana's cool poise that saved him from being spread-eagled and flogged when two of his mates were so treated; it was his lack of abandon that prevented him from taking up permanently with the sea, that prevented him from seeing more than one poetical spot, and more than one romantic spot on all the coast of Old California. Yet these apparent defects were his strength. They enabled him magnificently to write, and for all time, the picture of the sea-life of his time.

Written close to the middle of the last century, such has been the revolution worked in man's method of trafficking with the sea, that the life and conditions described in Dana's book have passed utterly away. Gone are the crack clippers, the driving captains, the hard-bitten but efficient foremast hands. Remain only crawling cargo tanks, dirty tramps, greyhound liners, and a sombre, sordid type of sailing ship. The only records broken today by sailing vessels are those for slowness. They are no longer built for speed nor are they manned before the mast by as sturdy a sailor stock, nor aft the mast are they officered by sail-carrying captains and driving mates.

Speed is left to the liners, who run the silk, and tea, and spices. Admiralty courts, boards of trade, and underwriters frown upon driving and sail-carrying. No more are the free-and-easy, dare-devil days, when fortunes were made in fast runs and lucky ventures, not alone for owners, but for captains as well. Nothing is ventured now. The risks of swift passages cannot be abided. Freights are calculated to the last least fraction of per cent. The captains do no speculating, no bargain-making for the owners. The latter attend to all this, and by wire and cable rake the ports of the seven seas in quest of cargoes, and through their agents make all business arrangements.

It has been learned that small crews only, and large carriers only, can return a decent interest on the investment. The inevitable corollary is that speed and spirit are at a discount. There is no discussion of the fact that in the sailing merchant marine the seamen, as a class, have sadly deteriorated. Men no longer sell farms to go to sea. But the time of which Dana writes was the heyday of fortune-making and adventure on the sea—with the full connotation of hardship and peril always attendant.

It was Dana's fortune, for the sake of the picture that the *Pilgrim* was an average ship, with an average crew and officers, and managed with average discipline. Even the *hazing* that took place after the California coast was reached, was of the average sort. The *Pilgrim* savored not in any way of a hell-ship. The captain, while not the sweetest-natured man in the world, was only an average down-east driver, neither brilliant nor slovenly in his seamanship, neither cruel nor sentimental in the treatment of his men. While, on the other hand, there were no extra liberty days, no delicacies added to the meager forecastle fare, nor grog or hot coffee on double watches, on the other hand the crew was not chronically crippled by the continual play of knuckle-dusters and belaying pins. Once, and once only, were men flogged or ironed—a very fair average for the year 1834, for at that time flogging on board merchant vessels was already well on the decline.

The difference between the sea-life then and now can no better be epitomized than in Dana's description of the dress of the sailor of his day:

"The trousers tight around the hips, and thence hanging long and loose around the feet, a superabundance of checked shirt, a low-crowned, well-varnished black hat, worn on the back of the head, with half a fathom of black ribbon hanging over the left-eye, and a peculiar tie to the black silk handkerchief."

Though Dana sailed from Boston only three-quarters of a century ago, much that is at present obsolete was then in full sway. For instance, the old word *larboard* was still in use. He was a member of the *larboard* watch. The vessel was on the *larboard* tack. It was only the other day, because of its similarity in sound to starboard, that *larboard* was changed to *port.* Try to imagine "All larboard bowlines on deck!" being shouted down into the forecastle of a present day ship. Yet that was the call used on the *Pilgrim* to fetch Dana and the rest of his watch on deck.

The chronometer, which is merely the least imperfect timepiece man has devised, makes possible the surest and easiest method by far of ascertaining longitude. Yet the *Pilgrim* sailed in a day when the chronometer was just coming into general use. So little was it depended upon that the *Pilgrim* carried only one, and that one, going wrong at the outset, was never used again. A navigator of the present would be aghast if asked to voyage for two years, from Boston, around the Horn to California, and back again, without a chronometer. In those days such a proceeding was a matter of course, for those were the days when dead reckoning was indeed something to reckon on, when running down the latitude was a common way of finding a place, and when lunar observations were direly necessary. It may be fairly asserted that very few merchant officers of today ever make a lunar observation, and that a large percentage are unable to do it.

"*Sept. 22nd.,* upon coming on deck at seven bells in the morning we found the other watch aloft throwing water upon the sails, and looking astern we saw a small, clipper-built brig with a black hull heading directly after us. We went to work immediately, and put all the canvas upon the brig which we could get upon her, rigging out oars for studding-sail yards; and continued wetting down the sails by buckets of water whipped up the mast head. . . . She was armed, and full of men, and showed no colors."

The foregoing sounds like a paragraph from *Midshipman Easy* or the *Water Witch*, rather than a paragraph from the soberest, faithfulest, and most literal chronicle of the sea ever written. And yet the chase by a pirate occurred, on board the brig *Pilgrim*, on September 22nd, 1834—something like only two generations ago.

Dana was the thorough-going type of man, not overbalanced and erratic, without quirk or quibble of temperament. He was efficient, but not brilliant. His was a general all-around efficiency. He was efficient at the law; he was efficient at college; he was efficient as a sailor; he was efficient in the matter of pride, when that pride was no more than the pride of a forecastle hand, at twelve dollars a month, in his seaman's task well done, in the smart sailing of his captain, in the cleanness and trimness of his ship.

There is no sailor whose cockles of the heart will not be warmed to Dana's description of the first time he sent down a royal yard. Once or twice he had seen it done. He got an old hand in the crew to coach him. And then, the first anchorage of Monterrey, being pretty *thick* with the second mate, he got him to ask the mate to be sent up the first time the royal yards were struck. "Fortunately," as Dana describes it, "I got through without any word from the officer; and heard the 'well done' of the mate, when the yard reached the deck, with as much satisfaction as I ever felt at Cambridge on seeing a 'bene' at the foot of a Latin exercise."

"This was the first time I had taken a weather ear-ring, and I felt not a little proud to sit astride of the weather yard-arm, past the ear-ring, and sing out 'Haul out to leeward!'" He had been over a year at sea before he essayed this able seaman's task, but he did it, and he did it with pride. And with pride, he went down a four-hundred foot cliff, on a pair of top-gallant studding-sail halyards bent together, to dislodge several dollars worth of stranded bullock hides, though all the acclaim he got from his mates was: "What a d———d fool you were to risk your life for half a dozen hides!"

In brief, it was just this efficiency in pride, as well as work, that enabled Dana to set down, not merely the photograph detail of life before the mast and hide-droghing on the coast of California, but of the unvarnished, simple psychology and ethics of the forecastle hands who droghed the hides, stood at the wheel, made and took in sail, tarred down the rigging, holystoned the decks, turned in all-standing, grumbled as they cut about the kid, criticized the seamanship of their officers, and estimated the duration of their exile from the cubic space of the hide-house.

Jack London
Glen Ellen, California
August 13, 1911

SELECTIONS FROM "JOHN BARLEYCORN"

⊕ ⊕ ⊕ ⊕ ⊕ ⊕ ⊕ ⊕ ⊕ ⊕ ⊕ ⊕

This twenty-five-hundred word excerpt from chapters 23, 25, and 26 of London's autobiographical *John Barleycorn* (New York: The Century Co., 1913), begins with his brief stint at the University of California at Berkeley which ended in the spring of 1897, and ends three years later at the beginning of his fabulous writing career.

Barleycorn is among London's most provocative works—one correctly regarded as an "autobiographical novel." Arthur Calder-Marshall has written that it "... is conceded by the few modern critics who have read it, to be 'a classic of alcoholism.' But in my view it is a literary masterpiece, not merely the greatest book which Jack London wrote but seen in its true setting, one of the most poignant documents of our century, a fortuitous work of inhibited and tortured genius." (*The Bodley Head Jack London,* vol. 2, p. 7.)

Irving Stone wrote that "The value of *John Barleycorn* as literature does not depend upon its conformity to the pattern of his life. *John Barleycorn* reads like a novel, is fresh, beautifully honest, simple and moving, contains magnificent writing about the White Logic, and remains as a classic on drinking." (*Sailor on Horseback,* p. 281.)

Biographer Andrew Sinclair says flatly that *Barleycorn* was "the book he wrote to exorcise his shame." (*Jack,* p. 174.)

And, in a letter written in September, 1913, London said: "The only trouble, I might say, about *John Barleycorn* is that I did not put in the whole truth. All that is in it is true; but I did not dare put in the whole truth." (*Letters From Jack London,* p. 401.)

Insofar as his recollections of the birth of his writing career, *Barleycorn* and *Martin Eden* are invaluable source works, if used with caution.

⊕ ⊕ ⊕ ⊕ ⊕ ⊕ ⊕ ⊕ ⊕ ⊕ ⊕

I completed the first half of my freshman year, and in January of 1897 took up my course for the second half. But the pressure from lack of money, plus a conviction that the university was not giving me all that I wanted in the time I could spare for it, forced me to leave. I was not very disappointed. For two years I had studied, and in those two years, what was far more valuable, I had done a prodigious amount of reading. Then, too, my grammar had improved. It is true, I had not yet learned that I must say "It is I"; but I no longer was guilty of the double negative in writing, though still prone to that error in excited speech.

I decided immediately to embark on my career. I had four preferences: first, music; second, poetry; third, the writing of philosophic, economic, and political essays; and fourth, and last, and least, fiction writing. I resolutely cut out music as impossible, settled down in my bedroom, and tackled my second, third and fourth choices simultaneously. Heavens, how I wrote! Never was there a creative fever such as mine from which the patient escaped fatal results. The way I worked was enough to soften my brain and send me to a mad-house. I wrote, I wrote everything—ponderous essays, scientific and sociological, short stories, humorous verse, verse of all sorts from triolets and sonnets to blank verse tragedy and elephantine epics in Spenserian stanzas. On occasion I composed steadily, day after day, for fifteen hours a day. At times I forgot to eat, or refused to tear myself away from my passionate outpouring in order to eat.

And then there was the matter of typewriting. My brother-in-law owned a machine which he used in the daytime. In the night I was free to use it. That machine was a wonder. I could weep now as I recollect my wrestlings with it. It must have been a first model in the year one of the typewriter era. Its alphabet was all capitals. It was informed with an evil spirit. It obeyed no known laws of physics, and overthrew the hoary axiom that like things performed to like things produce like results. I'll swear that machine never did the same thing in the same way twice. Again and again it demonstrated that unlike actions produce like results.

How my back used to ache with it! Prior to that experience, my back had been good for every violent strain put upon it in a none too gentle career. But that typewriter proved to me that I had a pipe-stem for a back. Also, it made me doubt my shoulders. They ached as with rheumatism after every bout. The keys of that machine had to be hit so hard that to one outside the house it sounded like distant thunder or some one breaking up the furniture. I had to hit the keys so hard that I strained my first fingers to the elbows, while the ends of my fingers were blisters burst and blistered again. Had it been my machine I'd have operated it with a carpenter's hammer.

The worst of it was that I was actually typing my manuscripts at the same time I was trying to master that machine. It was a feat of physical endurance and a brain storm combined to type a thousand words, and I was composing thousands of words every day which just had to be typed for the waiting editors.

Oh, between the writing and the typewriting I was well a-weary. I had brain- and nerve-fag, and body-fag as well, and yet the thought of drink never suggested itself. I was living too high to stand in need of an anodyne. All my waking hours, except those with that infernal type-writer, were spent in a creative heaven. And along with this I had no desire for drink, because I still believed in many things—in the love of all men and women in the matter of man and woman love; in fatherhood; in human justice; in art—in the whole host of fond illusions that keep the world turning around.

But the waiting editors elected to keep on waiting. My manuscripts made amazing round-trip records between the Pacific and the Atlantic. It might have been the weirdness of the typewriting that prevented the editors from accepting at least one little offering of mine. I don't know, and goodness knows the stuff I wrote was as weird as its typing. I sold my hard-bought school books for ridiculous sums to second-hand book-men. I borrowed small sums of money wherever I could, and suffered my old father to feed me with the meager returns of his failing strength.

It didn't last long, only a few weeks, when I had to surrender and go to work. Yet I was unaware of any need for the drink-anodyne. I was not disappointed. My career was retarded, that was all. Perhaps I did need further preparation. I had learned enough from the books to realize that I had touched only the hem of knowledge's garment. I still lived on the heights. My waking hours, and most of the hours I should have used for sleep, were spent with the books. . . .

After the laundry, my sister and her husband grubstaked me into the Klondike. It was the first gold rush into that region, the early fall rush of 1897. I was twenty-one years old, and in splendid physical condition. I remember, at the end of the twenty-eight mile portage across Chilkoot from Dyea Beach and Lake Linderman, I was packing up with the Indians and outpacking many an Indian. The last pack into Linderman was three miles. I back-tripped it four times a day, and on each forward trip carried one hundred and fifty pounds. This means that over the worst trails I daily traveled twenty-four miles, twelve of which were under a burden of one hundred and fifty pounds.

Yes, I had let career go hang, and was on the adventure-path again in quest of fortune. And, of course, on the adventure-path, I met John Barleycorn. Here were the chesty men again, rovers and adventurers, and while they didn't mind a grub famine, whisky they could not do without. Whisky went over the trail, while the flour lay cached and untouched by the trail-side.

As good fortune would have it, the three men in my party were not drinkers. Therefore I didn't drink save on rare occasions and disgracefully when with other men. In my personal medicine chest was a quart of whisky. I never drew the cork till six months afterward, in a lonely camp, where, without anesthetics, a doctor was compelled to operate on a man. The doctor and the patient emptied my bottle between them and then proceeded to the operation.

Back in California a year later, recovering from scurvy, I found that my father was dead and that I was the head and the sole bread-winner of a household. When I state that I had passed coal on a steamship from Behring Sea to British Columbia, and traveled in the steerage from there to San Francisco, it will be understood that I brought nothing back from the Klondike but my scurvy.

Times were hard. Work of any sort was difficult to get. And work of any sort was what I had to take, for I was still an unskilled laborer. I had no thought of career. That was over and done with. I had to find food for two mouths beside my own and keep a roof over our heads—yes, and buy a winter suit, my one suit being decidedly summery. I had to get some sort of work immediately. After that, when I had caught my breath, I might think about my future.

Unskilled labor is the first to feel the slackness of hard times, and I had no trades save those of sailor and laundryman. With my new responsibilities I didn't dare go to sea, and I failed to find a job at laundrying. I failed to find a job at anything. I had my name down in five employment bureaus. I advertised in three newspapers. I sought out the new friends I knew who might be able to get me work; but they were either uninterested or unable to find anything for me.

The situation was desperate. I pawned my watch, my bicycle, and a mackintosh of which my father had been very proud and which he had left to me. It was and is my sole legacy in this world. It had cost fifteen dollars, and the pawnbroker let me have two dollars on it. And—oh, yes— a water-front comrade of earlier years drifted along one day with a dress suit wrapped in newspapers. He could give no adequate explanation of how he had come to possess it, nor did I press for an explanation. I wanted the suit myself. No; not to wear. I traded him a lot of rubbish which, being unpawnable, was useless to me. I peddled the rubbish for several dollars, while I pledged the dress suit with my pawnbroker for five dollars. And for all I know, the pawnbroker still has the suit. I had never intended to redeem it.

But I couldn't get any work. Yet I was a bargain in the labor market. I was twenty-two years old, weighed one hundred and sixty-five pounds stripped, every pound of which was excellent for toil; and the last traces of my scurvy were vanishing before a treatment of potatoes chewed raw. I tackled every opening for employment. I tried to become a studio model, but there were too many fine-bodied young fellows out of jobs. I answered advertisements of elderly invalids in need of companions. And I almost became a sewing machine agent, on commission, without salary. But poor people don't buy sewing machines in hard times, so I was forced to forego that employment.

Of course, it must be remembered that along with such frivolous occupations, I was trying to get work as wop, lumper, and roustabout. But winter was coming on, and the surplus labor army was pouring into the cities. Also, I, who had romped along carelessly through the countries of the world and the kingdom of the mind, was not a member of any union.

I sought odd jobs. I worked days, and half-days, at anything I could get. I mowed lawns, trimmed hedges, took up carpets, beat them, and laid them again. Further, I took the civil service examinations for mail carrier and passed first. But alas, there was no vacancy, and I must wait. And while I waited, and in between the odd jobs I managed to procure, I started to earn ten dollars by writing a newspaper account of a voyage I had made, in an open boat down the Yukon, of nineteen hundred miles in nineteen days. I didn't know the first thing about the newspaper game, but I was confident I'd get ten dollars for my article.

But I didn't. The first San Francisco newspaper to which I mailed it never acknowledged receipt of the manuscript, but held on to it. The longer it held on to it, the more certain I was that the thing was accepted.

And here is the funny thing. Some are born to fortune, and some have fortune thrust upon them. But in my case I was clubbed into fortune, and bitter necessity wielded the club. I had long since abandoned all thought of writing as a career. My honest intention in writing that article was to earn ten dollars. And that was the limit of my intention. It would help to tide me along until I got steady employment. Had a vacancy occurred in the post office at that time, I should have jumped at it.

But the vacancy did not occur, nor did a steady job; and I employed the time between odd jobs with writing a twenty-one-thousand-word serial for the *Youth's Companion*. I turned it out and typed it in seven days. I fancy that was what was the matter with it, for it came back.

It took some time for it to go and come, and in the meantime I tried my hand at short stories. I sold one to the *Overland Monthly* for five dollars. The *Black Cat* gave me forty dollars for another. The *Overland*

Monthly offered me seven dollars and a half, pay on publication, for all the stories I should deliver. I got my bicycle, my watch, and my father's mackintosh out of pawn and rented a typewriter. Also, I paid up the bills I owed to the several groceries that allowed me a small credit. I recall the Portuguese groceryman who never permitted my bill to go beyond four dollars. Hopkins, another grocer, could not be budged beyond five dollars.

And just then came the call from the post office to go to work. It placed me in a most trying predicament. The sixty-five dollars I could earn regularly every month was a terrible temptation. I couldn't decide what to do. And I'll never be able to forgive the postmaster of Oakland. I answered the call, and I talked to him like a man. I frankly told him the situation. It looked as if I might win out at writing. The chance was good, but not certain. Now, if he would pass me by and select the next man on the eligible list, and give me a call at the next vacancy—

But he shut me off with: "Then you don't want the position?"

"But I do," I protested. "Don't you see, if you will pass me over this time—"

"If you want it you will take it," he said coldly.

Happily for me, the cursed brutality of the man made me angry.

"Very well," I said. "I won't take it."

. . . Having burned my one ship, I plunged into writing. I am afraid I always was an extremist. Early and late I was at it—writing, typing, studying grammar, studying writing and all the forms of writing, and studying the writers who succeeded in order to find out how they succeeded. I managed on five hours' sleep in the twenty-four, and came pretty close to working the nineteen waking hours left in me. My light burned till two and three in the morning, which led a good neighbor woman into a bit of sentimental Sherlock Holmes deduction. Never seeing me in the daytime, she concluded that I was a gambler, and that the light in my window was placed there by my mother to guide her erring son home.

The trouble with the beginner at the writing game is the long, dry spells, when there is never an editor's check and everything pawnable is pawned. I wore my summer suit pretty well through that winter, and the following summer experienced the longest, dryest spell of all, in the period when salaried men are gone on vacation and manuscripts lie in editorial offices until vacation is over.

My difficulty was that I had no one to advise me. I didn't know a soul who had written or who had ever tried to write. I didn't even know one reporter. Also, to succeed at the writing game, I found I had to unlearn about everything the teachers and university had taught me. I was very indignant about this at the time; though now I can understand it. They did not know the trick of successful writing in the years of 1895 and 1896.

They knew all about "Snow Bound" and "Sartor Resartus"; but the American editors of 1899 did not want such truck. They wanted the 1899 truck, and offered to pay so well for it that the teachers and professors of literature would have quit their jobs could they have supplied it.

I struggled along, stood off the butcher and the grocer, pawned my watch and bicycle and my father's mackintosh, and I worked. I really did work, and went on short commons of sleep. Critics have complained about the swift education one of my characters, Martin Eden, achieved. In three years, from a sailor with a common school education, I made a successful writer of him. The critics say this is impossible. Yet I was Martin Eden. At the end of three working years, two of which were spent in high school and the university and one spent at writing, and all three in studying immensely and intensely, I was publishing stories in magazines such as the *Atlantic Monthly,* was correcting proofs of my first book (issued by Houghton, Mifflin Co.), was selling sociological articles to *Cosmopolitan* and *McClure's,* had declined an associate editorship proffered me by telegraph from New York City, and was getting ready to marry.

Now the foregoing means work, especially the last year of it, when I was learning my trade as a writer. And in that year, running short on sleep and tasking my brain to its limit, I neither drank nor cared to drink. So far as I was concerned, alcohol did not exist. I did suffer from brain-fag on occasion, but alcohol never suggested itself as an ameliorative. Heavens! Editorial acceptances and checks were all the amelioratives I needed. A thin envelope from an editor in the morning's mail was more stimulating than half-a-dozen cocktails. And if a check of decent amount came out of the envelope, such incident in itself was a whole drunk.

Furthermore, at that time in my life I did not know what a cocktail was. I remember, when my first book was published, several Alaskans who were members of the Bohemian Club entertained me one evening at the club in San Francisco. We sat in most wonderful leather chairs, and drinks were ordered. Never had I heard such an ordering of liqueurs and of highballs of particular brands of Scotch. I didn't know what a liqueur or a highball was, and I didn't know that "Scotch" meant whisky. I knew only poor men's drinks, the drinks of the frontier and of sailor-town—cheap beer and cheaper whisky that was just called whisky and nothing else. I was embarrassed to make a choice, and the waiter nearly collapsed when I ordered claret as an after dinner drink.

TWO LETTERS TO WINSTON CHURCHILL

(March–April, 1913)

⊕ ⊕ ⊕ ⊕ ⊕ ⊕ ⊕ ⊕ ⊕ ⊕ ⊕ ⊕

Winston Churchill (1871–1947) was an American novelist and no relation to the more famous Winston Churchill of England.

Churchill's most famous works were *Richard Carvel* (1899), *The Crisis* (1901), *The Crossing* (1904), and *The Inside of the Cup* (1913).

These letters are reprinted from the *California Historical Society Quarterly* (Warren J. Titus, "Two Unpublished Letters of Jack London") 39, 1960.

⊕ ⊕ ⊕ ⊕ ⊕ ⊕ ⊕ ⊕ ⊕ ⊕ ⊕ ⊕

Mar 23, 1913

Jack London
Glen Ellen
Sonoma Co. Calif.

Mr. Winston Churchill,
    Dear Sir:
    I live in California—when I am not farther afield. I have published thirty-three books, as well as an ocean of magazine stuff, and yet I have never heard the rates that other writers receive.
    If it is not asking too much, may I ask you to tell me (confidentially, of course) what top rates, average rates, and minimum rates, you receive from (1) English magazines, (2) American magazines, (3) English book-publishers, (4) American book-publishers.

Sincerely yours,
Jack London

April 20, 1913

Jack London
Glen Ellen
Sonoma Co. Calif.

Dear Mr. Churchill:

In reply to your good letter of April 7, 1913, I certainly do appreciate the confidence you have given me, also the information. Concerning my own stuff, except for my first books I am getting twenty per cent. In the serialization, *The Cosmopolitan* cuts one of my novels to 100,000 words, for which it pays me for American and English rights, $13,200.00. Despite the fact that my novels are shorter than yours and that I am a quick worker, turning out two and three a year, I must say that your $30,000.00 for *The Inside of the Cup* is a splendid big price.

Of course, you can understand my situation that prompted me to write to you for information. I have always been so out of it that I had no line upon my own pay.

I was most astonished to find that you are located for some time in California.

Some time when you are up in the Bay region, won't you run up and visit us—this, of course, includes any one you may bring with you. Truly, I do not know whether you are married or not. It is as a born Californian that I dare to say to you that we will show you here a different California from any that you have so far seen.

Please always remember, also, that we are only camping out; but that nevertheless this is a dandy place for a man to loaf in and to work in.

Sincerely yours,
Jack London

LETTER TO MAX EASTMAN
(May 31, 1913)

⊕ ⊕ ⊕ ⊕ ⊕ ⊕ ⊕ ⊕ ⊕ ⊕ ⊕ ⊕

Max Eastman (1883-1969) was a leading American leftist of the early nineteenth century, editor of *The Masses* (1913-17), author of numerous political and psychological works. Among the latter were *The Enjoyment of Poetry* (1913) and *The Enjoyment of Laughter* (1936). His autobiography, *Love and Revolution,* appeared in 1965.

⊕ ⊕ ⊕ ⊕ ⊕ ⊕ ⊕ ⊕ ⊕ ⊕ ⊕ ⊕

Glen Ellen, Calif.
May 31, 1913

Dear Max Eastman:

Just a few lines of appreciation of your *Enjoyment of Poetry.*

It is a splendid presentation of the poet's case, especially so in view of the fact that the book is as full of common sense as it is of delicacy and distinction. In all of the book there is no nonsense, none of the absurd notions about poetry that have set most persons treating it in critique— notably Mr. Hudson Maxim. You are, moreover, fully sensitized to the poetic atmosphere, and show unerring taste in your conviction and likes (in my judgment likes and convictions being one and the same thing).

It seems to me that you reach your high-water mark on pages 116, 117 and 118. It would be hard to find elsewhere in literature a finer insight into matters that elude ordinary terms and dissections.

Again thanking you for your splendid contribution,

Sincerely yours,
Jack London

Reprinted from *Letters From Jack London* (1965).

FOUR LETTERS TO ASPIRING WRITERS

⊕ ⊕ ⊕ ⊕ ⊕ ⊕ ⊕ ⊕ ⊕ ⊕ ⊕ ⊕

The four letters that follow are typical of the direct, compassionate, and helpful advice London gave his aspiring writer correspondents. A hallmark of these, and hundreds of similar letters, is the brass-tacks admonition "serve your apprenticeship." London had limitless patience with the problems and questions of those who sought his advice, but would not countenance those who appeared seeking "instant success," knowing from his own experience that no such thing existed.

The letters are warm and open—but direct and at times blunt—messages from a brass-tacks man.

The letter to Max Feckler was reprinted under the title "Letter to a Young Writer."

All are reprinted from *Letters From Jack London* (1965).

⊕ ⊕ ⊕ ⊕ ⊕ ⊕ ⊕ ⊕ ⊕ ⊕ ⊕ ⊕

Glen Ellen, Calif.
Sept. 28, 1913

Dear friend Jess Dorman:

In reply to yours of Sept. 25, 1913. Assuming, to quote you, that you "have in mind an original virile story," that you are "capable of writing it," I should say, if you wrote it, at the rate of 1000 words a day, and sold it as an unknown at an unknown's price (which would be at least 2¢ for such a virile, original, well-written story), I leave the arithmetic to you.

If you are earning more than $20 a day, then leave it alone; if you are earning less than $20 a day, write the story.

Please know that I am answering your letter according to the very rigid stipulations that you laid down to me. Since, as you say, you know my career, you must know that I worked many a long month nineteen hours a day, without sleep, and sold a great deal of my stuff at 75¢ per 100 words for stories that were not original, that were not virile, that were not well written.

I plugged. Can you plug this way for 19 hours a day?

You say you cannot so plug. If you say truth, well, far be it from me to advise you to tackle such a game.

If you think you can jump in right now, without any apprenticeship, and lay bricks as well as a four, five, or six years' apprenticed bricklayer; if you think you can jump in on the floor and nail on shoes on ten horses as well as a man who has served a three, four, or five years' apprenticeship at shoeing horses on the floor; if you think you can jump in and nail laths, or spread plaster, or do concrete work, without previous experience, better or as well as the men who have served their three, four, and five years of apprenticeship;—in short, if you think that a vastly better-paid trade than that, namely, the writing-game, can be achieved in your first short story not yet written, or long story not yet written, why go ahead my boy and jump to it, and I'll pat you on the back—pat you on the back! the world will crush you in for the great genius that you are if you can do such a thing. In the meantime have a little patience and learn the trade.

If you know my career, you know that I am a brass-tack man. And I have given you brass tacks right here. If you can beat all the rest of us, without serving your apprenticeship, go to it. Far be it from us to advise you.

Sincerely yours,
Jack London

Oakland, Calif.
Oct. 26, 1914

Dear Max Feckler:

In reply to yours of recent date undated, and returning herewith your Manuscript. First of all, let me tell you that as a psychologist and as one who has been through the mill, I enjoyed your story for its psychology and point of view. Honestly and frankly, I did not enjoy it for its literary charm or value. In the first place, it has little literary value and practically no literary charm. Merely because you have got something to say that may be of interest to others does not free you from making all due effort to express that something in the best possible medium and form. Medium and form you have utterly neglected.

Anent the foregoing paragraph, what is to be expected of any lad of twenty, without practice, in knowledge of medium and form? Heavens on earth, boy, it would take you five years to serve your apprenticeship and become a skilled blacksmith. Will you dare to say that you have spent, not five years, but as much as five months of unimpeachable, unremitting toil in trying to learn the artisan's tools of a professional writer who can sell his stuff to the magazines and receive hard cash for same? Of course you cannot; you have not done it. And yet, you should be able to reason on the face of it that the only explanation for the fact that successful writers receive such large fortunes, is because very few who desire to write become successful writers. If it takes five years work to become a skilled blacksmith, how many years of work intensified into nineteen hours a day, so that one year counts for five—how many years of such work, studying medium and form, art and artisanship, do you think a man, with native talent and something to say, required in order to reach a place in the world of letters where he received a thousand dollars cash iron money per week?

I think you get the drift of the point I am trying to make. If a fellow harnesses himself to a star of $1000 a week, he has to work proportionately harder than if he harnesses himself to a little glowworm of $20.00 a week. The only reason there are more successful blacksmiths in the world than successful writers, is that it is much easier, and requires far less hard work to become a successful blacksmith than does it to become a successful writer.

It cannot be possible that you, at twenty, should have done the work at writing that would merit you success at writing. You have not begun your apprenticeship yet. The proof of it is the fact that you dared to write this manuscript, "A Journal of One Who Is to Die." Had you made any sort of study of what is published in the magazines you would have found that your short story was of the sort that never was published in the magazines. If you are going to write for success and money, you must deliver to the market marketable goods. Your short story is not marketable goods, and had you taken half a dozen evenings off and gone into a free reading room and read all the stories published in the current magazines, you would have learned in advance that your short story was not marketable goods.

Dear lad, I'm talking to you straight from the shoulder. Remember one very important thing: Your ennui of twenty, is your ennui of twenty. You will have various other and complicated ennuis before you die. I tell you this, who have been through the ennui of sixteen as well as the ennui of twenty; and the boredom, and the blaséness, and utter wretchedness of the ennui of twenty-five, and of thirty. And I yet live, am growing fat, am very happy, and laugh a large portion of my waking hours. You see, the disease has progressed so much further with me than with you that I, as a battle-scarred survivor of the disease, look upon your symptoms as merely the preliminary adolescent symptoms. Again, let me tell you that

I know them, that I had them, and just as I had much worse afterward of the same sort, so much worse is in store for you. In the meantime, if you want to succeed at a well-paid game, prepare yourself to do the work.

There's only one way to make a beginning, and that is to begin; and begin with hard work, and patience, prepared for all the disappointments that were Martin Eden's before he succeeded—which were mine before I succeeded—because I merely appended to my fictional character, Martin Eden, my own experiences in the writing game.

Any time you are out here in California, I should be glad to have you come to visit me on the ranch. I can meet you to the last limit of brass tacks, and hammer some facts of life into you that possibly so far have escaped your own experience.

Sincerely yours,
Jack London

Glen Ellen, Calif.
Dec. 11, 1914

My dear Miss Andersen:

In my opinion, three positive things are necessary for success as a writer. First a study and knowledge of literature as it is commercially produced today.

Second, a knowledge of life, and

Third, a working philosophy of life.

Negatively, I would suggest that the best preparation for authorship is a stern refusal to accept blindly the canons of literary art as laid down by teachers of high school English and teachers of university English and composition.

The average author is lucky, I mean the average successful author is lucky, if he makes twelve hundred to two thousand dollars a year. Many successful authors earn in various ways from their writings as high as twenty thousand dollars a year and there are some authors, rare ones, who make from fifty to seventy-five thousand dollars a year from their writings; and some of the most successful authors in some of their most successful years have made as high as a hundred thousand dollars or two hundred thousand dollars.

Personally, it strikes me that the one great special advantage of authorship as a means of livelihood is that it gives one more freedom than is given any person in business or in the various other professions. The author's office and business is under his hat and he can go anywhere and write anywhere as the spirit moves him.

Thanking you for your good letter,
Sincerely yours,
Jack London

Glen Ellen, Calif.
Feb. 5, 1915

My dear Ethel Jennings:

In reply to yours of January 12th, 1915:

By the way, January 12th, 1915 was my birthday—39 years old, if you please.

I am returning you herewith your manuscript. First of all, just a few words as to your story. A reader who knew nothing about you and who read your story in a book or magazine would wonder for a long time after beginning as to what part of the world was the locality of your story. You should have worked in artistically, and as a germane part of the story, right near the start, the locality of the story.

Your story, really, had no locality. Your story had no place as being distinctively different from any other place of the earth's surface. This is your first mistake in the story.

Let me tell you another mistake which I get from your letter, namely that you wrote this story at white heat. Never write any story at white heat. Hell is kept warm by unpublished manuscripts that were written at white heat.

Develop your locality. Get in your local color. Develop your characters. Make your characters real to your readers. Get out of youself and into your reader's minds and know what impression your readers are getting from your written words. Always remember that you are not writing for yourself but that you are writing for your readers. In connection with this let me recommend to you Herbert Spencer's "Philosophy of Style." You should be able to find this essay, "The Philosophy of Style," in Herbert Spencer's collected works in any public library.

On page 3 of your manuscript you stop and tell the reader how awful it is for a woman to live with a man outside of wedlock. I am perfectly willing to grant that it is awful for a woman to live with a man outside of wedlock, but as an artist I am compelled to tell you for heaven's sake, don't stop your story in order to tell your reader how awful it is. Let your reader get this sense of awfulness from your story as your story goes on.

Further I shall not go with you in discussing your manuscript with you except to tell you that no magazine or newspaper in the United States would accept your story as it now stands.

It has long been a habit of mine to have poems typed off in duplicate which I may send to my friends. I am sending you a few samples of said poems that I have on hand at the present time. I am sending them to you in order that you may study them carefully and try to know the fineness of utterance, the new and strong and beautiful way of expressing old, eternal things which always appear apparently as new things to new eyes who try to convey what they see to the new generations.

I am enclosing you also a letter to a young writer, a letter that I was compelled to write the other day. His situation is somewhat different from yours and yet the same fundamental truth and conditions underrun his situation and your situation. In line with this let me suggest that you study always the goods that are being bought by the magazines. These goods that the magazines publish are the marketable goods. If you want to sell such goods you must write marketable goods. Any time that you are down in this part of California look up Mrs. London and me on the ranch and I can tell you more in ten minutes than I can write you in ten years.

Sincerely yours,
Jack London

INTRODUCTION TO "THE CRY FOR JUSTICE"

⊕ ⊕ ⊕ ⊕ ⊕ ⊕ ⊕ ⊕ ⊕ ⊕ ⊕ ⊕

This book was subtitled "An Anthology of Literature of Social Protest" (Philadelphia: John C. Winston Co., 1915) and was edited by Upton Sinclair. Sinclair, in a digest version of the book published in 1944 by E. Haldeman-Julius of Girard, Kansas, wrote of London's introduction: "He read the manuscript on a steamer to Hawaii where he had gone seeking rest and recuperation. His words are a message to you and to all lovers of good literature and of justice, peace and kindliness among men. That the world needs such a message in this fifth year of universal war is something which can hardly be denied."

⊕ ⊕ ⊕ ⊕ ⊕ ⊕ ⊕ ⊕ ⊕ ⊕ ⊕ ⊕

This anthology, I take it, is the first edition, the first gathering together of the body of the literature and art of the humanist thinkers of the world. As well done as it has been done, it will be better done in the future. There will be much adding, there will be a little subtracting, in the succeeding editions that are bound to come. The result will be a monument of the ages, and there will be none fairer.

Since reading of the Bible, the Koran, and the Talmud has enabled countless devout and earnest right-seeking souls to be stirred and uplifted to higher and finer planes of thought and action, then the reading of this humanist Holy Book cannot fail similarly to serve the needs of groping, yearning humans who seek to discern truth and justice amid the dazzle and murk of the thought-chaos of the present-day world.

No person, no matter how soft and secluded his own life has been, can read this Holy Book and not be aware that the world is filled with a vast mass of unfairness, cruelty, and suffering. He will find that it has been observed, during all the ages, by the thinkers, the seers, the poets, and the philosophers.

And such person will learn, possibly, that this fair world so brutally unfair, is not decreed by the will of God nor by any iron law of Nature.

He will learn that the world can be fashioned a fair world indeed by the humans who inhabit it, by the very simple, and yet most difficult process of coming to an understanding of the world. Understanding, after all, is merely sympathy in its fine correct sense. And such sympathy, in its genuineness, makes toward unselfishness. Unselfishness inevitably connotes service. And service is the solution of the entire vexatious problem of man.

He, who by understanding becomes converted to the gospel of service, will serve truth to confute liars and make them truth-tellers; will serve kindness so that brutality will perish; will serve beauty to the erasement of all that is not beautiful. And he who is strong will serve the weak that they may become strong. He will devote his strength, not to the debasement and defilement of his weaker fellows, but to the making of opportunity for them to make themselves into men rather than into slaves and beasts.

One has but to read the names of the men and women whose words burn in these pages, and to recall that by far more than average intelligence have they won to their place in the world's eye and in the world's brain long after the dust of them has vanished, to realize that due credence must be placed in their report of the world herein recorded. They were not tyrants and wastrels, hypocrites and liars, brewers and gamblers, market-riggers and stock-brokers. They were givers and servers, and seers and humanists. They were unselfish. They conceived of life, not in terms of profit, but of service.

Life tore at them with its heart-break. They could not escape the hurt of it by selfish refuge in the gluttonies of brain and body. They saw, and steeled themselves to see, clear-eyed and unafraid. Nor were they afflicted by some strange myopia. They all saw the same thing. They are all agreed upon what they saw. The totality of their evidence proves this with unswerving consistency. They have brought the report, these commissioners of humanity. It is here in these pages. It is a true report.

But not merely have they reported the human ills. They have proposed the remedy. And their remedy is of no part of all the jangling sects. It has nothing to do with the complicated metaphysical processes by which one may win to other worlds and imagined gains beyond the sky. It is a remedy for this world, since worlds must be taken one at a time. And yet, that not even the jangling sects should receive hurt by the making fairer of this world for this own world's sake, it is well, for all future worlds of them that need future worlds, that their splendor be not tarnished by the vileness and ugliness of this world.

It is so simple a remedy, merely service. Not one ignoble thought or act is demanded of any one of all men and women in the world to make fair the world. The call is for nobility of thinking, nobility of doing. The call is for service, and, such is the wholesomeness of it, he who serves all, best serves himself.

Times change, and men's minds with them. Down the past, civilizations have exposited themselves in terms of power, of world-power or of other-world power. No civilization has yet exposited itself in terms of love-of-man. The humanists have no quarrel with the previous civilizations. They were necessary in the development of man. But their purpose is fulfilled, and they may well pass, leaving man to build the new and higher civilization that will exposit itself in terms of love and service and brotherhood.

To see gathered here together this great body of human beauty and fineness and nobleness is to realize what glorious humans have already existed, do exist, and will continue increasingly to exist until all the world beautiful be made over in their image. We know how gods are made. Comes now the time to make a world.

A LETTER EXCHANGE WITH JOSEPH CONRAD

⊕ ⊕ ⊕ ⊕ ⊕ ⊕ ⊕ ⊕ ⊕ ⊕ ⊕ ⊕

This charming exchange of letters begins with London's exultant encomium for Conrad's *Victory,* and ends with a "cordial handgrasp" across the Atlantic from Conrad.

The London letter is reprinted from *Letters From Jack London* (1965); the Conrad letter from *Letters in Manuscript* (selected and introduced by James Thorpe), San Marino, Calif.: The Huntington Library, 1971.

⊕ ⊕ ⊕ ⊕ ⊕ ⊕ ⊕ ⊕ ⊕ ⊕ ⊕ ⊕

Honolulu, T. H.
June 4, 1915

Dear Joseph Conrad:

The mynah birds are waking the hot dawn about me. The surf is thundering in my ears where it falls on the white sands of the beach, here at Waikiki, where the green grass at the roots of the coconut palm insists to the lip of the wave-wash. This night has been yours—and mine.

I had just begun to write when I read your first early work. I have merely madly appreciated you and communicated my appreciation to my friends through all these years. I never wrote you. I never dreamed to write you. But *Victory* has swept me off my feet, and I am inclosing herewith a carbon copy of a letter written to a friend at the end of this lost night's sleep.

Perhaps you will appreciate this lost night's sleep when I tell you that it was immediately preceded by a day's sail in a Japanese sampan of sixty miles from the Leper Settlement of Molokai (where Mrs. London and I had been revisiting old friends) to Honolulu.

On your head be it.

Aloha (which is a sweet word of greeting, the Hawaiian greeting, meaning "my love be with you").

Jack London

TO JACK LONDON

Capel House
Orlestone, North Ashford
September 10, 1915

My dear Sir:

I am immensely touched by the kindness of your letter—that apart from the intense satisfaction given me by the approval of an accomplished fellow craftsman and a true brother in letters—of whose personality and art I have been intensely aware for many years.

A few days before it reached me Percival Gibbon (a short-story writer and a most distinguished war corresp.) and I were talking you over endlessly, in the quiet hours of the night. Gibbon who had just returned after 5 months on the Russian front had been taking you in bulk, soaking himself in your prose. And we admired the vehemence of your strength and the delicacy of your perception with the greater sympathy and respect.

I haven't seen your latest yet. The reviews such as come my way are enthusiastic. The book is in the house but I wait to finish a thing (short) I am writing now before I sit down to read you. It'll be a reward for being a good industrious boy. For it is not easy to write here nowadays. At this very moment there is a heavy burst of gunfire in Dover. I can hear the quick firers and the big guns—and wonder where it is. The night before last a Zep passed over the house (not for the first time) bound west on that raid on London of which you would have read already in your papers. Moreover I've just now a gouty wrist. This explains my clumsy handwriting.

And so no more—this time. Keep me in your kind memory and accept a grateful and cordial handgrasp.

Yours Sincerely,
Joseph Conrad

LETTER TO MARY AUSTIN
(November 5, 1915)

⊕ ⊕ ⊕ ⊕ ⊕ ⊕ ⊕ ⊕ ⊕ ⊕ ⊕ ⊕

Mary Hunter Austin (1868–1934) was an American novelist, essayist, and dramatist, known chiefly for her studies of American Indian life. Among her works are *The Land of Little Rain* (1903), *The Basket Woman* (1904), *The Arrow Maker* (1911), and *A Woman of Genius* (1912). Her autobiography, *Earth Horizon* (1932) contains a valuable glimpse of London, George Sterling and the "literary tradition of Carmel."

The "Christ Story" Jack mentions is his chapter 17 of *The Star Rover* (1915).

⊕ ⊕ ⊕ ⊕ ⊕ ⊕ ⊕ ⊕ ⊕ ⊕ ⊕ ⊕

Glen Ellen, Calif.
Nov. 5, 1915

Dear Mary Austin:

In reply to yours of October 26, 1915:

Your letter strikes me that you are serious. Now, why be serious with this bone-head world? Long ere this, I know that you have learned that the majority of the people who inhabit the planet Earth are bone-heads. Wherever the bone of their heads interferes there is no getting through.

I have read and enjoyed every bit of your *Jesus Christ* book as published serially in the *North American Review*. What if it does not get across?

I have again and again written books that failed to get across. Long years ago, at the very beginning of my writing career, I attacked Nietzsche and his super-man idea. This was in *The Sea Wolf.* Lots of people read *The Sea Wolf,* no one discovered that it was an attack upon the super-man philosophy. Later on, not mentioning my shorter efforts, I wrote another novel that was an attack upon the super-man idea, namely my *Martin Eden.* Nobody discovered that this was such an attack. At another time I wrote an attack on ideas brought forth by Rudyard Kipling, and entitled my attack "The Strength of the Strong." No one was in the slightest way aware of the point of my story.

I am telling you all the foregoing merely to show that it is a very bone-head world indeed, and, also, that I never bother my head when my own books miss fire. And the point I am making to you is: why worry? Let the best effort of your heart and head miss fire. The best effort of my heart and head missed fire with you, as it has missed fire with practically everybody else in the world who reads, and I do not worry about it. I go ahead content to be admired for my red-blood brutality and for a number of other nice little things like that which are not true of my work at all.

Heavens, have *you* read *my* "Christ" story? I doubt that anybody has read this "Christ" story of mine, though it has been published in book form on both sides of the Atlantic. Said book has been praised for its redbloodedness and no mention has been made of my handling of the Christ situation in Jerusalem at all.

I tell you this, not because I am squealing, which I am not; but to show you that you are not alone in this miss-firing. Just be content with being called the "greatest American stylist."

Those who sit alone must sit alone. They must continue to sit alone. As I remember it, the prophets and seers of all times have been compelled to sit alone except at such times when they were stoned or burned at the stake. The world is mostly bone-head and nearly all boob, and you have no complaint if the world calls you the "great stylist" and fails to recognize that your style is merely the very heart and soul of your brain. The world has an idea that style is something apart from heart and brain. Neither you nor I can un-convince the world of that idea.

I do not know what more I can say except that, had I you here with me for half an hour I could make my point more strongly, namely, that you are very lucky, and that you should be content to receive what the world gives you. The world will never give you due recognition of your *Christ* book. I, who never read serials, read your serial of the *Christ* and turned always to it first when my *North American Review* came in. I am not the world, you are not the world. The world feeds you, the world feeds me, but the world knows damn little of either of us.

Affectionately yours,
Jack London

Reprinted from *Letters From Jack London* (1965).

LETTER TO ARMINE VON TEMSKY
(June 30, 1916)

⊕ ⊕ ⊕ ⊕ ⊕ ⊕ ⊕ ⊕ ⊕ ⊕ ⊕ ⊕

In her book, *Born in Paradise* (New York: Duell, Sloan & Pearce, 1940), Miss von Temsky tells of meeting Jack and Charmian London in July, 1907, during their *Snark* stopover on Hawaii: "Jack had a mind like a sword and when he grew eloquent about some subject which was close to his heart, the air crackled. Of course I shyly showed him a couple of my manuscripts. He was honest and straight from the shoulder. 'Writing's the hardest work in the world,' he told me. 'The stuff you're producing at present is clumsy incoherent tripe, but every so often there's a streak of fire on your pages. You're only a kid, but everything registers with you and you've a zest for life. If you're game enough to take all the lickings that will come to you, and keep on writing and writing, you'll make out.'"

Armine was then fourteen, the daughter of Louis von Temsky, manager of Haleakala Ranch on the slopes of Haleakala Volcano on Maui. She later wrote several novels, including *Hula* (1927), a book warmly reviewed by Charmian London.*

⊕ ⊕ ⊕ ⊕ ⊕ ⊕ ⊕ ⊕ ⊕ ⊕ ⊕ ⊕

Honolulu, T. H.
June 30, 1916

Dear Armine:

After long delay, for which I duly crave forgiveness, I am inclosing herewith the manuscripts.

Now I warned you to expect harsh treatment from me had you been able to come to see me for an hour or two during your last visit to Honolulu. Also, I got your permission to mark up your MSS. I have only marked the first fourteen pages of the "Lionel Pendragon" MS. I have

---

*A. Grove Day, *Jack London in the South Seas*, pp. 76–77.

not gone into any question of style, treatment, pitch, taste, handling; I have marked only for one particular thing.

And the harsh treatment I have led you to expect is connected with this one particular thing, which, necessarily, comes before all the other and bigger things in the writing game. This particular thing is slovenliness. There is no other name for it. In this, your case, it is utter, abject, arrant, and impudent. The editor does not exist who would read five pages of any manuscript so slovenly typed as these MSS of yours have been typed. I have in my time read many thousands of beginners' manuscripts. I have never yet read one so slovenly as these of yours.

Such slovenliness advertises to any editor, with a glance at a couple of pages, that you have no sincere regard for literature, no sincere desire to write literature; that either you are an abysmal fool or a very impudent young woman to submit such carelessly typed manuscript; that, in short, you are a self-advertised sloven.

Please believe that still I love you for all your other good qualities, but that such love for you does not mitigate the harshness of my chastisement of you for what you have done. If anybody ever merited such castigation, you have merited it by submitting such horrible, awful, and monstrous typed manuscript to me!

And further deponent sayeth not.

Affectionately yours,
Jack

P. S. Just the same, you ought to be damned well ashamed of yourself!

Reprinted from *Letters From Jack London* (1965).

EIGHT FACTORS OF LITERARY SUCCESS
(*The Silhouette*, February, 1917)

⊕ ⊕ ⊕ ⊕ ⊕ ⊕ ⊕ ⊕ ⊕ ⊕ ⊕ ⊕

Published posthumously (London died on November 22, 1916) in the Oakland "Quarterly Magazine of Stories in Profile," *The Silhouette*, London here reiterates the foundations of his own success as a writer.

⊕ ⊕ ⊕ ⊕ ⊕ ⊕ ⊕ ⊕ ⊕ ⊕ ⊕ ⊕

I was born in San Francisco in 1876. Almost the first thing I realized were responsibilities. I have no recollection of being taught to read or write, though I could do both at the age of five. As a ranch boy, I worked hard from my eighth year.

The adventure-lust was strong within me, and I left home. I joined the oyster pirates in the bay; shipped as sailor on a schooner; took a turn at salmon fishing; shipped before the mast and sailed for the Japanese coast on a seal-hunting expedition. After sealing for seven months I came back to California, and took odd jobs at coal shoveling and long-shoring, and also in a jute factory.

Later, I tramped through the United States from California to Boston, and up and down, returning to the Pacific coast by way of Canada, where I served a term in jail for vagrancy. My tramping experience made me a Socialist. Previously, I had been impressed by the dignity of labor. Work was everything; it was sanctification and salvation. I had fought my way from the open West, where the job hunted the man, to the congested labor centers of the Eastern states, where men hunted the job for all they were worth. I saw the workers in the shambles of the Social Pit; and I found myself looking on life from a new and totally different angle.

In my nineteenth year I returned to Oakland and started at the High School. I remained a year, doing janitor work as a means of livelihood. After leaving the High School, in three months of "cramming" by myself I took the three years' work for that time and entered the University of California. I worked in a laundry, and with my pen to help me, kept on.

The task was too much; when half way through my Freshman year, I had to quit.

Three months later, having decided that I was a failure as a writer, I gave it up and left for the Klondike to prospect for gold. It was in the Klondike that I found myself. There nobody talks. Everybody thinks. You get your true perspective. I got mine.

In answer to your question as to the greatest factors of my literary success, I will state that I consider them to be:

Vast good luck. Good health; good brain; good mental and muscular correlation, Poverty. Reading Ouida's "Signa" when I was eight years of age. The influence of Herbert Spencer's "Philosophy of Style." Because I got started twenty years before the fellows who are trying to start today.

Because, of all the foregoing, I have been *real,* and did not cheat reality any step of the way, even in so microscopically small, and cosmically ludicrous, a detail as the wearing of a starched collar when it would have hurt my neck had I worn it. My health was good—in spite of every liberty I took with it—because I was born with a strong body, and lived an open-air life, rough, hard, exercising.

I came of old American stock, of English and Welsh descent, but living in America for long before the French and Indian wars. Such accounts for my decent brain.

Poverty made me hustle. My vast good luck prevented poverty from destroying me. Nearly all my oyster-pirate comrades are long since hanged, shot, drowned, killed by disease, or are spending their declining years in prison. Any one of all these things might have happened to me before I was seventeen—save for my vast good luck.

Read Ouida's "Signa." I read it at the age of eight. The story begins: "It was only a little lad." The little lad was an Italian mountain peasant. He became an artist, with all Italy at his feet. When I read it, I was a little peasant on a poor California ranch. Reading the story, my narrow hill-horizon was pushed back, and all the world was made possible if I would dare it. I dared.

Read "Philosophy of Style." It taught me the subtle and manifold operations necessary to transmute thought, beauty, sensation and emotion into black symbols on white paper; which symbols, through the reader's eye, were taken into his brain, and corresponded with mine. Among other things, this taught me to know the brain of my reader, in order to select the symbols that would compel his brain to realize my thought, or vision, or emotion. Also, I learned that the right symbols were the ones that would require the expenditure of the minimum of my reader's brain energy, leaving the maximum of his brain energy to realize and enjoy the content of my mind, as conveyed to his mind.

A word as to the writer of today:

For one clever writer twenty years ago, there are, today, five hundred clever writers. Today, excellent writing is swamped in a sea of excellent writing. Or so it seems to me.

SELECTIONS FROM "MARTIN EDEN"

⊕ ⊕ ⊕ ⊕ ⊕ ⊕ ⊕ ⊕ ⊕ ⊕ ⊕ ⊕

Martin Eden (New York: The Macmillan Co., 1909), Jack London's immortal autobiographical novel, was begun in Honolulu in the summer of 1907 and completed in Papeete, Tahiti, in February, 1908. It was written in the harrowing circumstances of the trouble-dogged, near-calamitous *Snark* voyage.

The 13,350-word excerpt that follows is taken from seven chapters (24, 25, 27, 28, 29, 33, and 43), taking Martin from his numbing early days as a writer, combating hunger and seemingly nonexistent editors, to a bitter and unsatisfying success. (*Success,* indeed, was one of London's working titles for the book.)

That the book is heavily autobiographical is beyond dispute—"I was Martin Eden," London wrote on more than one occasion. Clearly too, *"The Transcontinental"* is the *Overland Monthly,* "Mr. Ends" is Roscoe Eames of the *Overland, "The White Mouse"* is *The Black Cat,* and similar thinly-disguised clues abound in the book.

In a letter to the editor of this volume, Dr. Howard Lachtman, the London scholar in Stockton, Calif., suggests that *Martin Eden* and *John Barleycorn* are two early examples in American literature of explorations of an author's state of mind—"Perhaps the tragedy of the thinking man in *Martin Eden* and the odyssey of the drinking man in *John Barleycorn* reflect the invention on London's part of the writer-as-character," Dr. Lachtman writes. "Certainly it has influenced in part the way later writers (Fitzgerald, Hemingway, Stein, Steinbeck, Mailer) portrayed or were portrayed as the fictive personas of their own experience."*

In the most valuable modern edition of *Martin Eden* (New York: Rinehart & Co., 1956), London scholar Sam Baskett writes in his introduction: "Actually, in writing *Martin Eden* London reversed the practice of his

---

*Letter to Dale L. Walker, March 26, 1977.

literary alter ego, beginning with his own life as the 'plot,' then attempting to examine the wider significance of the experience in which he was
enmeshed; and the relation between the particular and universal' in *Martin Eden* points up the purpose, achievement, and weakness of the novel."

⊕ ⊕ ⊕ ⊕ ⊕ ⊕ ⊕ ⊕ ⊕ ⊕ ⊕

. . . The weeks passed. Martin ran out of money, and publishers' checks were far away as ever. All his important manuscripts had come back and been started out again, and his hack-work fared no better. His little kitchen was no longer graced with a variety of foods. Caught in the pinch with a part sack of rice and a few pounds of dried apricots, rice and apricots was his menu three times a day for five days hand-running. Then he started to realize on his credit. The Portuguese grocer, to whom he had hitherto paid cash, called a halt when Martin's bill reached the magnificent total of three dollars and eighty-five cents.

"For you see," said the grocer, "you no catcha da work, I losa da mon'."

And Martin could reply nothing. There was no way of explaining. It was not true business principle to allow credit to a strong-bodied young fellow of the working class who was too lazy to work.

"You catcha da job, I let you have mora da grub," the grocer assured Martin. "No job, no grub. Thata da business." And then, to show that it was purely business foresight and not prejudice, "Hava da drink on da house—good friends justa da same."

So Martin drank, in his easy way, to show that he was good friends with the house, and then went supperless to bed.

The fruit store, where Martin had bought his vegetables, was run by an American whose business principles were so weak that he let Martin run a bill of five dollars before stopping his credit. The baker stopped at two dollars, and the butcher at four dollars. Martin added his debts and found that he was possessed of a total credit in all the world of fourteen dollars and eighty-five cents. He was up with his typewriter rent, but he estimated that he could get two months' credit on that, which would be eight dollars. When that occurred, he would have exhausted all possible credit.

The last purchase from the fruit store had been a sack of potatoes, and for a week he had potatoes, and nothing but potatoes, three times a day. An occasional dinner at Ruth's helped to keep strength in his body, though he found it tantalizing enough to refuse further helping when his appetite was raging at sight of so much food spread before it. Now and again, though afflicted with secret shame, he dropped in at his sister's at meal-time and ate as much as he dared—more than he dared at the Morse table.

Day by day he worked on, and day by day the postman delivered to him rejected manuscripts. He had no money for stamps, so the manuscripts accumulated in a heap under the table. Came a day when for forty hours he had not tasted food. He could not hope for a meal at Ruth's, for she was away to San Rafael on a two weeks' visit; and for very shame's sake he could not go to his sister's. To cap misfortune, the postman, in his afternoon round, brought him five returned manuscripts. Then it was that Martin wore his overcoat down into Oakland, and came back without it, but with five dollars tinkling in his pocket. He paid a dollar each on account to the four tradesmen, and in his kitchen fried steak and onions, made coffee, and stewed a large pot of prunes. And having dined, he sat down at his table-desk and completed before midnight an essay which he entitled "The Dignity of Usury." Having typed it out, he flung it under the table, for there had been nothing left from the five dollars with which to buy stamps.

Later on he pawned his watch, and still later his wheel, reducing the amount available for food by putting stamps on all his manuscripts and sending them out. He was disappointed with his hack-work. Nobody cared to buy. He compared it with what he found in the newspapers, weeklies, and cheap magazines, and decided that his was better, far better, than the average; yet it would not sell. Then he discovered that most of the newspapers printed a great deal of what was called "plate" stuff, and he got the address of the association that furnished it. His own work that he sent in was returned, along with a stereotyped slip informing him that the staff supplied all the copy that was needed.

In one of the great juvenile periodicals he noted whole columns of incident and anecdote. Here was a chance. His paragraphs were returned, and though he tried repeatedly he never succeeded in placing one. Later on, when it no longer mattered, he learned that the associate editors and sub-editors augmented their salaries by supplying those paragraphs themselves. The comic weeklies returned his jokes and humorous verse, and the light society verse he wrote for the large magazines found no abiding-place. Then there was the newspaper storiette. He knew that he could write better ones than were published. Managing to obtain the addresses of two newspaper syndicates, he deluged them with storiettes. When he had written twenty and failed to place one of them, he ceased. And yet, from day to day, he read storiettes in the dailies and weeklies, scores and scores of storiettes, not one of which would compare with his. In his despondency, he concluded that he had no judgment whatever, that he was hypnotized by what he wrote, and that he was a self-deluded pretender.

The inhuman editorial machine ran smoothly as ever. He folded the stamps in with his manuscript, dropped it into the letter-box, and from three weeks to a month afterward the postman came up the steps and handed him the manuscript. Surely there were no live, warm editors at the other end. It was all wheels and cogs and oil-cups—a clever mechanism operated by automatons. He reached stages of despair wherein he doubted if editors existed at all. He had never received a sign of the existence of one, and from absence of judgment in rejecting all he wrote it seemed plausible that editors were myths, manufactured and maintained by office boys, typesetters, and pressmen.

. . . He toiled on, miserable and well-nigh hopeless, it began to appear to him that the second battle was lost and that he would have to go to work. In doing this he would satisfy everybody—the grocer, his sister, Ruth, and even Maria, to whom he owed a month's room rent. He was two months behind with his typewriter, and the agency was clamoring for payment or for the return of the machine. In desperation, all but ready to surrender, to make a truce with fate until he could get a fresh start, he took the civil service examinations for the Railway Mail. To his surprise, he passed first. The job was assured, though when the call would come to enter upon his duties nobody knew.

It was at this time, at the lowest ebb, that the smooth-running editorial machine broke down. A cog must have slipped or an oil-cup run dry, for the postman brought him one morning a short, thin envelope. Martin glanced at the upper left-hand corner and read the name and address of the *Transcontinental Monthly*. His heart gave a great leap, and he suddenly felt faint, the sinking feeling accompanied by a strange trembling of the knees. He staggered into his room and sat down on the bed, the envelope still unopened, and in that moment came understanding to him how people suddenly fall dead upon receipt of extraordinarily good news.

Of course this was good news. There was no manuscript in that thin envelope, therefore it was an acceptance. He knew that story in the hands of the *Transcontinental*. It was "The Ring of Bells," one of his horror stories, and it was an even five thousand words. And, since first-class magazines always paid on acceptance, there was a check inside. Two cents a word—twenty dollars a thousand: the check must be a hundred dollars. One hundred dollars! As he tore the envelope open, every item of all his debts surged in his brain—$3.85 to the grocer; butcher, $4.00 flat; baker, $2.00; fruit store, $5.00; total $14.85. Then there was room rent, $2.50; another month in advance, $2.50; two months' typewriter, $8.00; a month in advance, $4.00; total, $31.85. And finally to be added, his pledges, plus interest, with the pawnbroker—watch, $5.50; overcoat,

$5.50; wheel, $7.75; suit of clothes, $5.50 (60% interest, but what did it matter?)–grand total, $56.10. He saw, as if visible in the air before him, in illuminated figures, the whole sum, and the subtraction that followed and that gave a remainder of $43.90. When he had squared every debt, redeemed every pledge, he would still have jingling in his pockets a princely $43.90. And on top of that he would have a month's rent paid in advance on the typewriter and on the room.

By this time he had drawn the single sheet of type-written letter out and spread it open. There was no check. He peered into the envelope, held it to the light, but could not trust his eyes, and in trembling haste tore the envelope apart. There was no check. He read the letter, skimming it line by line, dashing through the editor's praise of his story to the meat of the letter, the statement why the check had not been sent. He found no such statement, but he did find that which made him suddenly wilt. The letter slid from his hand. His eyes went lack-lustre, and he lay back on the pillow, pulling the blanket about him and up to his chin.

Five dollars for "The Ring of Bells"–five dollars for five thousand words! Instead of two cents a word, ten words for a cent! And the editor had praised it, too. And he would receive the check when the story was published. Then it was all poppycock, two cents a word for minimum rate and payment upon acceptance. It was a lie, and it had led him astray. He would have gone to work–to work for Ruth. He went back to the day he first attempted to write, and was appalled at the enormous waste of time–and all for ten words for a cent. And the other high rewards of writers, that he had read about, must be lies, too. His second-hand ideas of authorship were wrong, for here was the proof of it.

The *Transcontinental* sold for twenty-five cents, and its dignified and artistic cover proclaimed it as among the first-class magazines. It was a staid, respectable magazine, and it had been published continuously since long before he was born. Why, on the outside cover were printed every month the words of one of the world's great writers, words proclaiming the inspired mission of the *Transcontinental* by a star of literature whose first coruscations had appeared inside those self-same covers. And the high and lofty, heaven-inspired *Transcontinental* paid five dollars for five thousand words! The great writer had recently died in a foreign land–in dire poverty, Martin remembered, which was not to be wondered at, considering the magnificent pay authors receive.

Well, he had taken the bait, the newspaper lies about writers and their pay, and he had wasted two years over it. But he would disgorge the bait now. Not another line would he ever write. He would do what Ruth wanted him to do, what everybody wanted him to do–get a job. The thought of going to work reminded him of Joe–Joe, tramping through the land of nothing-to-do. Martin heaved a great sigh of envy. The reaction of nineteen hours a day for many days was strong upon him. But then, Joe was not in love, had none of the responsibilities of love, and he could afford to loaf through the land of nothing-to-do. He, Martin, had something to work for, and go to work he would. He would start out early next morning to hunt a job. And he would let Ruth know, too, that he had mended his ways and was willing to go into her father's office.

Five dollars for five thousand words, ten words for a cent, the market price for art. The disappointment of it, the lie of it, the infamy of it, were uppermost in his thoughts; and under his closed eyelids, in fiery figures, burned the "$3.85" he owed the grocer. He shivered, and was aware of an aching in his bones. The small of his back ached especially. His head ached, the top of it ached, the back of it ached, the brains inside of it ached and seemed to be swelling, while the ache over his brows was intolerable. And beneath the brows, planted under his lids, was the merciless "$3.85." He opened his eyes to escape it, but the white light of the room seemed to sear the balls and forced him to close his eyes, when the "$3.85" confronted him again.

Five dollars for five thousand words, ten words for a cent—that particular thought took up its residence in his brain, and he could no more escape it than he could the "$3.85" under his eyelids. A change seemed to come over the latter, and he watched curiously, till "$2.00" burned in its stead. Ah, he thought, that was the baker. The next sum that appeared was "$2.50." It puzzled him, and he pondered it as if life and death hung on the solution. He owed somebody two dollars and a half, that was certain, but who was it? To find it was the task set him by an imperious and malignant universe, and he wandered through the endless corridors of his mind, opening all manner of lumber rooms and chambers stored with odds and ends of memories and knowledge as he vainly sought the answer. After several centuries it came to him, easily, without effort, that it was Maria. With a great relief he turned his soul to the screen of torment under his lids. He had solved the problem; now he could rest. But no, the "$2.50" faded away, and in its place burned "$8.00." Who was that? He must go the dreary round of his mind again and find out.

How long he was gone on this quest he did not know, but after what seemed an enormous lapse of time, he was called back to himself by a knock at the door, and by Maria's asking if he was sick. He replied in a muffled voice he did not recognize, saying that he was merely taking a nap. He was surprised when he noted the darkness of night in the room. He had received the letter at two in the afternoon, and he realized that he was sick.

Then the "$8.00" began to smoulder under his lids again, and he returned himself to servitude. But he grew cunning. There was no need for him to wander through his mind. He had been a fool. He pulled a lever and made his mind revolve about him, a monstrous wheel of fortune, a merry-go-round of memory, a revolving sphere of wisdom. Faster and faster it revolved, until its vortex sucked him in and he was flung whirling through black chaos.

Quite naturally he found himself at a mangle, feeding starched cuffs. But as he fed he noticed figures printed on the cuffs. It was a new way of marking linen, he thought, until, looking closer, he saw "$3.85" on one of the cuffs. Then it came to him that it was the grocer's bill, and that these were his bills flying around on the drum of the mangle. A crafty idea came to him. He would throw the bills on the floor and so escape paying them. No sooner thought than done, and he crumpled the cuffs spitefully as he flung them upon an usually dirty floor. Ever the heap grew, and though each bill was duplicated a thousand times, he found only one for two dollars and a half, which was what he owed Maria. That meant that Maria would not press for payment, and he resolved generously that it would be the only one he would pay; so he began searching through the cast-out heap for hers. He sought it desperately, for ages, and was still searching when the manager of the hotel entered, the fat Dutchman. His face blazed with wrath, and he shouted in stentorian tones that echoed down the universe, "I shall deduct the cost of those cuffs from your wages!" The pile of cuffs grew into a mountain, and Martin knew that he was doomed to toil for a thousand years to pay for them. Well, there was nothing left to do but kill the manager and burn down the laundry. But the big Dutchman frustrated him, seizing him by the nape of the neck and dancing him up and down. He danced him over the ironing tables, the stove, and the mangles, and out into the wash-room and over the wringer and washer. Martin was danced until his teeth rattled and his head ached, and he marvelled that the Dutchman was so strong.

And then he found himself before the mangle, this time receiving the cuffs an editor of a magazine was feeding from the other side. Each cuff was a check, and Martin went over them anxiously, in a fever of expectation, but they were all blanks. He stood there and received the blanks for a million years or so, never letting one go by for fear it might be filled out. At last he found it. With trembling fingers he held it to the light. It was for five dollars. "Ha! Ha!" laughed the editor across the mangle. "Well, then, I shall kill you," Martin said. He went out into the wash-room to get the axe, and found Joe starching manuscripts. He tried to make him desist, then swung the axe for him. But the weapon remained posed in mid-air, for Martin found himself back in the ironing room in the midst of a snow-storm. No, it was not snow that was falling, but checks of large denomination, the smallest not less than a thousand dollars. He began to collect them and sort them out, in packages of a hundred, tying each package securely with twine.

He looked up from his task and saw Joe standing before him juggling flat-irons, starched shirts, and manuscripts. Now and again he reached out and added a bundle of checks to the flying miscellany that soared through the roof and out of sight in a tremendous circle. Martin struck at him, but he seized the axe and added it to the flying circle. Then he plucked Martin and added him. Martin went up through the roof, clutching at manuscripts, so that by the time he came down he had a large armful. But no sooner down than up again, and a second and a third time and countless times he flew around the circle. From far off he could hear a childish treble singing: "Waltz me around again, Willie, around, around, around."

He recovered the axe in the midst of the Milky Way of checks, starched shirts, and manuscripts, and prepared, when he came down, to kill Joe. But he did not come down. Instead, at two in the morning, Maria having heard his groans through the thin partition, came into his room, to put hot flat-irons against his body and damp cloths upon his aching eyes.

. . . The sun of Martin's good fortune rose. The day after Ruth's visit, he received a check for three dollars from a New York scandal weekly in payment for three of his triolets. Two days later a newspaper published in Chicago accepted his "Treasure Hunters," promising to pay ten dollars for it on publication. The price was small, but it was the first article he had written, his very first attempt to express his thought on the printed page. To cap everything, the adventure serial for boys, his second attempt, was accepted before the end of the week by a juvenile monthly calling itself *Youth and Age.* It was true the serial was twenty-one thousand words, and they offered to pay him sixteen dollars on publication, which was something like seventy-five cents a thousand words; but it was equally true that it was the second thing he had attempted to write and that he was himself thoroughly aware of its clumsy worthlessness.

But even his earliest efforts were not marked with the clumsiness of mediocrity. What characterized them was the clumsiness of too great strength—the clumsiness which the tyro betrays when he crushes butterflies with battering rams and hammers out vignettes with a warclub. So it was that Martin was glad to sell his early efforts for songs. He knew them for what they were, and it had not taken him long to acquire this knowledge. What he pinned his faith to was his later work. He had striven to be something more than a mere writer of magazine fiction. He had sought to equip himself with the tools of artistry. On the other hand, he had not sacrificed strength. His conscious aim had been to increase his strength by avoiding excess of strength. Nor had he departed from his love of reality. His work was realism, though he had endeavored to fuse with it the fancies and beauties of imagination. What he sought was an impassioned realism, shot through with human aspiration and faith. What he wanted was life as it was, with all its spirit-groping and soul-reaching left in.

He had discovered, in the course of his reading, two schools of fiction. One treated of man as a god, ignoring his earthly origin; the other treated of man as a clod, ignoring his heaven-sent dreams and divine possibilities. Both the god and the clod schools erred, in Martin's estimation, and erred through too great singleness of sight and purpose. There was a compromise that approximated the truth, though it flattered not the school of god, while it challenged the brute-savageness of the school of clod. It was his story, "Adventure," which had dragged with Ruth, that Martin believed had achieved his ideal of the true in fiction; and it was in an essay, "God and Clod," that he had expressed his views on the whole general subject.

But "Adventure," and all that he deemed his best work, still went begging among the editors. His early work counted for nothing in his eyes except for the money it brought, and his horror stories, two of which he had sold, he did not consider high work nor his best work. To him they were frankly imaginative and fantastic, though invested with all the glamour of the real, wherein lay their power. This investiture of the grotesque and impossible with reality, he looked upon as a trick—a skilful trick at best. Great literature could not reside in such a field. Their artistry was high, but he denied the worthwhileness of artistry when divorced from humanness. The trick had been to fling over the face of his artistry a mask of humanness, and this he had done in the half-dozen or so stories of the horror brand he had written before he emerged upon the high peaks of "Adventure," "Joy," "The Pot," and "The Wine of Life."

The three dollars he received for the triolets he used to eke out a precarious existence against the arrival of the *White Mouse* check. He cashed the first check with the suspicious Portuguese grocer, paying a dollar on account and dividing the remaining two dollars between the baker and the fruit store. Martin was not yet rich enough to afford meat, and he was on slim allowance when the *White Mouse* check arrived. He was divided on the cashing of it. He had never been in a bank in his life, much less been in one on business, and he had a naive and childlike desire to walk into one of the big banks down in Oakland and fling down his indorsed check for forty dollars. On the other hand, practical common sense rules that he should cash it with his grocer and thereby make an impression that would later result in an increase of credit. Reluctantly Martin yielded to the claims of the grocer, paying his bill with him in full, and receiving in change a pocketful of jingling coin. Also, he paid the other tradesmen in full, redeemed his suit and his bicycle, paid one month's rent on the typewriter, and paid Maria the overdue month for his room and a month in advance. This left him in his pocket, for emergencies, a balance of nearly three dollars.

In itself, this small sum seemed a fortune. Immediately on recovering his clothes he had gone to see Ruth, and on the way he could not refrain from jingling the little handful of silver in his pocket. He had been so long without money that, like a rescued starving man who cannot let the unconsumed food out of his sight, Martin could not keep his hand off the silver. He was not mean, nor avaricious, but the money meant more than so many dollars and cents. It stood for success, and the eagles stamped upon the coins were to him so many winged victories.

It came to him insensibly that it was a very good world. It certainly appeared more beautiful to him. For weeks it had been a very dull and sombre world; but now, with nearly all debts paid, three dollars jingling in his pocket, and in his mind the consciousness of success, the sun shone bright and warm, and even a rain-squall that soaked unprepared pedestrians seemed a merry happening to him. When he starved, his thoughts had dwelt often upon the thousands he knew were starving the world over; but now that he was feasted full, the fact of the thousands starving was no longer pregnant in his brain. He forgot about them, and being in love, remembered the countless lovers in the world. Without deliberately thinking about it, motifs for love-lyrics began to agitate his brain. Swept away by the creative impulse, he got off the electric car, without vexation, two blocks beyond his crossing.

. . . But success had lost Martin's address, and her messangers no longer came to his door. For twenty-five days, working Sundays and holidays, he toiled on "The Shame of the Sun," a long essay of some thirty thousand words. It was a deliberate attack on the mysticism of the Maeterlinck school—an attack from the citadel of positive science upon the wonder-dreamers, but an attack nevertheless that retained much of beauty and wonder of the sort compatible with ascertained fact. It was a little later that he followed up the attack with two short essays, "The Wonder-Dreamers" and "The Yardstick of the Ego." And on essays, long and short, he began to pay the travelling expenses from magazine to magazine.

During the twenty-five days spent on "The Shame of the Sun," he sold hack-work to the extent of six dollars and fifty cents. A joke had brought in fifty cents, and a second one, sold to a high-grade comic weekly, had fetched a dollar. Then two humorous poems had earned two dollars and three dollars respectively. As a result, having exhausted his credit with the tradesmen (though he had increased his credit with the grocer to five dollars), his wheel and suit of clothes went back to the pawnbroker.

The typewriter people were again clamoring for money, insistently pointing out that according to the agreement rent was to be paid strictly in advance. Encouraged by his several small sales, Martin went back to hack-work. Perhaps there was a living in it, after all. Stored away under his table were the twenty storiettes which had been rejected by the newspaper short-story syndicate. He read them over in order to find out how not to write newspaper storiettes and so doing, reasoned out the perfect formula. He found that the newspaper storiette should never be tragic, should never end unhappily, and should never contain beauty of language, subtlety of thought, nor real delicacy of sentiment. Sentiment it must contain, plenty of it, pure and noble, of the sort that in his own early youth had brought his applause from "nigger heaven"—the "For-God-my-country-and-the-Czar" and "I-may-be-poor-but-I-am-honest" brand of sentiment.

Having learned such precautions, Martin consulted "The Duchess" for tone, and proceeded to mix according to formula. The formula consists of three parts: (1) a pair of lovers are jarred apart; (2) by some deed or event they are reunited; (3) marriage bells. The third part was an unvarying quantity, but the first and second parts could be varied an infinite number of times. Thus, the pair of lovers could be jarred apart by misunderstood motives, by accident of fate, by jealous rivals, by irate parents, by crafty guardians, by scheming relatives, and so forth and so forth; they could be reunited by a brave deed of the man lover, by a similar deed of the woman lover, by change of heart in one lover or the other, by forced confession of crafty guardian, scheming relative, or jealous rival, by voluntary confession of same, by discovery of some unguessed secret, by lover storming girl's heart, by lover making long and noble self-sacrifice, and so on, endlessly. It was very fetching to make the girl propose in the course of being reunited, and Martin discovered, bit by bit, other decidedly piquant and fetching ruses. But marriage bells at the end was the one thing he could take no liberties with; though the heavens rolled up as a scroll and the stars fell, the wedding bells must go on ringing just the same. In quantity, the formula prescribed twelve hundred words minimum dose, fifteen hundred words maximum dose.

Before he got very far along in the art of the storiette, Martin worked out half a dozen stock forms, which he always consulted when constructing storiettes. These forms were like the cunning tables used by mathematicians, which may be entered from top, bottom, right, and left, which entrances consist of scores of lines and dozens of columns, and from which may be drawn, without reasoning or thinking, thousands of different conclusions, all unchallengeably precise and true. Thus, in the course of half an hour with his forms, Martin could frame up a dozen or so storiettes, which he put aside and filled in at his convenience. He found that he could fill one in, after a day of serious work, in the hour before going to bed. As he later confessed to Ruth, he could almost do it in his sleep. The real work was in constructing the frames, and that was merely mechanical.

He had no doubt whatever of the efficacy of his formula, and for once he knew the editorial mind when he said positively to himself that the first two he sent off would bring checks. And checks they brought, for four dollars each, at the end of twelve days.

In the meantime he was making fresh and alarming discoveries concerning the magazines. Though the *Transcontinental* had published "The Ring of Bells," no check was forthcoming. Martin needed it, and he wrote for it. An evasive answer and a request for more of his work was all he received. He had gone hungry two days waiting for the reply, and it was then that he put his wheel back in pawn. He wrote regularly, twice a week, to the *Transcontinental* for his five dollars, though it was only semi-occasionally that he elicited a reply. He did not know that the *Transcontinental* had been staggering along precariously for years, that it was a fourth-rater, or a tenth-rater, without standing, with a crazy circulation that partly rested on petty bullying and partly on patriotic appealing, and with advertisements that were scarcely more than charitable donations. Nor did he know that the *Transcontinental* was the sole livelihood of the editor and the business manager, and that they could wring their livelihood out of it only by moving to escape paying rent and by never paying any bill they could evade. Nor could he have guessed that the particular five dollars that belonged to him had been appropriated by the business manager for the painting of his house in Alameda, which painting he performed himself, on weekday afternoons, because he could not afford to pay union wages and because the first scab he had employed had had a ladder jerked out from under him and been sent to the hospital with a broken collar-bone.

The ten dollars for which Martin had sold "Treasure Hunters" to the Chicago newspaper did not come to hand. The article had been published, as he had ascertained at the file in the Central Reading-room, but no word could he get from the editor. His letters were ignored. To satisfy himself that they had been received, he registered several of them. It was nothing less than robbery, he concluded—a cold-blooded steal; while he starved, he was pilfered of his merchandise, of his goods, the sale of which was the sole way of getting bread to eat.

Youth and Age was a weekly, and it had published two-thirds of his twenty-one-thousand-word serial when it went out of business. With it went all hopes of getting his sixteen dollars.

To cap the situation, "The Pot," which he looked upon as one of the best things he had written, was lost to him. In despair, casting about frantically among the magazines, he had sent it to *The Billow*, a society weekly in San Francisco. His chief reason for submitting it to that publication was that, having only to travel across the bay from Oakland, a quick decision could be reached. Two weeks later he was overjoyed to see, in the latest number on the news-stand, his story printed in full, illustrated, and in the place of honor. He went home with leaping pulse, wondering how much they would pay him for one of the best things he had done. Also, the celerity with which it had been accepted and published was a pleasant thought to him. That the editor had not informed him of the acceptance made the surprise more complete. After waiting a week, two weeks, and half a week longer, desperation conquered diffidence, and he wrote to the editor of *The Billow*, suggesting that possibly through some negligence of the business manager his little account had been overlooked.

Even if it isn't more than five dollars, Martin thought to himself, it will buy enough beans and pea-soup to enable me to write half a dozen like it, and possibly as good.

Back came a cool letter from the editor that at least elicited Martin's admiration.

"We thank you," it ran, "for your excellent contribution. All of us in the office enjoyed it immensely, and, as you see, it was given the place of honor and immediate publication. We earnestly hope that you liked the illustrations.

"On rereading your letter it seems to us that you are laboring under the misapprehension that we pay for unsolicited manuscripts. This is not our custom, and of course yours was unsolicited. We assumed, naturally, when we received your story that you understood the situation, we can only deeply regret this unfortunate misunderstanding, and assure you of our unfailing regard. Again, thanking you for your kind contribution, and hoping to receive more from you in the near future, we remain, etc."

There was also a postscript to the effect that though *The Billow* carried no free list, it took great pleasure in sending him a complimentary subscription for the ensuing year.

After that experience, Martin typed at the top of the first sheet of all his manuscripts: "Submitted at your usual rate."

Some day, he consoled himself, they will be submitted at *my* usual rate.

He discovered in himself, at this period, a passion for perfection, under the sway of which he rewrote and polished "The Jostling Street," "The Wine of Life," "Joy," the "Sea Lyrics," and others of his earlier work. As of old, nineteen hours of labor a day was all too little to suit him. He wrote prodigiously, and he read prodigiously, forgetting in his toil the pangs caused by giving up his tobacco. Ruth's promised cure for the habit, flamboyantly labelled, he stowed away in the most inaccessible corner of his bureau. Especially during his stretches of famine he suffered from lack of the weed; but no matter how often he mastered the craving, it remained with him as strong as ever. He regarded it as the biggest thing he had ever achieved. Ruth's point of view was that he was doing no more than was right. She brought him the anti-tobacco remedy, purchased out of her glove money, and in a few days forgot all about it.

His machine-made storiettes, though he hated them and derided them, were successful. By means of them he redeemed all his pledges, paid most of his bills, and bought a new set of tires for his wheel. The storiettes at least kept the pot a-boiling and gave him time for ambitious work; while the one thing that upheld him was the forty dollars he had received from *The White Mouse.* He anchored his faith to that, and was confident that the really first-class magazines would pay an unknown writer at least an equal rate, if not a better one. But the thing was, how to get into the first-class magazines. His best stories, essays, and poems went begging among them, and yet, each month, he read reams of dull, prosy, inartistic stuff between all their various covers. If only one editor, he sometimes thought, would descend from his high seat of pride to write me one cheering line! No matter if my work is unusual, no matter if it is unfit, for prudential reasons, for their pages, surely there must be some sparks in it, somewhere, a few, to warm them to some sort of appreciation. And thereupon he would get out one or another of his manuscripts, such as the "Adventure," and read it over and over in a vain attempt to vindicate the editorial silence.

As the sweet California spring came on, his period of plenty came to an end. For several weeks he had been worried by a strange silence on the part of the newspaper storiette syndicate. Then, one day, came back to him through the mail ten of his immaculate machine-made storiettes. They were accompanied by a brief letter to the effect that the syndicate was overstocked, and that some months would elapse before it would be in the market again for manuscripts. Martin had even been extravagant on the strength of those ten storiettes. Toward the last the syndicate had been paying him five dollars each for them and accepting every one he sent. So he had looked upon the ten as good as sold, and he had lived accordingly, on a basis of fifty dollars in the bank. So it was that he entered abruptly upon a lean period, wherein he continued selling his earlier efforts to publications that would not pay and submitting his later work to magazines that would not buy. Also, he resumed his trips to the pawnbroker down in Oakland. A few jokes and snatches of humorous verse, sold to the New York weeklies, made existence barely possible for him. It was at this time that he wrote letters of inquiry to the several great monthly and quarterly reviews, and learned in reply that they rarely considered unsolicited articles, and that most of their contents were written upon order by well-known specialists who were authorities in their various fields.

. . . It was a hard summer for Martin. Manuscript readers and editors were away on vacation, and publications that ordinarily returned a decision in three weeks now retained his manuscript for three months or more. The consolation he drew from it was that a saving in postage was effected by the deadlock. Only the robber-publications seemed to remain actively in business, and to them Martin disposed of all his early efforts, such as "Pearl-diving," "The Sea as a Career," "Turtle-catching," and "The Northeast Trades." For these manuscripts he never received a penny. It is true, after six months' correspondence, he effected a compromise, whereby he received a safety razor for "Turtle-catching," and that *The Acropolis,* having agreed to give him five dollars cash and five yearly subscriptions for "The Northeast Trades," fulfilled the second part of the agreement.

For a sonnet on Stevenson he managed to wring two dollars out of a Boston editor who was running a magazine with a Matthew Arnold taste and a penny-dreadful purse. "The Peri and the Pearl," a clever skit of a poem of two hundred lines, just finished, white hot from his brain, won the heart of the editor of a San Francisco magazine published in the interest of a great railroad. When the editor wrote, offering him payment in transportation, Martin wrote back to inquire if the transportation was transferable. It was not, and so, being prevented from peddling it, he asked for the return of the poem. Back it came, with the editor's regrets, and Martin sent it to San Francisco again, this time to *The Hornet,* a pretentious monthly that had been fanned into a constellation of the first magnitude by the brilliant journalist who founded it. But *The Hornet's* light had begun to dim long before Martin was born. The editor promised Martin fifteen dollars for the poem, but, when it was published, seemed to forget about it. Several of his letters being ignored, Martin indicted an angry one which drew a reply. It was written by a new editor, who coolly informed Martin that he declined to be held responsible for the old editor's mistakes, and that he did not think much of "The Peri and the Pearl" anyway.

But *The Globe,* a Chicago magazine, gave Martin the most cruel treatment of all. He had refrained from offering his "Sea Lyrics" for publication, until driven to it by starvation. After having been rejected by a dozen magazines, they had come to rest in *The Globe* office. There were thirty poems in the collection, and he was to receive a dollar apiece for them.

The first month four were published, and he promptly received a check for four dollars; but when he looked over the magazine, he was appalled at the slaughter. In some cases the titles had been altered: "Finis," for instance, being changed to "The Finish," and "The Song of the Outer Reef" to "The Song of the Coral Reef." In one case, an absolutely different title, a misappropriate title, was substituted. In place of his own, "Medusa Lights," the editor had printed, "The Backward Track." But the slaughter in the body of the poems was terrifying. Martin groaned and sweated and thrust his hands through his hair. Phrases, lines, and stanzas not his own were substituted for his. He could not believe that a sane editor could be guilty of such maltreatment, and his favorite hypothesis was that his poems must have been doctored by the office boy or the stenographer. Martin wrote immediately, begging the editor to cease publishing the lyrics and to return them to him. He wrote again and again, begging, entreating, threatening, but his letters were ignored. Month by month the slaughter went on till the thirty poems were published, and month by month he received a check for those which had appeared in the current number.

Despite these various misadventures, the memory of the *White Mouse* forty-dollar check sustained him though he was driven more and more to hack-work. He discovered a bread-and-butter field in the agricultural weeklies and trade journals, though among the religious weeklies he found he could easily starve. At this lowest ebb, when his black suit was in pawn, he made a ten-strike—or so it seemed to him—in a prize contest arranged by the County Committee of the Republican Party. There were three branches of the contest, and he entered them all, laughing at himself bitterly the while in that he was driven to such straits to live. His poem won the first prize of ten dollars, his campaign song the second prize of five dollars, his essay on the principles of the Republican Party the first prize of twenty-five dollars. Which was very gratifying to him until he tried to collect. Something had gone wrong in the County Committee, and, though a rich banker and a state senator were members of it, the money was not forthcoming. While this affair was hanging fire, he proved that he understood the principles of the Democratic Party by winning the first prize for his essay in a similar contest. And, moreover, he received the money, twenty-five dollars. But the forty dollars won in the first contest he never received.

. . . Martin was steadily losing his battle. Economize as he would, the earnings from hack-work did not balance expenses. Thanksgiving found him with his black suit in pawn and unable to accept the Morses' invitation to dinner. Ruth was not made happy by his reason for not coming, and the corresponding effect on him was one of desperation. He told her that he would come, after all; that he would go over to San Francisco, to the *Transcontinental* office, collect the five dollars due him, and with it redeem his suit of clothes.

In the morning he borrowed ten cents from Maria. He would have borrowed it, by preference, from Brissenden, but that erratic individual had disappeared. Two weeks had passed since Martin had seen him, and he vainly cudgelled his brains for some cause of offense. The ten cents carried Martin across the ferry to San Francisco, and as he walked up Market Street he speculated upon his predicament in case he failed to collect the money. There would then be no way for him to return to Oakland, and he knew no one in San Francisco from whom to borrow another ten cents.

The door to the *Transcontinental* office was ajar, and Martin, in the act of opening it, was brought to a sudden pause by a loud voice from within, which exclaimed:—"But this is not the question, Mr. Ford." (Ford, Martin knew, from his correspondence, to be the editor's name.) "The question is, are you prepared to pay?—cash, and cash down, I mean? I am not interested in the prospects of the *Transcontinental* and what you expect to make it next year. What I want is to be paid for what I do. And I tell you, right now, the Christmas *Transcontinental* don't go to press till I have the money in my hand. Good day. When you get the money, come and see me."

The door jerked open, and the man flung past Martin with an angry countenance and went down the corridor, muttering curses and clenching his fists. Martin decided not to enter immediately, and lingered in the hallways for a quarter of an hour. Then he shoved the door open and walked in. It was a new experience, the first time he had been inside an editorial office. Cards evidently were not necessary in that office, for the boy carried word to an inner room that there was a man who wanted to see Mr. Ford. Returning, the boy beckoned him from halfway across the room and led him to the private office, the editorial sanctum. Martin's first impression was of the disorder and cluttered confusion of the room. Next he noticed a bewhiskered, youthful-looking man, sitting at a roll-top desk, who regarded him curiously. Martin marvelled at the calm repose of his face. It was evident that the squabble with the printer had not affected his equanimity.

"I—I am Martin Eden," Martin began the conversation, ("And I want my five dollars," was what he would have liked to say.)

But this was his first editor, and under the circumstances he did not desire to scare him too abruptly. To his surprise, Mr. Ford leaped into the air with a "You don't say so!" and the next moment, with both hands, was shaking Martin's hand effusively.

"Can't say how glad I am to see you, Mr. Eden. Often wondered what you were like."

Here he held Martin off at arm's length and ran his beaming eyes over Martin's second-best suit, which was also his worst suit, and which was ragged and past repair, though the trousers showed the careful crease he had put in with Maria's flat-irons.

"I confess, though, I conceived you to be a much older man than you are. Your story, you know, showed such breadth, and vigor, such maturity and depth of thought. A masterpiece, that story—I knew it when I had read the first half-dozen lines. Let me tell you how I first read it. But no; first let me introduce you to the staff."

Still talking, Mr. Ford led him into the general office, where he introduced him to the associate editor, Mr. White, a slender, frail little man whose hand seemed strangely cold, as if he were suffering from a chill, and whose whiskers were sparse and silky.

"And Mr. Ends, Mr. Eden. Mr. Ends is our business manager, you know."

Martin found himself shaking hands with a cranky-eyed, bald-headed man, whose face looked youthful enough from what little could be seen of it, for most of it was covered by a snow-white beard, carefully trimmed —by his wife, who did it on Sundays, at which times she also shaved the back of his neck.

The three men surrounded Martin, all talking admiringly and at once, until it seemed to him that they were talking against time for a wager.

"We often wondered why you didn't call," Mr. White was saying.

"I didn't have the carfare, and I live across the Bay," Martin answered bluntly, with the idea of showing them his imperative need for the money.

Surely, he thought to himself, my glad rags in themselves are eloquent advertisement of my need. Time and again, whenever opportunity offered, he hinted about the purpose of his business. But his admirers' ears were deaf. They sang his praises, told him what they had thought of his story at first sight, what they subsequently thought, what their wives and families thought; but not one hint did they breathe of intention to pay him for it.

"Did I tell you how I first read your story?" Mr. Ford said. "Of course I didn't. I was coming west from New York, and when the train stopped at Ogden, the train-boy on the new run brought aboard the current number of the *Transcontinental.*"

My God! Martin thought; you can travel in a Pullman while I starve for the paltry five dollars you owe me. A wave of anger rushed over him. The wrong done him by the *Transcontinental* loomed colossal, for strong upon him were all the dreary months of vain yearning, of hunger and privation, and his present hunger awoke and gnawed at him, reminding him that he had eaten nothing since the day before, and little enough then. For the moment he saw red. These creatures were not even robbers.

They were sneak-thieves. By lies and broken promises they had tricked him out of his story. Well, he would show them. And a great resolve surged into his will to the effect that he would not leave the office until he got his money. He remembered, if he did not get it, that there was no way for him to go back to Oakland. He controlled himself with an effort, but not before the wolfish expression of his face had awed and perturbed them.

They became more voluble than ever. Mr. Ford started anew to tell how he had first read "The Ring of Bells," and Mr. Ends at the same time was striving to repeat his niece's appreciation of "The Ring of Bells," said niece being a school-teacher in Alameda.

"I'll tell you what I came for," Martin said finally. "To be paid for that story all of you like so well. Five dollars, I believe, is what you promised me would be paid on publication."

Mr. Ford, with an expression on his mobile features of immediate and happy acquiescence, started to reach for his pocket, then turned suddenly to Mr. Ends, and said that he had left his money home. That Mr. Ends resented this, was patent; and Martin saw the twitch of his arm as if to protect his trousers pocket. Martin knew that the money was there.

"I am sorry," said Mr. Ends, "but I paid the printer not an hour ago, and he took my ready change. It was careless of me to be so short; but the bill was not yet due, and the printer's request, as a favor, to make an immediate advance, was quite unexpected."

Both looked expectantly at Mr. White, but that gentleman laughed and shrugged his shoulders. His conscience was clean at any rate. He had come into the *Transcontinental* to learn magazine-literature, instead of which he had principally learned finance. *The Transcontinental* owed him four months' salary, and he knew that the printer must be appeased before the associate editor.

"It's rather absurd, Mr. Eden, to have caught us in this shape," Mr. Ford preambled airily. "All carelessness, I assure you. But I'll tell you what we'll do. We'll mail you a check the first thing in the morning. You have Mr. Eden's address, haven't you, Mr. Ends?"

Yes, Mr. Ends had the address, and the check would be mailed the first thing in the morning. Martin's knowledge of banks and checks was hazy, but he could see no reason why they should not give him the check on this day just as well as on the next.

"Then it is understood, Mr. Eden, that we'll mail you the check to-morrow?" Mr. Ford said.

"I need the money today," Martin answered stolidly.

"The unfortunate circumstances—if you had chanced here any other day," Mr. Ford began suavely, only to be interrupted by Mr. Ends, whose cranky eyes justified themselves in this shortness of temper.

"Mr. Ford has already explained the situation," he said with asperity. "And so have I. The check will be mailed—"

"I also have explained," Martin broke in, "and I have explained that I want the money today."

He had felt his pulse quicken a trifle at the business manager's brusqueness, and upon him he kept an alert eye, for it was in that gentl' man's trousers pocket that he divined the *Transcontinental's* ready ca. was reposing.

"It is too bad—" Mr. Ford began.

But at that moment, with an impatient movement, Mr. Ends turne. as if about to leave the room. At the same instant Martin sprang for him, clutching him by the throat with one hand in such fashion that Mr. Ends' snow-white beard, still maintaining its immaculate trimness, pointed ceilingward at an angle of forty-five degrees. To the horror of Mr. White and Mr. Ford, they saw their business manager shaken like an Astrakhan rug.

"Dig up, you venerable discourager of rising young talent!" Martin exhorted. "Dig up, or I'll shake it out of you, even if it's all in nickels." Then, to the two affrighted onlookers: "Keep away! If you interfere, somebody's liable to get hurt."

Mr. Ends was choking, and it was not until the grip on his throat was eased that he was able to signify his acquiescence in the digging-up programme. All together, after repeated digs, his trousers pocket yielded four dollars and fifteen cents.

"Inside out with it," Martin commanded.

An additional ten cents fell out. Martin counted the result of his raid a second time to make sure.

"You next!" He shouted at Mr. Ford. "I want seventy-five cents more."

Mr. Ford did not wait, but ransacked his pockets, with the result of sixty cents.

"Sure that is all?" Martin demanded menacingly, possessing himself of it. "What have you got in your vest pockets?"

In token of his good faith, Mr. Ford turned two of his pockets inside out. A strip of cardboard fell to the floor from one of them. He recovered it and was in the act of returning it, when Martin cried:—

"What's that?—A ferry ticket? Here, give it to me. It's worth ten cents. I'll credit you with it. I've now got four dollars and ninety-five cents, including the ticket. Five cents is still due me."

He looked fiercely at Mr. White, and found that fragile creature in the act of handing him a nickel.

"Thank you," Martin said, addressing them collectively. "I wish you a good day."

"Robber!" Mr. Ends snarled after him.

"Sneak-thief!" Martin retorted, slamming the door as he passed out.

Martin was elated—so elated that when he recollected that *The Hornet* owed him fifteen dollars for "The Peri and the Pearl," he decided forthwith to go and collect it. But *The Hornet* was run by a set of clean-shaven, strapping young men, frank buccaneers who robbed everything and everybody, not excepting one another. After some breakage of the office furniture, the editor (an ex-college athlete), ably assisted by the business manager, an advertising agent, and the porter, succeeded in removing Martin from the office and in accelerating, by initial impulse, his descent of the first flight of stairs.

"Come again, Mr. Eden; glad to see you any time," they laughed down at him from the landing above.

Martin grinned as he picked himself up.

"Phew!" he murmured back. "The *Transcontinental* crowd were nanny-goats, but you fellows are a lot of prize-fighters."

More laughter greeted this.

"I must say, Mr. Eden," the editor of *The Hornet* called down, "That for a poet you can go some yourself. Where did you learn that right cross—if I may ask?"

"Where you learned that half-Nelson," Martin answered. "Anyway, you're going to have a black eye."

"I hope your neck doesn't stiffen up," the editor wished solicitously. "What do you say we all go out and have a drink on it—not the neck, of course, but the little rough-house?"

"I'll go you if I lose," Martin accepted.

And robbers and robbed drank together, amicably agreeing that the battle was to the strong, and that the fifteen dollars for "The Peri and the Pearl" belonged by right to *The Hornet's* editorial staff.

. . . "The Shame of the Sun" was published in October. As Martin cut the cords of the express package and the half-dozen complimentary copies from the publishers spilled out on the table, a heavy sadness fell upon him. He thought of the wild delight that would have been his had this happened a few short months before, and he contrasted that delight that should have been with his present uncaring coldness. His book, his first book, and his pulse had not gone up a fraction of a beat, and he was only sad. It meant little to him now. The most it meant was that it might bring some money, and little enough did he care for money.

He carried a copy out into the kitchen and presented it to Maria.

"I did it," he explained, in order to clear up her bewilderment. "I wrote it in the room there, and I guess some few quarts of your vegetable soup went into the making of it. Keep it. It's yours. Just to remember me by, you know."

He was not bragging, not showing off. His sole motive was to make her happy, to make her proud of him, to justify her long faith in him. She put the book in the front room on top of the family Bible. A sacred thing was this book her lodger had made, a fetich of friendship. It softened the blow of his having been a laundryman, and though she could not understand a line of it, she knew that every line of it was great. She was a simple, practical, hard-working woman, but she possessed faith in large endowment.

Just as emotionlessly as he had received "The Shame of the Sun" did he read the reviews of it that came in weekly from the clipping bureau. The book was making a hit, that was evident. It meant more gold in the money sack. He could fix up Lizzie, redeem all his promises, and still have enough left to build his grass-walled castle.

Singletree, Darnley & Co. had cautiously brought out an edition of fifteen hundred copies, but the first reviews had started a second edition of twice the size through the presses; and ere this was delivered a third edition of five thousand had been ordered. A London firm made arrangements by cable for an English edition, and hot-footed upon this came the news of French, German, and Scandinavian translations in progress. The attack upon the Maeterlinck school could not have been made at a more opportune moment. A fierce controversy was precipitated. Saleeby and Haeckel indorsed and defended "The Shame of the Sun," for once finding themselves on the same side of a question. Crookes and Wallace ranged up on the opposing side, while Sir Oliver Lodge attempted to formulate a compromise that would jibe with his particular cosmic theories, Maeterlinck's followers rallied round the standard of mysticism. Chesterton set the whole world laughing with a series of alleged nonpartisan essays on the subject, and the whole affair, controversy and controversialists, was well-nigh swept into the pit by a thundering broadside from George Bernard Shaw. Needless to say the arena was crowded with hosts of lesser lights, and the dust and sweat and din became terrific.

"It is a most marvellous happening," Singletree, Darnley & Co. wrote Martin, "a critical philosophic essay selling like a novel. You could not have chosen your subject better, and all contributory factors have been unwarrantedly propitious. We need scarcely to assure you that we are making hay while the sun shines. Over forty thousand copies have already been sold in the United States and Canada, and a new edition of twenty thousand is on the presses. We are overworked, trying to supply the demand. Nevertheless we have helped to create that demand. We have already spent five thousand dollars in advertising. The book is bound to be a record-breaker.

"Please find herewith a contract in duplicate for your next book which we have taken the liberty of forwarding to you. You will please note that we have increased your royalties to twenty per cent, which is about as high as a conservative publishing house dares go. If our offer is agreeable to you, please fill in the proper blank space with the title of your book. We make no stipulations concerning its nature. Any book on any subject. If you have one already written, so much the better. Now is the time to strike. The iron could not be hotter.

"On receipt of signed contract we shall be pleased to make you an advance on royalties of five thousand dollars. You see, we have faith in you, and we are going in on this thing big. We should like, also, to discuss with you the drawing up of a contract for a term of years, say ten, during which we shall have the exclusive right of publishing in book-form all that you produce. But more of this anon."

Martin laid down the letter and worked a problem in mental arithmetic, finding the product of fifteen cents times sixty thousand to be nine thousand dollars. He signed the new contract, inserting "The Smoke of Joy" in the blank space, and mailed it back to the publishers along with the twenty storiettes he had written in the days before he discovered the formula for the newspaper storiette. And promptly as the United States mail could deliver and return, came Singletree, Darnley & Co.'s check for five thousand dollars.

"I want you to come down town with me, Maria, this afternoon about two o'clock," Martin said, the morning the check arrived. "Or, better, meet me at fourteenth and Broadway at two o'clock. I'll be looking out for you."

At the appointed time she was there; but *shoes* was the only clue to the mystery her mind had been capable of evolving, and she suffered a distinct shock of disappointment when Martin walked her right by a shoe-store and dived into a real estate office. What happened thereupon resided forever after in her memory as a dream. Fine gentlemen smiled at her benevolently as they talked with Martin and one another; a typewriter clicked; signatures were affixed to an imposing document; her own landlord was there, too, and affixed his signature; and when all was over and she was outside on the sidewalk, her landlord spoke to her, saying, "Well, Maria, you won't have to pay me no seven dollars and a half this month."

Maria was too stunned for speech.

"Or next month, or the next, or the next," her landlord said.

She thanked him incoherently, as if for a favor. And it was not until she had returned home to North Oakland and conferred with her own kind, and had the Portuguese grocer investigate, that she really knew that she was the owner of the little house in which she had lived and for which she had paid rent so long.

"Why don't you trade with me no more?" the Portuguese grocer asked Martin that evening, stepping out to hail him when he got off the car; and Martin explained that he wasn't doing his own cooking any more, and then went in and had a drink of wine on the house. He noted it was the best wine the grocer had in stock.

"Maria," Martin announced that night, "I'm going to leave you. And you're going to leave here yourself soon. Then you can rent the house and be a landlord yourself. You've a brother in San Leandro or Haywards, and he's in the milk business. I want you to send all your washing back unwashed—understand?—unwashed, and to go out to San Leandro tomorrow, or Haywards, or wherever it is, and see that brother of yours. Tell him to come to see me. I'll be stopping at the Metropole down in Oakland. He'll know a good milk-ranch when he sees one."

And so it was that Maria became a landlord and the sole owner of a dairy, with two hired men to do the work for her and a bank account that steadily increased despite the fact that her whole brood wore shoes and went to school. Few persons ever meet the fairy princes they dream about; but Maria, who worked hard, never dreaming about fairy princes, entertained hers in the guise of an ex-laundryman.

In the meantime the world had begun to ask: "Who is this Martin Eden?" He had declined to give any biographical data to his publishers, but the newspapers were not to be denied. Oakland was his own town, and the reporters nosed out scores of individuals who could supply information. All that he was and was not, all that he had done and most of what he had not done, was spread out for the delectation of the public, accompanied by snapshots and photographs—the latter procured from the local photographer who had once taken Martin's picture and who promptly copyrighted it and put it on the market. At first, so great was his disgust with the magazines and all bourgeois society, Martin fought against publicity; but in the end, because it was easier than not to, he surrendered. He found that he could not refuse himself to the special writers who travelled long distances to see him. Then again, each day was so many hours long, and, since he no longer was occupied with writing and studying, those hours had to be occupied somehow; so he yielded to what was to him a whim, permitted interviews, gave his opinions on literature and philosophy, and even accepted invitations of the bourgeoisie. He had settled down into a strange and comfortable state of mind. He no longer cared. He forgave everybody, even the cub reporter who had painted him red and to whom he now granted a full page with specially posed photographs.

He saw Lizzie occasionally, and it was patent that she regretted the greatness that had come to him. It widened the space between them.

Perhaps it was with the hope of narrowing it that she yielded to his persuasions to go to night school and business college and to have herself gowned by a wonderful dressmaker who charged outrageous prices. She improved visibly from day to day, until Martin wondered if he was doing right, for he knew that all her compliance and endeavor was for his sake. She was trying to make herself of worth in his eyes—of the sort of worth he seemed to value. Yet he gave her no hope, treating her in brotherly fashion and rarely seeing her.

"Overdue" was rushed upon the market by the Meredith-Lowell Company in the height of his popularity, and being fiction, in point of sales it made even a bigger strike than "The Shame of the Sun." Week after week his was the credit of the unprecedented performance of having two books at the head of the list of bestsellers. Not only did the story take with the fiction-readers, but those who read "The Shame of the Sun" with avidity were likewise attracted to the sea-story by the cosmic grasp of mastery with which he had handled it. First, he had attacked the literature of mysticism, and had done it exceedingly well; and, next, he had successfully supplied the very literature he had exposited, thus proving himself to be that rare genius, a critic and a creator in one.

Money poured in on him, fame poured in on him; he flashed, comet-like, through the world of literature, and he was more amused than interested by the stir he was making. One thing was puzzling him, a little thing that would have puzzled the world had it known. But the world would have puzzled over his bepuzzlement rather than over the little thing that to him loomed gigantic. Judge Blount invited him to dinner. That was the little thing, or the beginning of the little thing, that was soon to become the big thing. He had insulted Judge Blount, treated him abominably, and Judge Blount, meeting him on the street, invited him to dinner. Martin bethought himself of the numerous occasions on which he had met Judge Blount at the Morses' and when Judge Blount had not invited him to dinner. Why had he not invited him to dinner then? he asked himself. He had not changed. He was the same Martin Eden. What made the difference? The fact that the stuff he had written had appeared inside the covers of books? But it was work performed. It was not something he had done since. It was achievement accomplished at the very time Judge Blount was sharing this general view and sneering at his Spencer and his intellect. Therefore it was not for any real value, but for a purely fictitious value that Judge Blount invited him to dinner.

Martin grinned and accepted the invitation, marvelling the while at his complacence. And at the dinner, where, with their womenkind, were half a dozen of those that sat in high places, and where Martin found himself quite the lion, Judge Blount, warmly seconded by Judge Hanwell, urged privately that Martin should permit his name to be put up for the Styx—the ultra-select club to which belonged, not the mere men of wealth, but the men of attainment. And Martin declined, and was more puzzled than ever.

He was kept busy disposing of his heap of manuscripts. He was overwhelmed by requests from editors. It had been discovered that he was a stylist, with meat under his style. *The Northern Review,* after publishing "The Cradle of Beauty," had written him for half a dozen similar essays, which would have been supplied out of the heap, had not *Burton's Magazine,* in a speculative mood, offered him five hundred dollars each for five essays. He wrote back that he would supply the demand, but at a thousand dollars an essay. He remembered that all these manuscripts had been refused by the very magazines that were now clamoring for them. And their refusals had been cold-blooded, automatic, stereotyped. They had made him sweat, and now he intended to make them sweat. *Burton's Magazine* paid his price for five essays, and the remaining four, at the same rate, were snapped up by *Mackintosh's Monthly, The Northern Review* being too poor to stand the pace. Thus went out to the world "The High Priests of Mystery," "The Wonder-Dreamers," "The Yardstick of the Ego," "Philosophy of Illusion," "God and Clod," "Art and Biology," "Critics and Test-tubes," "Star-dust," and "The Dignity of Usury,"—to raise storms and rumblings and mutterings that were many a day in dying down.

Editors wrote to him telling him to name his own terms, which he did, but it was always for work performed. He refused resolutely to pledge himself to any new thing. The thought of again setting pen to paper maddened him. He had seen Brissenden torn to pieces by the crowd, and despite the fact that him the crowd acclaimed, he could not get over the shock nor gather any respect for the crowd. His very popularity seemed a disgrace and a treason to Brissenden. It made him wince, but he made up his mind to go on and fill the money-bag.

He received letters from editors like the following: "About a year ago we were unfortunate enough to refuse your collection of love-poems. We were greatly impressed by them at the time, but certain arrangements already entered into prevented our taking them. If you still have them, and if you will be kind enough to forward them, we shall be glad to publish the entire collection on your own terms. We are also prepared to make a most advantageous offer for bringing them out in book form."

Martin recollected his blank-verse tragedy, and sent it instead. He read it over before mailing, and was particularly impressed by its sophomoric amateurishness and general worthlessness. But he sent it; and it was published, to the everlasting regret of the editor. The public was indignant and incredulous. It was too far a cry from Martin Eden's high standard to that serious bosh. It was asserted that he had never written it, that the magazine had faked it very clumsily, or that Martin Eden was emulating the elder Dumas and at the height of success was hiring his writing done for him. But when he explained that the tragedy was an early effort of his literary childhood, and that magazine had refused to be happy unless it got it, a great laugh went up at the magazine's expense and a change in the editorship followed. The tragedy was never brought out in book-form, though Martin pocketed the advance royalties that had been paid.

Coleman's Weekly sent Martin a lengthy telegram, costing nearly three hundred dollars, offering him a thousand dollars an article for twenty articles. He was to travel over the United States, with all expenses paid, and select whatever topics interested him. The body of the telegram was devoted to hypothetical topics in order to show him the freedom of range that was to be his. The only restriction placed upon him was that he must confine himself to the United States. Martin sent his inability to accept and his regrets by wire "collect."

"Wiki-Wiki," published in *Warren's Monthly,* was an instantaneous success. It was brought out forward in a wide-margined, beautifully decorated volume that struck the holiday trade and sold like wildfire. The critics were unanimous in the belief that it would take its place with those two classics by two great writers, "The Bottle Imp" and "The Magic Skin."

The public, however, received the "Smoke of Joy" collection rather dubiously and coldly. The audacity and unconventionality of the storiettes was a shock to bourgeois morality and prejudice; but when Paris went mad over the immediate translation that was made, the American and English reading public followed suit and bought so many copies that Martin compelled the conservative house of Singeltree, Darnley & Co. to pay a flat royalty of twenty-five per cent for a third book, and thirty per cent flat for a fourth. These two volumes comprised all the short stories he had written and which had received, or were receiving, serial publication. "The Ring of the Bells" and his horror stories constituted one collection; the other collection was composed of "Adventure," "The Pot," "The Wine of Life," "The Whirlpool," "The Jostling Street," and four other stories. The Lowell-Meredith Company captured the collection of all his essays, and the Maxmillian Company got his "Sea Lyrics" and his "Love-Cycle," the latter receiving serial publication in the *Ladies Home Companion* after the payment of an extortionate price.

Martin heaved a sigh of relief when he had disposed of the last manuscript. The grass-walled castle and the white, coppered schooner were very near to him. Well, at any rate he had discovered Brissenden's contention that nothing of merit found its way into the magazines. His own success demonstrated that Brissenden had been wrong. And yet, somehow, he had a feeling that Brissenden had been right, after all. "The Shame of the Sun" had been the cause of his success more than the stuff he had written. That stuff had been merely incidental. It had been rejected right and left by the magazines. The publication of "The Shame of the Sun" had started a controversy and precipitated the landslide in his favor. Had there been no "Shame of the Sun" there would have been no landslide, and had there been no miracle in the go of "The Shame of the Sun" there would have been no landslide. Singletree, Darnley & Co. attested that miracle. They had brought out a first edition of fifteen hundred copies and been dubious of selling it. They were experienced publishers and no one had been more astounded than they at the success which had followed. To them it had been in truth a miracle. They never got over it, and every letter they wrote him reflected their reverent awe of that first mysterious happening. They did not attempt to explain it. There was no explaining it, It had happened. In the face of all experience to the contrary, it had happened.

So it was, reasoning thus, that Martin questioned the validity of his popularity. It was the bourgeoisie that bought his books and poured its gold into his money-sack, and from what little he knew of the bourgeoisie it was not clear to him how it could possibly appreciate or comprehend what he had written. His intrinsic beauty and power meant nothing to the hundreds of thousands who were acclaiming him and buying his books. He was the fad of the hour, the adventurer who had stormed Parnassus while the gods nodded. The hundreds of thousands read him and acclaimed him with the same brute non-understanding with which they had flung themselves on Brissenden's "Ephemera" and torn it to pieces— a wolf-rabble that fawned on him instead of fanging him. Fawn or fang, it was all a matter of chance. One thing he knew with absolute certitude: "Emphemera" was infinitely greater than anything he had in him. It was a poem of centuries. Then the tribute the mob paid him was a sorry tribute indeed, for that same mob had wallowed "Ephemera" into the mire. He sighed heavily and with satisfaction. He was glad the last manuscript was sold and that he would soon be done with it all.

JACK LONDON: A CHRONOLOGY

1876   Born at 615 Third Street, San Francisco, California, January 12. Son of Flora Wellman (born Massillon, Ohio, August 17, 1843) and William Henry Chaney (born near present-day Chesterville, Maine, January 13, 1821). Chaney, an itinerant astrologer, lives with Flora Wellman 1874–75 but deserts his common-law wife upon learning of her pregnancy and later (1897) denies to London that he can have been his father.

On September 7, Flora (who uses the name Chaney) marries John London, a native of Pennsylvania and a Union Army veteran, a widower with two daughters. John London accepts Flora's son as his own, and he is named John Griffith London, the middle name deriving from a favorite nephew of Flora Wellman's, Griffith Everhard.

1891   Completes grammar school. Works in a cannery.

1892   Purchases the sloop *Razzle-Dazzle* with three hundred dollars borrowed from his former wet nurse, "Mammy Jenny" Prentiss and becomes "Prince of the Oyster Pirates" on San Francisco Bay. Serves as officer in the fish patrol on the Bay.

1893   Serves several months aboard the sealing schooner *Sophia Sutherland* in the Bering Sea and the North Pacific. Returns in summer, and on November 12 wins first prize in the San Francisco *Call*'s Best Descriptive Article Contest for "Story of a Typhoon Off the Coast of Japan."

1894   Joins the western detachment of Coxey's Army—Kelly's Army— to march to Washington, D.C. Leaves the ragtag "army" in the Midwest and rides the rails eastward. Is arrested for vagrancy in Niagara Falls, N.Y., in June and serves one month in the Erie County Penitentiary. These experiences he will later chronicle in *The Road* (1907).

1895   Finishes high school education at Oakland High School, where he writes sketches and stories for the student magazine *Aegis*.

1896   Joins Socialist Labor Party. Passes entrance examinations and attends the University of California at Berkeley for one semester.

1897   Joins Klondike gold rush and spends winter in the Yukon.

      John London dies in Oakland on October 14.

1898   Returns from Alaska by two-thousand-mile-boat trip down the Yukon River.

1899   Publishes first "professional" story, "To the Man on Trail," in *Overland Monthly*. Begins writing for a living.

      December 21 signs contract with Houghton Mifflin Co., for a book of short stories.

1900   "An Odyssey of the North" is published in the *Atlantic Monthly*. Marries Bessie Maddern April 7; on the same day his first published book, *The Son of the Wolf*, a collection of northland fiction, appears.

1901   First daughter, Joan, is born.

1902   Travels to London where he lives six weeks in the city's East End ghetto and there gathers material for his brilliant sociological study *The People of the Abyss* (a phrase credited to H. G. Wells).

      Second daughter, Bess, is born.

      First novel, *A Daughter of the Snows,* is published by Lippincott's.

1903   W. H. Chaney dies January 8.

      The Kempton-Wace Letters, an epistolary exchange with coauthor Anna Strunsky on the subject of love, is published by Macmillan.

      Separates from Bessie London.

      The Call of the Wild is published, an instantaneous success.

1904   Sails for Japan and Korea as war correspondent for the Hearst syndicate in the Russo-Japanese War.

      The Sea Wolf is published.

1905   Divorces Bessie Maddern London. Marries Charmian Kittredge November 20 in Chicago.

      Purchases ranch near Glen Ellen, California.

      Lectures in Midwest and East.

1906   Lectures at Yale in January on "The Coming Crisis."

      Reports on the San Francisco earthquake and fire, April 18, for *Collier's*.

Begins building the *Snark* (named after Lewis Carroll's creation), to sail around the world.

White Fang, written as a companion volume to *The Call of the Wild*, is published.

1907 Sails April 23 from San Francisco in *Snark*, visiting Hawaii—including the leper colony at Molokai—the Marquesas, and Tahiti.

1908 Returns to California aboard the *Mariposa* to straighten out financial affairs. Continues *Snark* voyage to Samoa, Fiji Islands, New Hebrides, and the Solomons.

The Iron Heel is published.

1909 Is hospitalized in Sydney, Australia, with a series of tropical ailments. Abandons *Snark* voyage and returns to California on the Scots collier *Tymeric*, via Pitcairn Island, Ecuador, Panama, New Orleans, and Arizona. Arrives home on July 24.

Martin Eden, a semiautobiographical novel, is published.

1910 Devotes energies and funds to building up his "Beauty Ranch."

Wolf House, London's baronial mansion, is begun.

Birth and death of Charmian's and Jack's first child, a daughter named Joy.

1911 With his wife and servant drives a four-horse carriage through northern California and Oregon.

1912 Sails March 2 from Baltimore around Cape Horn to Seattle aboard the four-masted barque *Dirigo*, a 148-day voyage.

The London's second baby lost in miscarriage.

1913 Wolf House, on August 21, is mysteriously destroyed by fire, a seventy-thousand-dollar loss.

John Barleycorn, semiautobiographical novel-treatise on alcoholism, is published.

1914 Becomes correspondent for *Collier's* at eleven hundred dollars a week, in Mexican revolution.

1915 Returns to Hawaii, this time for health purposes.

His last great work, *The Star Rover*, is published.

Is warned by doctors of his excesses in drink and diet.

1916 Resigns from Socialist party "because of its lack of fire and fight, and its loss of emphasis on the class struggle."

Dies 7:45 p.m., November 22, of uremic poisoning. Suicide, as suggested by biographical novelist Irving Stone (in his *Sailor on Horseback*), by a calculated lethal dose of morphine and atropine sulphates, a possibility, but in no way conclusive.

1922 Flora Wellman London dies January 4.

1947 Bessie Maddern London dies September 7.

1955 Charmian Kittredge London dies January 13.

1965 *Letters From Jack London,* most important of all source books on London's life and thought, is published.

1970 *Jack London Reports,* a collection of London's war correspondence, prizefight reporting, and miscellaneous newspaper writing, is published by Doubleday, edited by King Hendricks and Irving Shepard.

1971 Joan London dies January 18.

SUGGESTED READING

Calder-Marshall Arthur, ed. *The Bodley Head Jack London.* London: The Bodley Head, 1963, four volumes.

Day, A. Grove. *Jack London and the South Seas.* New York: Four Winds Press, 1971.

Hendricks, King, and Shepard, Irving. *Jack London Reports.* Garden City, N.Y.: Doubleday, 1970.

Hendricks, King, and Shepard, Irving. *Letters From Jack London.* New York: The Odyssey Press, 1965.

Labor, Earle. *Jack London* New York: Twayne Publications, 1974.

London, Charmian K. *The Book of Jack London.* New York: The Century Co., 1921, two volumes.

London, Joan. *Jack London and His Times.* New York: Doubleday, Doran & Co., 1939; reissued with new introductory material by University of Washington Press, Seattle, 1968.

McClintock, James I. *White Logic: Jack London's Short Stories.* Grand Rapids, Mich.: Wolf House Books, 1975.

O'Connor, Richard. *Jack London: A Biography.* Boston: Little, Brown & Co., 1964.

Sherman, Joan R. *Jack London: A Reference Guide.* Boston: G. K. Hall & Co., 1977.

Sinclair, Andrew. *Jack: A Biography of Jack London.* New York: Harper & Row, 1977.

Stone, Irving. *Sailor on Horseback: The Biography of Jack London.* New York: Houghton Mifflin Co., 1938; revised edition published with 28 London stories, Doubleday (New York), 1977.

Walcutt, Charles C. *Jack London.* Minneapolis: University of Minnesota Press, 1966, monograph.

Walker, Dale L., ed. *Curious Fragments: Jack London's Tales of Fantasy Fiction.* Port Washington, N.Y.: Kennikat Press, 1975.

Walker, Dale L., and Sisson, James E., III. *The Fiction of Jack London: A Chronological Bibliography.* El Paso, Tx.: Texas Western Press of The University of Texas at El Paso, 1972.

Walker, Franklin. *Jack London & The Klondike.* San Marino, Calif.: Huntington Library, 1966.

Woodbridge, Hensley C.; London, John; and Tweney, George H. *Jack London: A Bibliography.* Georgetown, Calif.: The Talisman Press, 1966; revised and expanded edition, Kraus Reprints (Millwood, N.J.), 1973.